Praise for Nick Bollettieri

"Nick, I've spent time with Vince Lombardi, Bob Knight, Tommy Lasorda, Joe Torre, Larry Brown, Casey Stengel, and Cus D'Amato—just to name a few—and they're all successful and they're all different."

"The key thing for a coach and for a human being is to be yourself, and Nick, this is the characteristic you share with all those Hall of Fame coaches. You are yourself. You're the consummate coach. You care about the game, about the way it is played, and about the person who is playing it. You don't quite demand perfection, but you damn well want it."

"You coached me through the book we wrote together. Of all the people I've worked with on books—Joe Namath, Joe Montana, Billy Crystal, Bo Jackson, Tom Seaver, Dave DeBusschere, and Jerry Kramer—nobody drove me as hard as you did, nobody cared more about the final product, nobody tried harder to give and share. You called me at any hour from any place to make suggestions and to offer information, even after the book had gone to press, and I think I found out what it was like to be a tennis player coached by Nick Bollettieri. All you asked was everything, and that's you, and that's terrific."

"Nick, you remind me of the first time I met George Allen. I walked into his Redskins training camp in Carlisle, Pennsylvania, and before I could ask him anything about football, he pointed to the cooler of bottled water and launched into a lecture on the unmatchable virtues of that particular kind of bottled water. George Allen wanted everything to be the best—down to the bottled water. You include dark tans and bright teeth in your repertoire.

And one more thing: Larry Brown's ultimate term of respect is to call someone Coach—as in Coach Holzman or Coach Smith. You are Coach Bollettieri."

—Dick Schaap
Author and host of ESPN's *The Sports Reporter*

"My definition of coaching is the ability of an individual to get maximum efficiency out of each athlete who comes under his or her guidance. Developing a positive attitude and maximizing the performance of each athlete are key components of all successful coaches. Coaching is the ability to communicate your concepts and your beliefs into making that athlete the best possible performer he or she can become. Once you develop the individuals' talents so they can excel in their own areas of expertise, the next factor is to blend the individuals into a winning team. It is vital that coaches convey to their athletes the necessity of having a sense of pride in themselves because that plays a big role in forming a winning attitude. Pride can be broken down as follows: P for perseverance, R for respect, I for intelligence, D for the four Ds of life—desire, dedication, determination, and discipline of body and mind—and E for enthusiasm. If a coach can develop players with PRIDE and get each athlete to perform to the best of his or her ability, then that coach has succeeded and has earned the right to feel like a championship coach."

"Nick Bollettieri has always been a man with great vision and a charismatic personality who energizes everyone in his presence. I have watched Nick coach athletes of all abilities, from beginners to professionals. His positive teachings, with his energetic approach, lead to the development of successful tennis players."

—Dick Vitale

ABC and ESPN basketball analyst

"When I moved in with Nick at the age of 13, he became a surrogate father to me. Nick stressed discipline and self-control, but most of all he believed in me. Nick has the uncanny ability to know what each player needs to be motivated. For me, it was praise. The most lasting impression that I have about Nick is simply the feeling that came over me whenever he was on the court with me. Even to this day, if I'm playing tennis and Nick is there, the adrenaline starts to flow, and I leave the court sure that I can conquer the world."

—Jimmy Arias

After Jim Courier's five-set victory over Greg Rusedski in the fifth and final match of the Davis Cup tie versus Great Britain, Nick sent this fax:

Dear Jim,

Your success is not an accident. You work. You fight. You do anything you have to in order to win. I'm proud of you.

Your friend,
Nick Bollettieri

Jim sent the following fax in response:

Dear Nick,

Thanks for your kind fax. The qualities you pointed out in your fax—the hard work, the fighting—are qualities that were molded in your backyard.

Thank you for giving the opportunity to hundreds of dreamers like me. There are a lot of us out here doing this for a living who would be working elsewhere if it weren't for you.

All my very best,
Jim Courier

"Not only has Nick has been a great help to our tennis game, but he has also been a close friend of the family for years. His friendship and instruction have been invaluable to us."

—Venus Williams

"I really think that Nick is not just a coach, but also a friend and someone that you can talk to. As a coach, he really knows what to tell the player so the player will be able to take the next step to be on the top. He has personally helped me to realize that I need the small things more than the large things. In the end, Nick is a great person and my friend."

—Serena Williams

"Not only is Nick a terrific coach but also a great motivator. He makes you feel good on the court no matter what. Also, knowing him for the past few years, he's not only a coach to me but a great friend with a big heart. He'll always be special."

—Tommy Haas

In March 1999, Martina Hingis was interviewed by Associated Press sports writer Steven Wine. The headline of the resulting newspaper article read, "Hingis rolls into semis, will face Serena." Last year, Wine wrote, "Hingis lost in the semi-finals of the French Open, Wimbledon, and the U.S. Open, then lost the No. 1 ranking to Davenport. Chastened, she prepared for 1999 by training with Nick Bollettieri in Bradenton." He continued, "Fit and trim again, Hingis has regained her remarkable sense of anticipation. Her serve and forehand, meanwhile, are more powerful than before. . . That was the first time after a long time I really worked for two weeks, day after day, three or four hours of tennis. You can see it, I mean, I'm back to No. 1. The scores tell it."

—Martina Hingis

"Nick has shown his comprehensive knowledge of tennis and the industry. If anyone has seen it all and done it all—and has the right to say it all—it's my friend and respected colleague, Nick Bollettieri."

—Tim Heckler
Late CEO of USPTA

"Nick has made his mark in the tennis world. He pioneered the concept of a full-time tennis academy, has nurtured the careers of many players, and is the consummate salesman of his profession."

—Dennis Van der Meer
President of USPTR Van der Meer Tennis University

"Bollettieri is a coach's coach. His instincts are legendary. His head for success is uncanny. He lets us all in on his secrets. Most important, he shares one of the most compelling life lessons: Bypass the big serve, the flashy footwork, the killer backhand. Those are merely surface. Laser in on what's under the surface—in the heart and mind. That's where the real stuff of winners, their potential for greatness, lives."

—Harvey Mackay
Author of *Swim With the Sharks* and *Pushing the Envelope*

Nick Bollettieri's Tennis Handbook

Second Edition

Nick Bollettieri

Human Kinetics

Library of Congress Cataloging-in-Publication Data
Bollettieri, Nick.
   [Bollettieri's tennis handbook]
   Nick Bollettieri's tennis handbook / Nick Bollettieri. -- Second Edition.
       pages cm
   Includes index.
   Revised edition of: Bollettieri tennis handbook. 2001.
   1. Tennis--Handbooks, manuals, etc. I. Title.
   GV995.B68347 2015
   796.342'2--dc23

                                    2014043804

ISBN: 978-1-4504-8943-0 (print)

The web addresses cited in this text were current as of June 2015, unless otherwise noted.

Acquisitions Editor: Justin Klug; **Developmental Editor:** Laura Pulliam; **Managing Editor:** Nicole Moore; **Copyeditor:** Patricia L. MacDonald; **Indexer:** Katy Balcer; **Graphic Designer:** Angela K. Snyder; **Cover Designer:** Keith Blomberg; **Photograph (cover):** Casey Brooke-Lawson; **Photographs (interior):** © Human Kinetics; **Visual Production Assistant:** Joyce Brumfield; **Photo Production Manager:** Jason Allen; **Art Manager:** Kelly Hendren; **Associate Art Manager:** Alan L. Wilborn; **Illustrations:** © Human Kinetics; **Printer:** Sheridan Books

We thank the IMG Academy in Bradenton, Florida, for assistance in providing the location for the photo shoot for this book.

Human Kinetics books are available at special discounts for bulk purchase. Special editions or book excerpts can also be created to specification. For details, contact the Special Sales Manager at Human Kinetics.

The video contents of this product are licensed for private home use and traditional, face-to-face classroom instruction only. For public performance licensing, please contact a sales representative at www.HumanKinetics.com/SalesRepresentatives.

Printed in the United States of America

10 9 8 7 6 5 4 3 2 1

The paper in this book is certified under a sustainable forestry program.

Human Kinetics
Website: www.HumanKinetics.com

United States: Human Kinetics
P.O. Box 5076
Champaign, IL 61825-5076
800-747-4457
e-mail: humank@hkusa.com

Canada: Human Kinetics
475 Devonshire Road Unit 100
Windsor, ON N8Y 2L5
800-465-7301 (in Canada only)
e-mail: info@hkcanada.com

Europe: Human Kinetics
107 Bradford Road
Stanningley
Leeds LS28 6AT, United Kingdom
+44 (0) 113 255 5665
e-mail: hk@hkeurope.com

Australia: Human Kinetics
57A Price Avenue
Lower Mitcham, South Australia 5062
08 8372 0999
e-mail: info@hkaustralia.com

New Zealand: Human Kinetics
P.O. Box 80
Mitcham Shopping Centre, South Australia 5062
0800 222 062
e-mail: info@hknewzealand.com

E6279

I would like to dedicate this book to all of the students and coaches throughout the world who I've had the pleasure and privilege of working with over the years. Especially the students and coaches at IMG Academy, who support me and who we continue to learn from each day.

Contents

Video Contents

Fundamentals of Athletic Development
Athletic foundation
Drop step and drive
Forward sprint footwork
Closed stance
Neutral stance
Semi-open and open stance
Running open stance

Racket Grips

Forehands
Aggressive forehands

Backhands
One-handed backhand shot
One-handed backhand slice
Two-handed backhand shot

Serves
Serve fundamentals

Returns
Return-of-serve stance
Sonic return
Defensive return

Accessing the Online Video

This book includes access to online video that includes 26 clips demonstrating tennis fundamentals and 13 clips of commentary from Nick on some of his former students. Throughout the book, fundamentals marked with this play button icon indicate where the content is enhanced by online video clips: ▶

Take the following steps to access the video. If you need help at any point in the process, you can contact us by clicking on the Support link under Customer Service on the right side of the screen.

1. Visit www.HumanKinetics.com/NickBollettierisTennisHandbook.
2. Click on the **View online video** link next to the book cover.
3. You will be directed to the screen shown in figure 1. Click the **Sign In** link on the left or top of the page. If you do not have an account with Human Kinetics, you will be prompted to create one.

Figure 1

4. If the online video does not appear in the list on the left of the page, click the **Enter Pass Code** option in that list. Enter the pass code that is printed here, including all hyphens. Click the Submit button to unlock the online video. After you have entered this pass code the first time, you will never have to enter it again. For future visits, all you need to do is sign in to the book's website and follow the link that appears in the left menu.

Pass code for online video: BOLLETTIERI-SK9M-OV

5. Once you have signed into the site and entered the pass code, select **Online Video** from the list on the left side of the screen. You'll then see an Online Video page with information about the video, as shown in the screenshot in figure 2. You can go straight to the accompanying videos for each topic by clicking on the links at the bottom of the page.

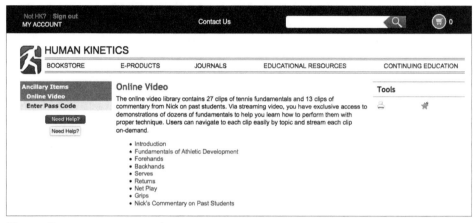

Figure 2

6. You are now able to view video for the topic you selected on the previous screen, as well as all others that accompany this product. Across the top of this page, you will see a set of buttons that correspond to the topics on the text that have accompanying video, as shown in figure 3.

Figure 3

Once you click on a topic, a player will appear. In the player, the clips for that topic will appear vertically along the right side. Select the video you would like to watch and view it in the main player window. You can use the buttons at the bottom of the main player window to view the video full screen, turn captioning on and off, and to pause, fast-forward, or reverse the clip.

Preface

I have created this volume of work with one purpose—to share the experiences of my career of almost 60 years. I describe my concepts on teaching players at all levels, from beginner to top-ranked in the world. I relate stories about many of the players I've worked with. I describe their strengths, idiosyncrasies, fears, and paranoid behaviors. One look at the table of contents shows the range of topics the book covers, from physical conditioning to parenting to the composition and tension of your racket strings. I hope that we have included something for everyone. If the players, coaches, administrators, and parents who read this book feel that a light went on, that they learned something new, I will consider the thousands of hours of production time to have been worthwhile. The book is the product of curious people who attempt to remain on the cutting edge of the tennis industry.

At the outset, I want to be clear that the opinions expressed in this handbook are born of the experience acquired over more than five decades of instructing. I don't profess to be right, and I don't accuse anyone whose methods are different of being wrong. In numerous instances I show a variety of techniques for comparison. *Nick Bollettieri's Tennis Handbook* contains far more than the fundamentals of hitting a ball. It includes world-class techniques from IMG Academy and the nuances that can make a good player great. The book is organized in such a way that you can seek specific information—finding the right program for you, beginning your training, developing the physical and mental skills for a successful tennis career, and much more. I have recounted the growth experiences of some of the greatest players, including Agassi, Krickstein, Courier, Horvath, Bassett, Sampras, Seles, Pierce, Majoli, Rios, Hingis, Haas, Philippoussis, Becker, Janković, and the Williams sisters. I hope you enjoy reading about these players as much as I enjoyed compiling the material. Throughout my coaching career, I have interacted with people from all walks of life. So before you end up with regrets, start keeping a diary today. Diaries become treasures in which you recall the minutiae of an event, those details that make it worth remembering in the first place.

I have had the pleasure of witnessing the complete metamorphosis of tennis. From a tennis teacher to a coach, I've had to adjust to new styles of play. If I had not adjusted, my students would have been victimized by other players' advancements in physical fitness and mental toughness and the improvements in equipment, strategy, and tactics. However, hard work, dedication, and willingness to accept responsibility for failure have always been the underpinnings of a champion. Practicing with purpose and performing drills repeatedly allow an athlete to achieve absolute confidence. Repetition translates into championship performance. Players must hit thousands of times to create the muscle memory, which increases the chance of hitting those shots during matches.

All a coach can hope to achieve is to enable students to reach the maximum level of their abilities. This is not easy! Coaches who understand their students—their moods, fears, and needs—can gain their confidence and trust. These coaches have a chance of lifting their students to their potential. Indeed, the ability to understand the student may be the defining characteristic of a coach, the quality that differentiates a coach from a teacher or instructor.

A coach develops an understanding of the true personality and hidden nuances of the student. This description is not intended to diminish the value of an instructor, who plays a vital role. But the road to exceptional, outstanding, or world-class performance is littered with the casualties of talented individuals who took to the road without a coach and other specialists.

My Perfect Athlete

My perfect athlete would win far more often than lose. No one wins all the time—not Michael Jordan, not Serena Williams, not Muhammad Ali, not Roger Clemens, and not even Derek Jeter. But my perfect athlete does not lose often. She plays to win. The athlete increases the chance of winning by preparing long before the actual battle begins.

When my perfect athlete wins, he would win fairly and graciously, abiding by the written rules and the unwritten ones, neither antagonizing nor demeaning the opponent. When my player loses, she would realize that she was outplayed and didn't fail to give total effort. The athlete would then be determined to make the necessary adjustments to win the next time.

Individuals like Billie Jean King and Arthur Ashe exemplify the term *pioneer*. Billie Jean was the driving force in elevating the women's game. Even today, she continues to give, promote, and elevate.

Arthur was likely the greatest ambassador for our sport. He was a gentleman and a fierce competitor, yet a warrior who invested his private time in fighting for human rights.

Wayne Gretzky's retirement solidified his position as one of the most respected athletes of all time. I'll never forget a comment he made at an interview once, a comment that explains his immense popularity. He said that in every game, every exhibition, every charity performance, every practice session, he did exactly the same thing—he gave his very best. We could all learn from his attitude.

Chris Evert left her mark on tennis. She exemplifies the word *respect*. And who can forget Bjorn Borg? His focus allowed him to win Wimbledon six times as a baseliner. His sole objective was to hit the last ball over the net. I could not end my list of almost-perfect athletes without Arnold Palmer. He is a standout performer, the quintessential gentleman, and a fine model for all of us.

My perfect athlete both in sport and in life is a person who goes into competition with the attitude of planning, even expecting, to win! This athlete is prepared to give all to be in the winners' circle. But there can be many types of winners: winners according to the score and winners who gave it their all but lost the battle. These are winners by effort!

The most outstanding coach in the history of the NFL, Vince Lombardi, said, "My teams never lost. They just ran out of time."

Chapter 1

Teaching Philosophy

There is no substitute for hard work. There will be disappointments, but the harder you work, the luckier you will get. Never be satisfied with less than your best effort. If you strive for the top and miss, you'll still "beat the pack."

Former President Gerald R. Ford made this comment, which applies as much to sports and coaching as it does to any other human endeavor. These words apply to athletics, coaching, raising children, going to school, or just getting out of bed on a cold, dreary morning. The dreams attached to any athletic contest cannot be manifested without the application of an uncommon work ethic. The single greatest component of success in sports is discipline.

Looking at the Past and Into the Future

I have heard about strokes and grips for many years. In the early stages of my career (the late 1950s and 1960s), there were only a few types of grips and swings. The following was the conventional wisdom about ground-stroke grips at the time:

- For the forehand, players used the eastern forehand grip. For the backhand, players used the eastern backhand grip. The majority of players were one-handed.

- The strokes were very quiet. For the most part, players did little running around when choosing to hit a forehand or backhand. Today, players tend to hit as many forehands as possible.
- Players assumed ready position at the center hash mark. The only time there was a choice of which stroke to use was when the ball came down the middle of the court.
- At contact and recovery, players had to finish the stroke, avoid jumping, keep the back foot behind them, and so on. They were then to recover and return to the center-court position.
- Players were expected to meet the ball in front of the lead foot.

Even so, Harold Solomon and Eddie Dibbs were hitting two-hand backhands at the time. Harold had a funny grip (full semiwestern to western). In hindsight, it is now clear that Solomon and Dibbs were ahead of their time in their choice of grips. At the same time Jimmy Evert was teaching his daughter, Chris, a two-hand backhand.

40 years later there is an entirely new view. This chapter will give you a look at what is going on today. Even though the look has changed, some principles seem to be eternal. When I first started teaching the game, my knowledge was limited. Today, I realize that the lack of technical knowledge contributed to both my successes and my failures. I let my students do what came naturally to them. I knew almost nothing about the volley, but somehow Brian Gottfried, one of my students in the early 1960s, became one of the best volleyers in the game. Accidents happen.

In 1996 Bjorn Borg visited IMG Academy to get ready for the senior 35 tour. In talking to Bjorn, I realized that his style of play was not taught. He did it naturally. I came to understand that his fantastic career was a result of working with natural talent and instinct, especially his western grip. He would run for every ball (his trademark). He hit with heavy spin, looped backhands with two hands, and at times would hit with two hands and follow through with one. He was unique. Those who said he couldn't win on grass were silenced by his six Wimbledon titles. Borg knew how to win. I thought the same thing when I saw Martina Hingis at age 11. Her strokes were somewhat iffy, but she knew what to do with the ball. Her mom deserves a Golden Ball award for not letting someone else teach her.

Nick's Tip

Life is built on strengths and weaknesses; you must blend them for success!

During Borg's few months at the academy, he told me he liked to play rather than just hit; he simply liked doing what felt natural to him. Bjorn would also run down anything that wasn't nailed to the court. This is the philosophy that I try to implant in all my students. Two students that come to mind are Jimmy Arias and Andre Agassi. Both of their dads told them simply to "hit the hell out of the ball."

Basic rules are necessary no matter what type of player a coach works with. All players are different. Even with the fundamentals, there might be slight differences. I often repeat myself by saying that hitting a ball is not enough to reach your potential. Every player has assets and liabilities. Life is built on strengths and weaknesses; you must blend them for success. Few fundamentals can be put aside if a player is to reach higher levels.

In the end, people will usually play in a fashion that is consistent with their personalities. Take Aaron Krickstein, for example. He was a quiet and introspective player. During matches he would play exactly like that, although he was extraordinarily competitive. Another example is Monica Seles. Her quiet demeanor belied her aggressive nature. She was almost Jekyll and Hyde in contrast. Carling Bassett was always the same, both on and off the court. She was aggressive but used a style that won people over to become fans. Jimmy Arias had an unwavering personality. He would bet on anything and was always coming at others, both on and off the court. Andre Agassi was an extremely competitive player, but not as loud as Arias in his words and actions. On court, however, he was relentless and often enjoyed punishing players by keeping them on the court much longer than he had to. Martina Hingis has an engaging smile and is quiet, but don't let that fool you. She is the most dangerous kind of player, a professional assassin with a smile.

Helping the Student's Game

I have always had a simple, uncomplicated approach to tennis and life. On and off court, in good times and bad, the art of reducing problems to their simplest form has served me well. As with life, teaching well can be simplified by reducing it to its basic elements. My experience has shown that at its simplest level, tennis can be divided into three sections: technique, mental ability, and physical conditioning.

I also try to identify and include in the equation inherited athletic traits; athletic background of the family; statistical analysis of playing characteristics; and testing to determine size, nutrition, and so on.

Before getting into grips, swings, and other intricate parts of the game, here are some key expressions used by coaches when teaching, by commentators when calling a match, and even by parents as they speak to their children.

Keeping the Ball in Play

Keeping the ball in play is known as consistency. The player should always have the goal of hitting the ball over the net one more time than the opponent does. Impatient players may want to go for a big shot early. Coaches can allow this, but they should make sure the player earns it by putting a specific number of balls in play before going for a winner. It is important to instill this idea in players who seek to take their game to another level. Examples of instructions to players are the following:

- Keep the ball in play but don't push.
- Keep the ball in play for a certain number of strokes, then go for the winner without waiting for margin of error.
- Keep the ball in play until the opponent misses.

Hitting to a Certain Spot

Hitting to a certain location is known as placement. The first priority is keeping the ball in play. The next challenge is to place the ball to selected areas.

Keeping the Opponent Deep

Depth prevents a player from gaining control. The player must achieve depth early in the development of a point. Adding more height clearance over the net will produce deeper balls.

Putting Action on Balls

Action on balls is known as variations of spin. Hitting the ball the same way all the time may not be enough to beat a good opponent, especially if the opponent tunes in to the player's single style of play. Adding spins to the ball can create a major weapon!

Having Power, or "Controlled Power"

Players must understand that power does not come about by sheer physical energy. Marcelo Rios was only five foot nine, yet he generated great power on serves and ground strokes. This power came from lots of practice, with timing and increased racket-head speed being the primary ingredients.

In sports, all athletes dream of being the best, but many underestimate the hard work, dedication, knowledge, and sacrifices it takes to excel in a sport. Anyone can have the dream, but only a special few have the talent it takes and consistently put in the work day after day, year after year. That's what players like Maria Sharapova are willing to do.

Players need to be familiar with the elements of their sport. In some fun way they must learn the feel and flow of the object of the sport, be it a ball, a puck, the water, or even a horse. For young tennis players, I first allow them to have fun while they develop their motor skills, their confidence, and an understanding of how and why balls bounce. This rhythm, this idea of becoming one with the ball, teaches the discipline needed to succeed at a game, a project, or a career. Children are sponges and acquire most of their knowledge in their first three years.

Beginners and even accomplished tennis players experimenting with new shots should not concern themselves initially that they are spraying balls all over the court. Rather, they should learn how the ball feels, how it bounces, and what it can do.

The level of understanding is simple:

1. Knowing something about the ball
2. Knowing how to get ready for the ball and how to move toward it
3. Knowing what happens at contact
4. Coordinating the racket, the body, and timing with the ball

This simplicity is evident in beginners and advanced players. The beginner should focus on contact rather than the construction of the shot. Consider the example of an advanced student being taught how to hit a slice. Before the student can perfect the shot, she must first know how it bounces, changes direction, moves forward or backward, and the rationale behind hitting a slice.

Nick's Tip

Coaches should teach one segment of the game; when that is understood, then go to the next adjustment or correction.

Only when the student understands all these concepts can a coach devise a practice session that will spill over effectively into matches. My most profound advice is to get to know the ball. It's impossible to have success with any sport, car, computer, mathematical problem, whatever, until you are completely at ease with the fundamentals. For instance, Dale Earnhardt Sr., once one of the best race-car drivers in the world, had a staff possessing the best mechanical expertise money can buy. Still, Earnhardt could tell you the amount of air in his tires and how the engine worked. It's the same story with Microsoft chairman Bill Gates. He can discuss every aspect of his business, from invention to sales.

I play simple games with my students to get them started. I ask them to see the ball as soon as they can and react to it. How a player reacts is indicative of the playing level:

- A *lower intermediate player* reacts to the ball after it bounces on his side.
- A *solid intermediate player* reacts to the ball as it crosses the net.

- An *advanced player* reacts to the ball when it leaves the opponent's racket.
- A *top player* can anticipate with accuracy what type of ball will cross the net and where it is likely to go by looking at the racket face, the level of contact, and the opponent's body position.

Racing experts say that Michael Schumacher knew his automobile so well and was so in tune with the feel and sounds that he knew how fast he's going within two miles per hour without looking at the speedometer. This quality made him among the best in the world.

The more a player can identify his opponent's tendencies, the more effective he'll be by not having to overanalyze every situation. Note the following:

- Players should be quick to read what type of ball they are receiving and where in the court they need to position themselves.
- Players should mentally track the tendencies of opponents—their favorite shots, habits under pressure, and preferred patterns of play.

Every player has a certain style. Pete Sampras hit the forehand relatively flat. On the backhand he could hit flat down the line and crosscourt with some spin. Monica Seles hit the ball early and had spin on both sides. Marcelo Rios hit the ball early and relatively flat on both sides. If the experts are largely predictable, at any lesser level it should be a snap to anticipate ball direction. Players should note these tips for picking up the ball early:

- Check the book on the opponent's preferences before the match.
- Observe the opponent's position, stance, and preparation.
- Note the angle of the racket.
- Notice whether the swing is low to high or high to low.
- Note the speed of the swing.

There are various ways a player can anticipate which type of serve is coming. These factors include the following:

- Height of the toss (i.e., does it vary with certain serves)
- Direction of the toss
- Variety of leg use
- Amount of hip and shoulder rotation

By looking for these clues, the player will be able to pick up the ball earlier. Baseball scouts are ahead of the field in this art. In an effort to anticipate what type of ball the pitcher will throw, they videotape pitchers and look for small differences on each pitch. It's the same for quarterbacks or backfield men in football. Running backs may set up in a different way if they are to block rather than carry the ball. By observing multiple repetitions, opponents or scouts can detect the little moves one makes without the ball. In a 1997 playoff game, the New England Patriots picked up on the signals of Dan Marino. They sacked him repeatedly or intercepted him. Result: Miami lost.

Through my years of teaching, one obvious standard has emerged. Students who give 100 percent have a better chance to reap the benefits. We tell all our students—full time, short time, adults, juniors, and professionals—that the two important tips to improving without taking a lesson are as follows:

- Never think you can't reach a ball. If you try for every ball, even the impossible ones, you'll reach balls you never thought possible.

- Never let the ball bounce twice in practice. If you train yourself in this manner, you will learn to pick up the ball earlier.

Making Changes for Long-Term Improvement

In almost every area of human endeavor, people are reluctant to change and may even fight it. The mere suggestion of change indicates that something is wrong with the status quo, a concept that most people have difficulty accepting. Changing the status quo may be unacceptable, especially for people who have had some success. More important, almost everyone is comfortable with the status quo.

If you ask someone to change, you must first be aware of the fear that change engenders. From a coach's point of view, allow me to share my experiences. A change in the grip, for example, will definitely be uncomfortable. No one knows if the change will be successful. As in all changes, much depends on the eagerness and determination of the one making the changes. But, as a coach, if you believe you are doing what is best for the student, you must take the challenge and face the risk. With most students, you must be prepared to deal with the student and their parents.

In making changes, consider the approach of making small adjustments so that the student isn't even aware that changes are being made. A good model is the dentist who distracts the patient when administering an uncomfortable shot. That is, you can prevent a student from thinking about the big changes by making small but gradual changes.

Some students are fearful of any change. With these students, major changes come about only if the coach is willing to do some ancillary work. In particular, the coach must first discuss with the student and the parents what the changes involve and what will likely happen to the student's game. Consider what happens when changing an extreme western grip to an eastern grip:

- A loss of power will occur. The extreme western grip offers the feeling of strength, great racket speed, and lots of spin, with the face of the racket closing very quickly.

- With the new grip the racket face will not close as quickly, and the ball will probably go high and out. The eastern grip may be too much change to effect in one step because strength issues, lack of racket speed, face on contact, and spin will result in all sorts of hits, including balls going high, deep, and far out of play.

- Physical discomfort (blisters) and mental anxiety (loss of confidence) will occur.

- The process may take a long time. The coach must realize it could require changing the student's practice sets and tournament play. The two options are making the change all at once or making the change in small segments to limit the trauma to the student.

Before making any changes, it is necessary to consider many factors:

Age of the student

Athletic ability of the student

Goals of the student

Rest of the student's game

Type of game the student plays

Present results as a player

Mental attitude of the student

Parents' ability to accept change

For instance, Pete Sampras accepted the wisdom of Dr. Fischer, a far older coach. Fischer advised Sampras that to compete at the top of the world one day, he needed to augment his God-given talents. Primarily, he had to change from a two-hand backhand to a one-hand backhand. This decision was difficult because Sampras had done reasonably well with his two-hand backhand. The discussion has been much talked about because Pete was only 14 at the time. It took two years of losses and the loss of his junior standing for Sampras to achieve his goal. You decide if it was worth it.

As someone who has changed many players, I find the method of making changes a little at a time the most interesting and most challenging. Trying to get a student to the next level by effecting some small change, particularly when the student fears change or is satisfied with success, is one of the most challenging obstacles any coach can confront. Our way is to accept their intransigence as a fact and to work indirectly.

For example, a student comes to us with a high circular backswing. We notice that on the run he has difficulty hitting a forehand crosscourt. The first thing we do is get the student to admit he has "some" difficulty hitting crosscourt. We use the word *some* because it's important not to destroy confidence or challenge the ego. The next step should be a discussion that contains the following elements:

1. Define the situation.
2. Be sure that both player and coach agree that a problem exists.
3. Determine the recommended solution.

Using this example, difficulty in hitting on-the-run crosscourt shots is usually caused by using too big a backswing; preparing too late, often caused by using a circular backswing that is too high or a double backswing; or allowing movement to upset timing. We counteract this by instructing the student to place the racket in a complete backswing before starting to run. Now the student need only swing forward to hit crosscourt. This invariably increases the chance of making the shot.

After considering all these factors, a coach must be patient and positive, working as much with a student's mental attitude as with the technicalities of change. Help from an outside source may be needed.

Conclusion

Coaches, educators, parents, and business people must understand the entire picture before considering changes and adjustments. In the next chapter, you will learn about the fundamentals of the game and be able to apply what is best for your game and the game of your student(s) remember, no two students are alike. What is beneficial for one student may be detrimental for another student.

Chapter 2

Fundamentals of Athletic Development

Tennis is a game of movement. You can't hit what you can't reach.

At IMG Academy, our tennis program includes instruction in the areas of technique, competition, physical conditioning, nutrition, mental conditioning, injury prevention and body management, leadership, life skills, and college preparation. You don't have to be a professional tennis player or a tennis superstar to be a total athlete. All players can maximize their performance by incorporating these elements into their training.

This chapter highlights all the keys that are imperative to becoming a well-rounded and successful player. As you progress through this book, if you are having trouble executing any of the skills, this is the chapter you'll want to return to for reviewing technique. From developing a solid athletic foundation and timing, to adaptability, stances, and grips, becoming a total athlete begins here! Each coach has their own approach to teaching the techniques of the game. In addition, there are students who are very successful with unorthodox strokes, physical, and mental parts of their games. I've learned over the years that there is no one right way to play the game. This chapter, however, will explain the foundations of the game, which apply no matter what style of game you play.

Nick's Tip

Adjustments and changes to technique are best implemented between the ages of 10 through 14.

Athletic Foundation

When players are just starting out, they develop with different styles and at different levels. As players develop, especially in the last few years of their junior development, their progress depends on one single factor: the presence of a strong and disciplined athletic foundation. The ability to maintain and defend a strong athletic foundation is the measure of a great tennis athlete and one of the most critical components in the evolution from junior to professional. Strangely enough, very few players and coaches put enough priority into specifically developing this athletic foundation and mastering the movement skills. As a result, the athletic foundation remains the most underdeveloped quality in most players, severely limiting their potential.

The construction of a house or building starts with a strong foundation. In the same way, when building a tennis player, you start with the foundation. It is a critical element for successful development. To better understand the concept of the athletic foundation, begin by exploring the design aspects involved in auto racing. The structural design and component aspects of any vehicle tell the story of the vehicle's intended function and determine its performance capabilities. Consider the Formula 1 racing car. Beneath the car's flashy exterior lies a sturdy frame reinforced by a very tight suspension for razor-sharp handling. The car's center of gravity hovers inches above the ground. The width of the wheelbase is proportionately very wide. Together, the wide base and low center of gravity enable the car to perform sharp turns at high speeds and achieve maximum stability against the forces that cause rollovers.

At the opposite end of the spectrum is a farm tractor. A tractor's design reflects the specific needs of a farmer. Acceleration, speed, and handling aren't requirements to succeed in farming. The tractor needs plenty of ground clearance and a high center of gravity to navigate a muddy field and stay above the crops without damaging them. Now imagine a Formula 1 car attempting to perform the off-road tasks of a tractor. Instantly, it gets stuck in the mud. Conversely, envision a tractor traveling at top speed through a road course. It's a rollover on the first corner. The point is exactly the same in understanding movement on the court. A player's form must be designed for optimal function.

The four essential structural features of the athletic foundation (figure 2.1) are:

Figure 2.1 Athlete in a proper athletic foundation.

1. Wide base of support
2. Low center of gravity
3. Balance on the balls of the feet
4. Reinforced back posture

Wide Base of Support

For quicker reaction time as well as better power and control in stroke production, the optimal footwork base is one and a half to three shoulder widths apart. With a wider base it becomes easier to keep the center of gravity low to the ground. If the footwork base is too narrow, it's difficult to remain low enough, and fatigue occurs much more quickly. A very narrow base leads to inefficient first-step reactions and typically results in

Nick's Tip

An athletic position gives you a burst of energy for a quicker start. Remember, this is not long-distance running. Tennis requires short, quick bursts of movement and recovery similar to short-distance sprinters.

too much upward launching through the stroke. The end result is a loss of power and control in stroke production.

Many players aren't comfortable establishing a wider footwork base because they believe it slows down their first-step reaction. However, there are techniques that top players develop to achieve explosive first-step reactions from a wider base.

Low Center of Gravity

The actual location of the center of gravity in humans varies by body type. In females, the center of gravity tends to be between the hips, whereas in males it tends to be slightly higher. The difference is nominal, so we typically refer to the hips as the reference point for the center of gravity.

When you are down in the athletic foundation position, you establish what is referred to as your "athletic height."

- Your athletic height should measure approximately 6 to 12 inches (15 to 30 cm) below your normal standing height.
- You achieve this low-to-the-ground position by bending your knees to lower your hips while maintaining upright back posture.

Most players have trouble maintaining a low enough athletic height during play simply because they haven't developed all the corresponding movement techniques associated with being low to the ground. In addition, it requires more leg strength and stamina to play low. Being able to maintain a consistent athletic height in your movement produces that smooth and fluid look of the champions. Great athletes make movement look effortless, although it takes a considerable amount of effort to create that look.

Some players try hard to play low but just can't seem to maintain the low athletic height. Coaches yell at them to "stay low," often to no avail. The fact is, if you've never practiced and trained your body how to move while maintaining a low center of gravity, you are not equipped with the athletic techniques to get the job done. In the long run, playing too upright is very inefficient. It produces poor results (on court) and causes fatigue much more quickly over the course of a match.

Nick's Tip

Because it is not easy to stay low and perform at the ideal athletic height, most players succumb to playing too upright much of the time. As a result, they develop inefficient movement habits that correspond with a high center of gravity. They end up moving more like that tractor.

Balance on the Balls of the Feet

Another skill you must learn is how to center your balance on the balls of the feet. Great athletes develop the ability to quickly use tiny adjustment steps to best position their feet and their balance to generate the stroke. Centering balance off the heels and onto the balls of the feet creates a lean of momentum forward for better reaction.

Reinforced Back Posture

Can a person's self-confidence be accurately assessed merely by observing body language? Most certainly. Typically, people tend to display low self-esteem and lack of confidence through poor back posture. Conversely, a person with high self-esteem and confidence tends to maintain strong, upright posture. Beyond being a measure of your self-confidence, strong back posture offers enormous physical benefits. It is the final link to reinforcing your entire athletic foundation:

- Intensely reinforced back posture efficiently channels the power generated from the lower body up to the shoulders to produce powerful strokes.
- Posture ensures that the shoulders remain level and stable during stroke production, especially critical when sliding on clay. The head should remain still and centered between the shoulders.

From a movement perspective, intensely reinforced back posture works like a tight suspension in a Formula 1 car. It enables quicker reactions and sharp changes of direction while resisting the forces of inertia that cause strokes to break down.

You've learned that when lifting heavy objects you should keep the back straight to avoid injury. This holds true when competing in sports such as tennis, where moving vigorously and creating powerful strokes are required. Learning to activate your back muscles with intensity to reinforce your posture creates an ideal support system for the shoulder mechanics.

Nick's Tip

The risk of injury increases dramatically when players misuse the back muscles and maintain weak posture. In addition to strong back muscles, great athletes need strength in the core muscles of the abdomen and around the hips.

Powerful Lower Body Muscles

The legs are the primary power source of movement, acting like the super-charged engine of the Formula 1 car. Powerful fast-twitch muscles generate explosive movement. The quads and thighs also serve as the essential braking mechanisms of movement. If you look at the top professional players, you'll notice their thighs and backsides are very well developed. This gives you an indication of how important lower body strength is to a tennis athlete's performance. Your quadriceps and gluteus must be in great shape to perform low to the ground like a Formula 1 car.

Tennis athletes develop a variety of footwork patterns that allow them to move quickly in any direction. Similar to the first gear in a Formula 1 car, the footwork strides must be short and quick to achieve rapid acceleration.

Laws of Physics and the Dynamics of Movement

Newton's laws of motion will help you better understand the dynamics of movement. The concepts of *mass, center of gravity, base of support, inertia,* and *momentum* explain how the laws of physics influence our ability to move and dictate the techniques that are most efficient.

The human body is an object that has mass and a center of gravity. The greater the size and weight of your body, the greater your mass. Objects with greater mass are harder to move. Your body's center of gravity is located between the hips and is the exact point where your body weight would be naturally balanced if you were lying down horizontally.

While standing, your base of support is the distance of your footwork base. The width of the base of support, relative to the height of the center of gravity, determines the degree of stability. Lying flat on the ground creates the greatest stability because the base of support is the entire length of your body and your center of gravity is barely off the ground. Standing upright with your feet close together results in the least stability because the base of support is very narrow and the center of gravity is in its highest position.

Inertia can be described as the tendency for an object at rest to remain at rest, until acted upon by another object or force. When force and acceleration are applied in a given direction, the body in motion establishes what is referred to as momentum—the tendency for an object to continue moving in the same direction unless acted on by a force, such as friction, or another object.

According to these principles of inertia, when your body is at rest or standing still, it has a natural tendency to remain there and not want to move. The greater your mass, the more strength and force required to get your body from at rest into motion, and once in motion, the more difficult it is for you to stop and reverse your body's momentum. When changing directions you are reversing the direction of momentum, which is the most demanding task of all. That is why your total body weight has such an impact on your quickness and agility. The bigger and heavier you are, the more lower-body strength is required to start, stop, and change directions. Reversing momentum is the ultimate test of the integrity of your athletic foundation, especially your back posture, to fight the forces of inertia as you put on the brakes and change directions.

By bending the knees and lowering the hips you lower your center of gravity. A position low to the ground enables you to better access the strength of your lower body muscles and achieve greater stability and control over your body mass. A wide footwork base creates less of a load on the leg muscles by distributing the body weight more into the hips and gluteus muscles. When you lower your center of gravity with your feet too close together, the load of your body weight distributes into the lower thighs just above the knees. A narrow base makes it more difficult to stay down, causing your leg muscles to fatigue more quickly. Learning to manage a consistently low center of gravity throughout play creates the fluid, smooth, and agile look of a pro. A wider footwork base of two or three shoulder widths enables you to go from at rest into motion more explosively, generate more power in your stroke production, and reverse directions more quickly.

Timing

Using lateral movement technique, how far can a player expect to move in less than two seconds? At an average rally speed, the ball travels from baseline to baseline in less than two seconds. Specifically, the average ball travel time from baseline to baseline is 1.5 seconds for juniors, 1.25 seconds for WTA players, and 1.1 seconds for ATP players. So, this means you have less than two seconds to react, move to the ball, and execute, followed by less than two seconds to fully recover.

Quick Start

Getting a quick start is far less important for a marathon runner in a 26-mile (42 km) race than for a sprinter running just 100 yards or meters. Explosive reaction time off the gun is critical in a very short race. Tennis could be considered nothing more than a series of short multidirectional sprints ranging from a few feet to less than 10 yards. So, like the sprinter, it is extremely important to react explosively off the opponent's strike of the ball and recover as quickly as possible if you want to stay ahead of the pace in a high-powered rally.

Tempo

The magic in great dancing is the synergy of moving in sync with the tempo and timing of the music. Tennis is as rhythmic and timing-based as dancing. If you listen to the sound of two players rallying back and forth, you'll hear a consistent rhythmic beat like the tick-tock tempo of a metronome or clock. Bounce–hit . . . bounce–hit . . . and so on. That bounce–hit rhythm sets the tempo for the timing of movement. A tempo that's out of rhythm results in the following:

- Players who are slow to react fall behind the tempo of the rally, which forces them to rush their movement to catch up.
- Late starts limit a player's range of effective court coverage and result in missed opportunities to play offensively.
- Slow reactions and sluggish recoveries create the look of a player whose timing is out of sync, always on the defensive and scrambling out of control to keep up with the rally.

Movement specialists such as Roger Federer, Rafa Nadal, and Novak Djokovic have mastered the skill of precisely timing their movement to stay slightly ahead of the pace of the rally. Federer's explosive, well-timed reactions; agile and smooth footwork; and instantaneous changes of direction on recovery enable him to look effortless in his work. He makes playing tennis look as fluid and artistic as ballet. It is that combination of technique and timing that makes it happen.

Recovery Time

The recovery phase is the time it takes for the ball to travel from your racket to your opponent. Recovery for the everyday player is normally nonexistent. At IMG Academy, our coaches focus a lot of time on this important skill.

To fully recover, you must position yourself at the midpoint of possible shots—that's halfway between the opponent's best shot options—before your opponent executes his next shot. So, once your shot reaches your opponent's racket, the recovery phase has expired and you must be prepared to react to the opponent's next shot. If you don't make it back to recovery position in time, you leave your court open for attack. When you continue to recover beyond the recovery time frame, it affects your ability to react to the opponent's next shot and can leave you vulnerable to shots hit behind you. Here are a few key points about recovery:

- Recovery positions change based on the direction and depth of your shots (more about recovery technique later in the chapter).
- Your shot selection affects your ability to recover as well. That's why you'll often see players pulled wide in a rally hit back crosscourt to continue the point because it provides the shortest distance to full recovery.

Adaptability

What makes professional tennis different from nearly every other sport is the fact that tennis pros have to compete on such a wide variety of playing surfaces. To be successful, you must learn how to quickly adapt every aspect of your game as conditions change (e.g., surface and speed changes, playing outdoors versus indoors, altitude changes). When Jimmy Connors was asked what adjustments he made in the transition of playing on hard courts, moving to clay, then to grass, he replied, "I get lower to the ground to play on clay and make myself play down even lower for the grass." The height of ball bounces off of clay, hard, and grass courts are all different. Each player must react to the bounce by utilizing the lower foundation, using the legs to get down to the level of the ball.

Let's take a look at this example: Years ago, most cars were rear-wheel drive. It was common in snowy conditions to see people strapping tire chains on the rear tires and loading sandbags into the trunk of the car to add weight and improve traction. Front-wheel-drive cars became a popular option because of improved performance and less hassle in the snow. Having the weight of the heavy engine directly above the front tires powering the car maximizes traction and handling. In reviewing the first-step reaction techniques, you will see how movement specialists incorporate the "front-wheel drive" concept into their movement. When on clay and grass, players with less efficient skills struggle like rear-wheel-drive cars in the snow.

Nick's Tip

The first-step reaction techniques that work best on clay and grass work best on all surfaces. That's why those players who are movement specialists on clay tend to be the best movers on all surfaces.

Reaction Techniques

Hitting the ball is only one part of the tennis puzzle. The first problem to solve is how to get to the ball in order to hit it.

Pre-Reaction Techniques

To stay up with the speed of play at the higher levels of tennis, players must anticipate well and rely on what we refer to as pre-reaction techniques. To better understand the concept, think of how sprinters position to start the race with their feet in starting blocks and their hands on the ground. It is the most powerful position of forward momentum so that when the gun sounds, they can achieve the quickest reaction and acceleration up to speed. Choosing to start in blocks is an example of a pre-reaction technique.

In tennis, players are typically positioned near the baseline during play, which leaves the short court vulnerable to attack from drop shots, angles, and mis-hit balls by the opponent. This is why high-level players use a variety of pre-reaction techniques, such as the drop-back, elevated splits, and combinations of the two, to defend the court and manage momentum more effectively.

Drop-Back

The drop-back maneuver (see figure 2.2, *a-b*) is commonly used by top players to position the upper body with forward momentum. When a player is positioned in the back court well behind the baseline, the short court is the most vulnerable against attack because it is farther away than balls to the left or right. The drop-back technique involves dropping the feet backward to position the upper body on a lean forward. It occurs not only during baseline rallies but also around the net when recovering after a volley.

Figure 2.2 Drop-back.

Elevated Split Step

The elevated split step (see figure 2.3, *a-b*) is a technique that movement specialists often use just before returning the serve and when moving laterally, timed with the opponent's point of contact. It is nothing more than a split step that elevates the body off the ground. When perfectly timed to the opponent's contact point, the defensive player elevates off the ground, determining where the next ball is going. By the time the feet hit the ground, the defensive player has already adjusted to land left foot then right to move right, or right foot then left to move left. The elevated split step enables players to ward off inertia and hit the ground moving with momentum in the right direction.

Drop-Back and Elevated Staggered Split

The drop-back and elevated staggered split landing of the feet can occur simultaneously (see figure 2.4, *a-b*). This is used for return of wide serves and when reacting to wide, fast shots from a stationary position.

First-Step Reaction Techniques

There is a natural tendency for your body at rest to resist reaction into motion. Overcoming this state of inertia requires strong fast-twitch

Figure 2.3   Elevated split step.

Figure 2.4   Drop-back and elevated staggered split.

muscles and efficient movement techniques. Equally as important, you must maintain a motivated mind-set to want to be explosive to make it happen.

Establishing upper body momentum in the direction of movement is essential for an explosive first-step reaction. Note the following:

- When your center of gravity is low, it is much more natural to establish upper body momentum in your reaction and movement technique.

- When your center of gravity is high, it is more likely you'll over-stride in your first step and be very slow to establish upper body momentum.

No matter what direction you are moving, you want your upper body leading the way and maintaining momentum until you begin to adjust your feet for the stroke. As you adjust your feet for the stroke, your upper body momentum should become more neutral, centering your balance on the balls of the feet. The width of the footwork base, the height of the center of gravity at the moment of reaction, and the conditions of the playing surface will determine which variation of first-step reaction technique a player may use.

Step-Out

The step-out move is acceptable when moving a very short distance, like stepping out to return a serve that is barely out of reach. But as a first-step reaction for balls more than a step or two away, the step-out reaction is very inefficient.

Too narrow a reaction base (approximately shoulder-width distance) and too high a center of gravity tend to produce the slowest first-step reaction maneuver. This step-out reaction tendency is common among recreational players. To better explain this inefficient movement, imagine a player positioned with a high center of gravity and narrow base reacting to his right to hit a forehand as follows:

1. The step-out footwork means the player pushes hardest with the left foot as he steps out and reaches with the right foot to move to the right.

2. As a result, this first-step reaction move fails to establish a position of upper body momentum, making it difficult to get the body into motion.

3. In addition, as his body weight shifts off the left foot, the left foot will often lose traction on clay, thwarting his first-step move. This common reaction flaw compares closely to the analogy of the rear-wheel-drive car in the snow.

Inside-Foot Pivot and Drive

When reacting from a wider footwork base, the inside-foot pivot and drive maneuver is the predominant first-step reaction technique top players use, particularly on hard court and carpet surfaces where traction is not an issue (see figure 2.5, *a-d*). You'll see this technique commonly used to set up a lunge transfer on return of serve, when reacting on volleys, or during ground-stroke rallies, as follows:

1. From a reaction footwork base equal to approximately two shoulder widths, you begin the maneuver with a quick, hard push off the outside foot (the foot opposite from the direction of movement), as the inside foot (the foot nearest to the direction of movement) pivots the toes to point in the direction of movement.

2. The outside foot essentially drives the body weight toward the inside foot until the body weight is positioned and loaded over the inside foot.

3. From this loaded position, the upper body is prepared to establish momentum in the direction of movement. With the body weight centered over the inside foot, the inside foot is in a position to drive hard with maximum traction.

Figure 2.5   Inside-foot pivot and drive.

You must use added caution when attempting the foot pivot and drive technique on more slippery surfaces. If you drive too hard off the outside foot and for too long, you'll risk losing traction as your body weight shifts off the outside foot. Also, be careful not to allow your inside foot to step out and reach toward the direction you want to move or it will slow your first-step reaction considerably. All you want to do is pivot the inside foot and use it to drive your body into motion.

▶ Drop Step and Drive

Many top players are reacting from footwork bases as broad as three shoulder widths, especially when playing on clay and grass. From such a wide base, the foot pivot and drive technique is not as effective at managing footwork traction or as quick at establishing upper body momentum. The drop step and drive is the quickest technique for reacting from a very wide base (see figure 2.6, *a-c*). It is a preferable maneuver, particularly on more slippery surfaces and when reacting to very challenging balls that are more than just a few steps away. It is commonly used on reaction during the heated rally exchanges. You'll also see the drop step and drive technique as a primary recovery maneuver when players are pulled wide off the court and must reverse momentum, then cover a significant distance very quickly.

Figure 2.6   Drop step and drive.

Here's an example:

1. The outside foot begins the maneuver by creating a controlled push, shifting the body weight toward the direction of movement as the inside foot slides under the torso, establishing upper body momentum in the direction of movement.

2. With the full weight of the body over the inside foot and the shoulders leading in the direction of movement, the inside foot has maximum traction for a powerful drive into motion.

Specialty Footwork Patterns

As a child, one of the first physical skills you learn is how to walk. When you walk, your base of support is narrow, about shoulder width. The center of gravity is high. Your stride lengths are slightly wider than shoulder width. These elements are analogous to the structural characteristics of the tractor. But in tennis, you'll never reach your athletic potential performing like a tractor. Instead you need to develop the performance characteristics of the race car.

The greatest tennis players are movement specialists: athletes who have learned how to transform their body structure to more resemble the design characteristics of a Formula 1 vehicle.

Top players use their movement strengths as weapons to dominate the opposition. They are explosive on reaction and quickly accelerate to cover every inch of court and maximize offensive opportunities. Fluid and agile footwork enables them to efficiently track down balls and smoothly execute their strokes, even under forcing pressure. Instantaneous changes of direction and sharp recovery skills are their weapons for defending the court, minimizing open-court opportunities for the opponent.

▶ Forward Sprint Footwork

To become quicker in your forward movement, maintain a low center of gravity, with your upper body momentum leading the way as you limit the length of your strides. Players who are very quick use first-gear footwork (see figure 2.7, *a-c*), meaning they run primarily on the balls of the feet using short, choppy strides while the feet remain approximately shoulder-width apart. The concept is to take shorter steps but more of them and pump the legs very rapidly to drive the body weight forward. It is similar to racing off the start in first gear on a 10-speed bike, which pumps the legs quickly. Traveling the same distance, a quicker player may take 15 push-off driving strides, whereas a slower player might take only 10 longer strides. The difference is the RPMs, or how quickly you can pump the legs.

Figure 2.7   Forward sprint footwork.

Lateral Sprint Footwork

The demands of tennis call for quickness in nearly every direction, but the majority of movement is lateral. Although it may be quicker just to turn sideways and sprint when running down a wide forehand, tennis players need to get to the ball not only in time but also in optimal position to execute the stroke. In situations where turning and sprinting is the best option to get to the ball, it is important to angle your upper body as you get close to the ball so that your shoulders turn toward the net as you set up. Lateral movement techniques enable you to flow more smoothly into the optimal hitting stance and execute. Let's look at the various lateral-movement footwork patterns.

Crossover

Crossover footwork is the quickest and most commonly used lateral footwork pattern. In this technique, the opposite foot crosses over in front of the foot nearest to the direction of movement (see figure 2.8, *a-c*). Think of it as

Figure 2.8   Crossover.

sprinting footwork except the core body remains more aligned toward the direction of the net rather than totally facing the direction you are running as you would to sprint. Although your shoulders are not completely turned in the direction you are running, you still want the shoulders leading the way to provide upper body momentum as you cross over. The crossover pattern is effective for covering greater distances laterally, whether you are moving to the ball or moving back on recovery.

Shuffle

Shuffle footwork is a lateral movement technique where the feet come together in the movement but never cross over, used primarily on recovery (see figure 2.9, *a-c*). There is definitely a time and place for shuffle

Figure 2.9   Shuffle.

footwork in everyone's game. When you have to move a greater distance on recovery, you should use the crossover pattern for the first couple of strides and then transition into the shuffle footwork as you get closer to recovery position. Using a combination of footwork patterns enables you to initially cover more ground; as you get nearer to recovery position and reaction, shuffling allows you to neutralize your body momentum as you continue to move and flow seamlessly into the reaction split-footwork base.

Because it naturally limits body momentum, shuffle footwork is effective only for moving shorter distances. Too many players use shuffle footwork when they should be using crossover footwork. For instance, from a wide position in the court, they try to shuffle the whole way back on recovery, which is too slow to be effective. Only when the ball is within one or two steps would you want to use shuffle footwork to get there.

Cross-Behind

In the cross-behind pattern, the opposite foot crosses behind the foot nearest to the direction of movement. Not as commonly used as the crossover, the cross-behind step is still a very versatile technique. This footwork helps you maintain sideways alignment to the net when moving back to cover deep balls and on the follow-through when moving forward through slice approach shots. You'll also use the cross-behind step to move one step laterally, to quickly position and simultaneously load the body weight for the runaround forehand.

Kick Step

A variation of the cross-behind step in forward movement is the kick step. It is called a kick step because the shin of the rear leg often collides into the calf of the front leg, almost kicking the front leg forward. The kick step is an effective maneuver on both the forehand and backhand side for moving one stride forward in a neutral hitting stance to hit a shorter ball.

What Are Adjustment Steps?

When you are watching the top players, their adjustment steps happen so quickly you may not always see them, but on the hard courts you can definitely hear them—those chirping squeak noises as the player sets up the stance to strike the ball. Adjustment steps slow down the body's directional momentum as well as arrange the feet into an optimal hitting stance. What triggers the feet to set up for the stroke is a natural process involving a relationship between the hands and the feet.

Essentially, the feet adjust and set up automatically based on the position of the dominant hand in racket preparation. For example, on a right-handed forehand, if the right hand reaches out, the right foot will set up beneath it, triggering an open stance. Now, if the right hand goes back behind the body into a deep backswing, the right foot will stay back with the right hand, causing the left foot to set up in a closed stance. So for setting up the optimal stance for every situation, your racket should be prepared ahead of your body as you close into position and before you begin your adjustment steps to allow yourself enough time to set your feet for the shot. When the backswing is too large and gets behind your back, the butt of the racket points toward the side fence, sending the wrong message down to the feet, triggering the feet to set up in a less preferable closed stance. When your racket preparation positions the racket in front of your body, the butt of the racket will point in the direction of the net, which sends the correct message to the feet that you need a stance that enables you to create power in that direction.

Hitting Stances

There are differences of opinions in the coaching community as to which stances should be used when hitting the ball. No matter what your level of play, different court surfaces, lack of time, or difficult positioning will result in the need to use different hitting stances. For this reason, I suggest that players learn all the variations including the closed, neutral, and open stances. I have had the best success starting young children with the neutral stance, but first I always see what they do naturally without direction, and if that's successful, I let it be.

▶ Closed Stance

When the front foot points in the direction of the side fence with the feet spread apart parallel to the baseline, it is considered a closed stance (see figure 2.10). This applies to one- and two-hand backhands. However, there are many problems associated with the closed stance as it relates to all strokes, one being that it restricts the core rotation required to power those strokes and makes it more difficult for recovery. In addition, especially out wide in the court, you need to present a triple threat in the mind of the opponent: capable of striking crosscourt, to the middle, or down the line with equal control and power.

A fully closed stance limits a player's shot options, making shot selection more predictable under pressure as balance, control, power, and direction are compromised by the stance. And worse yet, because of the high degree of torque and twisting the body must endure, the potential for repetitive injury in the lower body increases dramatically. Stress fractures of the feet, strained tendons in the ankles, torn ligaments in the knees, and even many lower back injuries can be attributed to the stress associated with the habits of repetitively hitting from a fully closed stance.

Figure 2.10   Closed stance.

Many years ago when I was working with Monica Seles, she developed a lower back strain from hitting with a closed stance. We worked to get her front foot to point to the target area, which solved the problem. To break the habit of hitting from the closed stance, you must make changes in your racket preparation to ensure the dominant hand is leading ahead of your body as your feet begin the adjustment steps.

▶ Neutral Stance

When the stance is perpendicular to the baseline and the front foot points toward the net, it is called a neutral stance (see figure 2.11). When you have time to set up, the optimal choice is to set up the back foot and then drive forward into a neutral stance. It is considered the ideal hitting stance for situations when you have the opportunity to step forward to hit and time permits. The weight transfer in a neutral stance starts on the back foot, and as the swing starts forward the weight drives to the front foot before contact.

When performed optimally, the weight transfer generates a pivoting turn of the core body to help power the stroke. So the power achieved in a neutral stance comes more from the pivoting action than from the linear back-to-front movement. It is very important to maintain your athletic foundation to manage the weight transfer. Be sure to take your wide recovery step, which will also help you rotate your hips and shoulders, and then push off to start your recovery.

Figure 2.11   Neutral stance.

▶ Semi-Open Stance

The semi open stance is between the neutral stance and the open stance (see figure 2.12). The position on the court and the difficulty of the oncoming ball will cause the player to naturally adjust their stance without even thinking about it.

Figure 2.12   Semi-open stance.

▶ Open Stance

When the feet and hips are aligned parallel to the baseline, similar to a traditional split step, it is called the open stance (see figure 2.13). In situations where you are under pressure with very little time to set up, the open stance is your best option. Being able to effectively execute from the open stance is a required element in today's fast-paced game on both the forehand and backhand sides.

Figure 2.13 Open stance.

The open stance is most commonly used in situations where time to set up is very limited, especially when pushed very wide in the court, when hitting a half volley inside the baseline, when hitting a return of a high-velocity first serve, or when in a ready position close to the baseline.

For many players, the open stance is their preferred stance even when there is time to step forward into the neutral. To hit the open stance effectively, you have to load the body weight on the foot closest to the ball and avoid transferring your body weight toward the other foot. In addition, it is important to pivot your hips and shoulders to face contact in the loading process. Variations on the finish include hitting static from the open stance, transferring with a lunge to strike, or transferring to the neutral stance after contact. Have your coach make sure your outside knee is pointed to the opposite side. If it is not, you will have difficulty with your balance and stroke.

Loading Up

The concept of loading up refers not just to creating the right stance for a situation but also to positioning the core body weight properly in the stance. Following are guidelines for each of the stances:

- For an open stance, stay low in your athletic foundation, and load the body weight over the foot nearest to the ball so that the heel of that foot naturally elevates slightly off the ground. Hips and shoulders should be turned to face contact.
- For a neutral stance, your athletic foundation and body weight should be loaded into the back foot, prepared to transfer forward into the stroke.
- For a closed stance, it is much more difficult to load up because your weight is parallel to the net. If you have to hit from a closed stance, have your weight and body going in the same direction towards the target. It's very difficult to hit standing still from a closed stance.

Hitting on the Run

One shortfall of tennis instruction in many parts of the world is that conventional teaching methods usually have young players standing still as they learn the strokes. The moment players try to rally or play a match, their strokes tend to break down easily because they haven't learned the skills of moving and hitting. In some parts of the world such as the Czech Republic and Spain, they approach it very differently. They introduce beginners to moving and hitting from day one. Young players quickly become comfortable with the flow of movement into a stroke and find earlier success sustaining rallies. At IMG Academy, we focus a tremendous amount of time and effort on the development of efficient movement technique at every level of play.

Nick's Tip

Teachers need to determine the method that best fits the student. Young players between ages four and seven do better when they learn the stroke first and then integrate the movement. With young children, movement to the ball should be limited. Once they have the concept of the stroke technique, they can begin movement.

The running open stance and the load and lunge are two advanced running stances that will help transition a player from a running position into a hitting position.

▶ Running Open Stance

The running open stance (see figure 2.14, *a-c*) is basically a hard-surface technique. It enables players to maintain control of their momentum, flowing seamlessly through the stroke. On the run, the last step before the hit sets up a loaded open stance. As the swing starts forward, the outside leg starts to cross in front of the body to counterbalance the weight

Figure 2.14   Running open stance.

of the stroke. It happens too fast in real play for the naked eye, but on video you can see that the crossing foot does not touch ground until after contact is made with the ball. That's why it is not considered hitting from a closed stance.

Braking

Recovering while hitting on the run requires that you put on the brakes and reverse direction as rapidly and efficiently as possible. At the pro level, braking techniques are some of the most stressful movements in tennis, which is why it is important that they be clearly understood. If not done correctly, this can be the cause of many injuries, especially when you add sliding into hitting on the run.

Stroke and Skid

The stroke and skid is one of the most stressful moves in tennis. This maneuver can easily turn an ankle if the upper body momentum doesn't reverse itself enough in the course of the stroke. Even when done efficiently, skidding on hard courts can create stress fractures and strain ankle, knee, and hip ligaments. It is typically employed on clay courts, but some pro players are increasingly using this braking technique on hard courts as well.

Nick's Tip

To be a more effective clay court player, you have to be able to slide into your strokes. Those who can't slide tend to run through the stroke like on hard court, skidding to a stop well after the stroke. This adds distance to the recovery and wastes time and energy.

Kick-Out Steps

Sliding or skidding far on hard courts should be avoided because of risk of injury. Kick-out steps are a safer alternative. This technique works like antilock brakes in a car. The speed and force moving into the stroke will determine whether it takes more than one kick-out step to stop and reverse your momentum. Sometimes it's better to take another step or two in the same direction after hitting the ball.

Players should try to point their foot into the kick-out or skid to reduce the possibility of rolling the ankle. Work to keep your body upright or leaning back toward the center of the court to minimize the force into the braking foot and prevent having to push off the outside foot too hard on recovery.

Load and Lunge

The load and lunge (see figure 2.15, *a-d*) is a more extreme variation of the running open stance that creates an explosive burst of momentum toward contact to begin the forward swing, turning running shots into weapons. Be careful, however, only a few can do this.

The load and lunge transfers upper body momentum into extra loading in the rear leg. The timing of the leg crossing works exactly in sync with the start of the forward swing. This in turn drives the body diagonally forward toward contact even when the player is moving to the side. This technique works equally well on both the forehand and backhand sides, and for both the one- and two-hand backhands.

Figure 2.15   Load and lunge.

Built-in Recovery

If I were pinned down to offering just two tips to help players improve, one of those tips would be related to recovery. It is extremely important for the player to get back into position after hitting a shot. As I watch juniors, adults, and even some pros, I can't help but notice how little recovery techniques are implemented, especially among everyday players.

One way to become quicker at getting back for the next shot is to develop what is called built-in recovery. That means when you are stretched wide and have a long way to travel back, you build a lower body change of direction into the follow-through. Depending on the situation and surface, there are a few common variations of the built-in recovery.

Open-Stance Slalom Recovery

For the open-stance slalom recovery, like a downhill skier changing directions in the turn around the slalom flag, the lower body shifts underneath the core to reverse directional momentum in the course of the stroke (see figure 2.16, *a-b*). By the time follow-through is complete, your upper body is positioned for momentum to lead the way back.

Neutral-Stance Pivot Recovery

The neutral-stance pivot is another common recovery pattern, particularly when the player is coming forward on a diagonal (see figure

Figure 2.16 Open-stance slalom recovery.

Figure 2.17 Neutral-stance pivot recovery.

2.17, *a-b*). This pattern occurs when you are deep in the court and are chasing a ball that is short on the other side of your court. With this breaking pattern, the body weight drives forward into the neutral stance. The weight drives into the front foot as it touches down, forcing the dominant side to pivot around so the body is facing the net on the finish. The result is that the back leg swings around into a split-step ready position to begin recovery.

Lateral Recovery

The key to the lateral recovery movement back toward the middle when you've been stretched out wide is shoulder alignment facing the net with an upper body lean in the direction of movement (see figure 2.18, *a-b*). Players must resist the temptation to turn and sprint back to the middle. Although sprinting may be the fastest way to move, keeping the chest facing the net and using lateral movement keeps you prepared to quickly change directions if the opponent hits behind you. Move as quickly as possible using crossover and shuffle footwork until you reach a full recovery position or until the opponent is about to make contact. Whether you reach full recovery position in time or not, you need to split-step at the opponent's contact to react on time to the next shot. If you fail to split-step on time, you will be late on reaction to the next shot.

Figure 2.18   Lateral recovery.

▶ Racket Grips

In my early days of teaching, I went to the books. The experts defined and described the grips, and that was it. I'm happy I don't follow directions well because I quickly realized each person's style and grips would be individual to that person. No more going by those books. Many factors come into play when selecting grips:

- Dealing with bounces off different court surfaces
- Handling balls of varying heights
- Adding spins to the ball
- Having weapons with minor grip changes
- Hitting the ball on the rise
- Using one hand versus two hands

Certain grips seem to perform better on certain shots. If I had to give you only one grip for each part of the game, here's what they would be:

- *Forehand*: Semiwestern
- *One-hand backhand*: Strong eastern or semiwestern for more spin
- *Two-hand backhand*: Strong eastern for the top hand and a continental for the bottom hand
- *Serve*: Continental to eastern

Keep in mind, however, that the age of the player would also influence the grip I recommend for some shots. For example, for very young kids I would recommend an eastern forehand grip for the serve. When players hit specialty shots their grips will change—there are grips that handle the slice, drop shot, volley, and kick serve better than others.

Grips will have a major influence on just about everything, including the following:

- The ability to develop spin
- The ability to hit flat drives
- The ability to handle high or low balls
- The ability to develop angles, drop shots, and lobs

You name it and the grip will make a difference. For example, player A has an eastern forehand grip. Player B has a semiwestern grip, and his style of play is hitting high, looping, and heavy topspin shots that bounce high in the air. Player A with his eastern grip will have a difficult time trying to consistently bring those balls back down into the court with any pace.

To locate each grip, place the base knuckle of the index finger and the heel pad of the palm on the numbered bevel shown in figure 2.19. This will ensure that the hand is correctly aligned on the grip. For example, the continental grip is located by placing the base knuckle on bevels 1 and 2 (top bevel and top right bevel) and the heel pad of the palm on bevel 2.

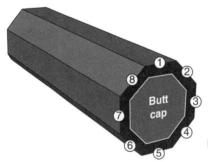

Figure 2.19   Bevels on a racket.

Table 2.1 provides an overview of all grips for both right- and left-handed players. We hope you find it useful in gaining a greater understanding of each grip.

In addition, using the proper grip pressure is important, regardless of your grip. Holding the grip too tightly, a common problem, will restrict your flexibility. Keep your hand relaxed, especially between shots, and let the racket do the work. (Try squeezing hard on a tennis ball. See how quickly you begin to lose feeling and how quickly your arm becomes tired.) A baseball pitcher doesn't hold the ball with a death grip, nor does a golfer hold the club too tightly.

Table 2.1 Grip Reference Chart

One-hand grips	Right-handed player		Left-handed player	
	Base knuckle	Heel pad	Base knuckle	Heel pad
Continental	2	1-2	8	1-8
Eastern forehand	3	2-3	7	7-8
Eastern backhand	1	1-8	1	1-2
Semiwestern forehand	4	4	6	6
Semiwestern backhand	8	8	2	2
Western forehand	5	5	5	5

Two-hand grips	Right-handed player				Left-handed player			
	Bottom hand		Top hand		Bottom hand		Top hand	
	Base knuckle	Heel pad	Base knuckle	Heel pad	Base knuckle	Heel pad	Base knuckle	Heel pad
Eastern forehand/ eastern forehand	2	2-3	7	7-8	7	7-8	3	2-3
Eastern forehand/ semiwestern forehand	3	2-3	6	6	6	6-7	4	4
Eastern forehand/ western forehand	3	2-3	5	5	7	7-8	5	5
Eastern backhand/ semiwestern forehand	1-8	8	6	6	1-2	2	4	4
Continental/eastern forehand	2	1-2	7	7-8	8	1-8	2	2-3
Continental/semiwestern forehand	2	1-2	6	6	8	1-8	4	4
Continental/western forehand	2	1-2	5	5	8	1-8	5	5

One-Hand Grips

Players use four basic one-hand grips:

- Continental
- Eastern
- Semiwestern
- Western

Each of these grips has advantages and disadvantages. Ultimately, players need to use a grip that provides a blend of consistency, control, and power for their style of play.

Continental Grip

The continental grip was once the universal grip used to hit forehands, backhands, specialty shots, volleys, overheads, and the serve. It originated on the soft, low-bouncing clay courts of Europe. Although it has been superseded in today's game, it still serves as the foundation grip for the drop shot, volley, serve, and overhead for most players. The continental grip is my preferred grip for teaching the volley to advanced players; it does not require a grip change, and it offers the most support to the wrist when hitting forehand and backhand volleys. In today's game, it is the preferred grip for most top professionals for the drop shot, volley, serve, and overhead. Don't forget that top players use this grip when stretched out wide hitting on the run in order to gain time by hitting a slow underspin slice deep to their opponent's court. See table 2.2 for a list of the advantages, disadvantages, and recommended uses for this grip.

Table 2.2 Continental Grip: Advantages, Disadvantages, and Recommended Uses

Advantages	• Low balls and stretch balls • Control • Transition to the net • Drop shot • Spin on serve • Underspin on volleys • Serve and volley
Disadvantages	• High balls • Cannot generate a lot of topspin • Difficult to generate power • Specialty shots—topspin angles and lobs • Weak forearm • Requires impeccable timing
Recommended for	• Volleys—grip provides support for both the forehand and backhand volley and can apply touch and spin • Drop shots—grip is used very effectively for drop shots, one of the biggest weapons on the tour today. • Slices—grip can be used for offensive slices, but I think the eastern grip is a little better for the backhand slices • Defensive shots—grip can be used when pulled out wide to buy time by applying slice to the forehand or backhand • Serve—grip can be used for the serve
Not recommended for	• Backhand baseline rallies

This grip allows the net player to execute the drop shot, serve, overhead, and forehand and backhand volleys without changing grips. To locate the continental grip, place the base knuckle of the index finger on bevels 1 and 2 and the heel pad of the palm on bevel 2 (see figure 2.20).

Continental Forehand

As tennis has evolved, the continental forehand grip has become forgotten. It has almost been eliminated from the modern game; in fact, I forbid it. It requires an exceptionally strong forearm and impeccable timing. Many old-timers, however, still use this grip. In today's game, if you use this grip, you'll have to exaggerate your follow-through and move back when facing high balls so you can hit your shot from low to high.

Continental Backhand

The continental backhand grip is used less often today to hit the power backhand; it's just about obsolete except among old-timers. Although effective for producing a slice backhand, the continental grip does not provide the strength or stability in the racket head to handle powerful ground strokes from an opponent. It is difficult to produce topspin, and I recommend it only to players who are learning to slice.

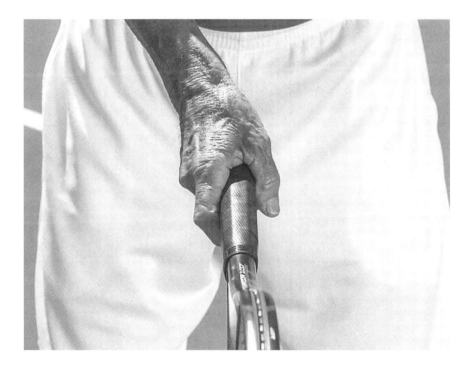

Figure 2.20   Continental grip.

Eastern Grip

The Eastern grips evolved from the Continental grips, which were extensively used in the early part of the 20th century. As court surfaces changed from predominately grass and low bouncing surfaces to hard and higher bouncing surfaces and players envisioned hitting more aggressive ground strokes with higher margins for errors, the Eastern grips became more popular.

See table 2.3 for a list of the advantages, disadvantages, and recommended uses for this grip.

Eastern Forehand

The eastern forehand is the classic forehand grip. The eastern grip originated on the medium-bouncing courts in the eastern United States. The eastern grip offers flexibility for individual styles, comfort for beginners, and versatility for all surfaces. This is the simplest grip to learn and use. To locate the eastern forehand grip, position the base knuckle of the index finger on bevel 3 and the heel pad of the palm on bevels 2 and 3 (see figure 2.21, *a-b*).

Table 2.3   Eastern Grip: Advantages, Disadvantages, and Recommended Uses

Advantages	• Easy for beginners • Fairly easy to generate power • Waist-high balls • Adaptable for different surfaces • Variety—topspin, underspin, flat drive
Disadvantage	• Difficult for very high balls
Recommended for	• Serve—grip can be used on the serve to apply spin and kick • Slice • Drop shots
Not recommended for	• Young players

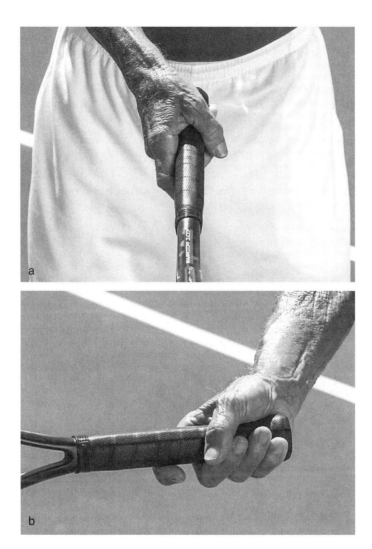

Figure 2.21   Eastern forehand grip: (a) front and (b) side.

Nick's Tip

Some players naturally adopt "the hammer grip" on the forehand, with all the fingers together and the thumb touching the index finger. When using that grip, most players experience a loss of feel and control. I instruct my students to spread the index finger out to improve both feel and racket-head stability at contact. If a student has success with the hammer grip, though, let it be.

Eastern Backhand

The eastern backhand, the classic backhand grip, offers stability and allows the player to drive the ball and hit with topspin. Pete Sampras and Petr Korda are among the past professionals who employed this grip. Today Roger Federer and others have chosen a semiwestern for the most part but keep the eastern for slices, drop shots, and some volleys. I recommend to most players that they adopt a strong eastern grip on topspin backhands. To locate the eastern backhand grip, position the base knuckle of the index finger on bevel 1 and the heel pad of the palm on bevels 1 through 8 (see figure 2.22, *a-b*). Essentially, from the eastern forehand grip, a quarter turn to the left yields the eastern backhand. The base knuckle of the index finger should move from bevel 3 to bevel 1. The heel pad should move from bevels 2 and 3 to bevels 1 through 8.

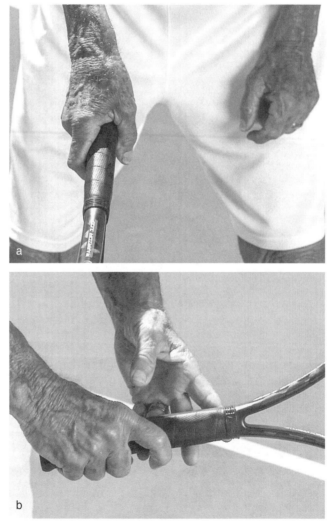

Figure 2.22 Eastern backhand grip: (*a*) front and (*b*) side.

Semiwestern Grip

The game has become much more powerful, including defending against deep, heavy, and penetrating rollers and kick serves. Many of the top players have adjusted their grips to handle these shots with a semiwestern grip. This grip also allows the player to hit the ball on the rise and come over high bouncing balls by applying excessive racket-head acceleration.

See table 2.4 for a list of the advantages, disadvantages, and recommended uses for this grip.

Table 2.4   Semiwestern Grip: Advantages, Disadvantages, and Recommended Uses

Semiwestern forehand	
Advantages	• Shoulder-high balls • Heavy topspin ground strokes • Hitting the big, heavy-spin power ball • Swinging volleys with power and spin • Disguise on shots
Disadvantages	• Low balls • Difficult to apply slice on drop shots • Difficult to volley very low balls • Major grip change required
Recommended for	• Majority of groundstrokes
Not recommended for	• Touch shots, slices and drop shots
Semiwestern backhand	
Advantages	• Applying topspin • Specialty shots—angles and topspin lobs from medium-height balls • Heavy spin from high rally balls
Disadvantages	• Difficult to apply underspin • Difficult to hit drop shots • Difficult to hit the flat drive • Difficult to hit very low balls
Recommended for	• Majority of groundstrokes
Not recommended for	• Touch shots, slices, and drop shots

Semiwestern Forehand

This grip offers both strength and control to the forehand. Beginners feel comfortable with it because the palm of the hand supports the racket and provides additional racket-head stability at contact. It is especially suited for hitting powerful topspin and loop forehands. To locate the semiwestern forehand grip, position the base knuckle of the index finger on bevel 4 and the heel pad of the palm on bevel 4 (see figure 2.23, *a-b*).

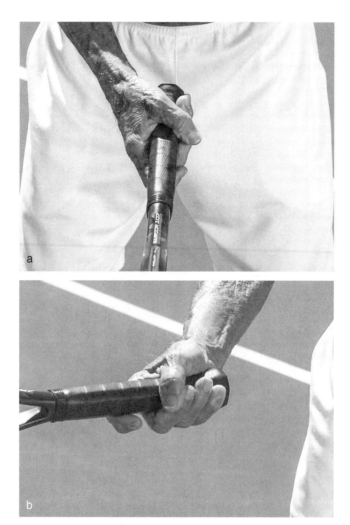

Figure 2.23   Semiwestern forehand grip: (*a*) front and (*b*) side.

Semiwestern Backhand

The semiwestern backhand is the same as the semiwestern forehand in reference to the hand and the racket, but reversed. This grip offers considerable topspin but requires strength and ability to accelerate the racket on contact. This grip tends to cause the player to lead with the elbow during the forward swing. A more advanced player might consider this grip. Professional players use it frequently when hitting topspin lobs and angle shots. I do not recommend this grip for the majority of players. To locate the semiwestern backhand grip, position the base knuckle of the index finger on bevel 8 and the heel pad of the palm on bevel 8 (see figure 2.24, *a-b*).

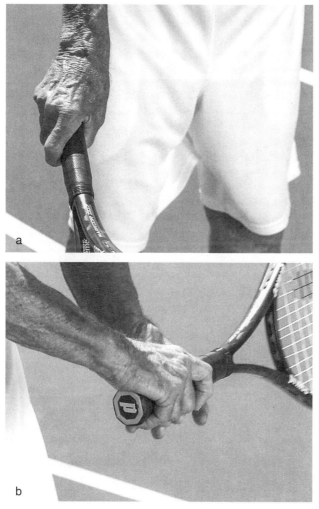

Figure 2.24   Semiwestern backhand grip: (*a*) front and (*b*) side.

Western Grip

This grip originated on the high-bouncing cement courts of the western United States. The drawback of this grip is that it closes the racket face too soon before contact. This is an excellent grip for high balls and topspin but is awkward for low balls and underspin. To play with this grip successfully demands a very strong hitting foundation, a strong forearm, excessive racket-head acceleration, and a follow-through out toward the target and finishing around waist high. To locate the western forehand grip, position the base knuckle of the index finger on bevel 5 and the heel pad of the palm on bevel 5 (see figure 2.25, *a-b*). Note that the western backhand grip is extremely difficult to be successful with. I'd say 99.9 percent of players should never use this grip (see figure 2.26, *a-b*).

See table 2.5 for a list of the advantages, disadvantages, and recommended uses for this grip.

Figure 2.25   Western forehand grip: (*a*) front and (*b*) side.

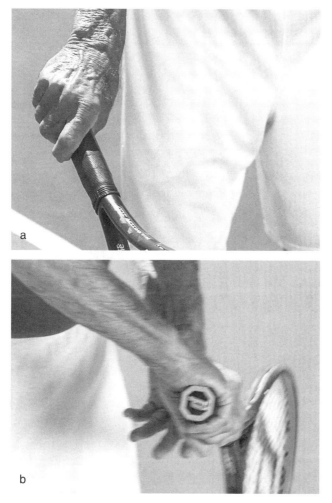

Figure 2.26 Western backhand grip: (a) front and (b) side.

Nick's Tip

For several reasons, the semiwestern and western grips are more common than in years past. While you are young, these grips may seem the most comfortable. As your game develops, you should use grips that complement the style of play you like best. A grip adjustment requires patience and hard work and for the most part should be done between ages 11 and 14. After that, be careful with drastic changes, but I stand firm that a semiwestern grip for forehands would be my choice.

Table 2.5   Western Grip: Advantages, Disadvantages, and Recommended Uses

Advantages	• Best for very high balls • Can attack high balls • Can generate immense racket-head speed • Can produce considerable topspin • Good for topspin lobs and angles from medium-height balls
Disadvantages	• Very difficult to lift low balls • Cannot slice, chip, or hit drop shots • Very large grip change required • Difficult to drive the ball—passing shots
Recommended for	• Forehand baseline rallies—can be used effectively on the forehand to provide a lot of spin and easily hit high bouncing balls
Not recommended for	• Very difficult to execute on low bouncing balls, volleys, and one-hand backhands

Two-Hand Grips

I will go on record by saying this: Coaches must be open to just about everything, as I was when becoming the coach of Monica Seles. So many of the experts thought I would change her two-hand grips, but I stayed with them and the results speak for themselves. The two-hand grips, however, in general require the player to stay closer to the baseline. The two-hand backhand gives you less reach when you are stretched out wide and come forward for short balls. Monica Seles stood right on the baseline.

Pancho Segura, Monica Seles, Jan-Michael Gambill, and Fabrice Santoro were a few of the players who had success using a two-hand forehand. Gambill and Santoro were outstanding players who used two hands on both sides but varied in style of play. Jan-Michael was much more aggressive and hit with less spin, whereas Fabrice was a counterpuncher with many specialty shots.

Nick's Tip

When discussing two-hand grips, it is important to understand that depending on the grip set, the roles of each hand can work differently.

If a player hits with two hands off both sides and does not change the position of the hands, the top hand is not able to play the same role on both sides. For example, Monica Seles as a left-hander had a traditional two-hand backhand. On her forehand side, because she didn't switch her hands, it was a cross-handed grip set. That meant to generate power, her top right hand worked to pull the racket head through contact as the bottom hand anchored the butt end. On her true backhand side, the top right hand worked to drive the racket head forward and was her stronger side as a result.

With an eastern backhand bottom hand (like Borg and Mats Wilander) and even in some versions of the continental where both arms are fully extended at contact (like Agassi), the bottom hand can work in a see-saw-like fashion to drive the racket head into contact. That means the role of the top hand is to provide support in the leverage action, the same way a fulcrum supports the plank of a seesaw. In continental grip swings that have the bottom arm bent at contact, and all forehand bottom-hand grip varieties, the bottom hand merely provides an anchoring pivot point in the moments leading into contact, while the top hand drives the racket head action into contact.

With most of my players, I encouraged the use of the continental grip with the bottom hand because I find it to be most versatile. I find the eastern backhand grip on the bottom hand tends to be a little too wristy. I want the bottom hand to be the support hand to make sure the butt of the racket goes through the contact point and continues out toward the target.

In most grip sets today, the top hand is driving the power. However, players who aren't naturally coordinated with the nondominant arm will take much longer to develop coordination. Most players today are using either an eastern or a semiwestern grip on the top hand.

Several variations of grips are used today when hitting with two hands. They apply to both the two-hand forehand and two-hand backhand. The grip variations for the two-hand forehand and the two-hand backhand are essentially the same. The only difference is whether the right or left hand is on top. Note that the photos are of a right-handed player, but the grip reference table (table 2.1) will help you locate grips for the left hand.

Table 2.6 shows various combinations available; note, however, that I cover only a few of our favorites.

Let's look at the most common grip sets we recommend.

Two-Hand Backhand Grip: Eastern Backhand–Eastern Forehand

Figure 2.27 shows the bottom hand with a continental and the top hand with an eastern.

Table 2.6 Two-Hand Grip Combinations

Bottom hand	Top hand
Eastern forehand	Eastern forehand
Eastern backhand	Semiwestern forehand
Eastern forehand	Western forehand
Eastern forehand	Semiwestern forehand
Continental	Eastern forehand
Continental	Semiwestern forehand
Continental	Western forehand

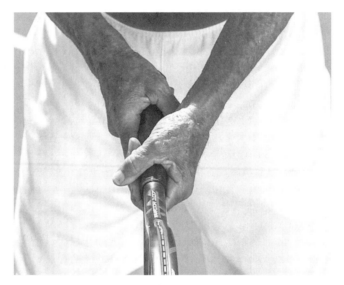

Figure 2.27 Eastern backhand–eastern forehand.

Two-Hand Backhand Grip: Eastern Backhand–Semiwestern Forehand

This not so common grip combination enables the player to become balanced in dominance, and perhaps even more dominant with the bottom hand. It works well for players looking to feature their naturally dominant side. The eastern backhand grip on the bottom hand creates leverage similar to how a hockey stick works. The semiwestern grip of the top hand provides an ideal amount of support as the bottom hand works to drive the racket head forward.

To locate the eastern backhand–semiwestern grip, position the bottom-hand base knuckle of the index finger on bevel 1 and the heel pad of the palm on bevel 8. Place the top-hand base knuckle of the index finger on bevel 6, with the heel pad of the palm on bevel 6.

Two-Hand Backhand Grip: Continental–Eastern Forehand

This grip allows the player to let go with the top hand on contact and hit a one-hand slice, drop shot, or volley with a continental grip. Although the top hand does not provide as much support as it does with a semiwestern grip, this grip combination will serve the player well.

To locate the continental–eastern grip, position the bottom-hand base knuckle of the index finger on bevel 2 and the heel pad of the palm on bevels 1 and 2. Place the top-hand base knuckle of the index finger on bevel 7, with the heel pad of the palm on bevels 7 and 8.

Two-Hand Backhand Grip: Continental–Semiwestern Forehand

This is my grip recommendation for the two-hand backhand. The top hand in a semiwestern grip is in an ideal position to play the dominant role, with the palm of the hand being under the grip, providing maximum support. The continental grip of the bottom hand gives the player the option to slice, drop-shot, volley, and reach wide balls when the top hand is released.

To locate the continental–semiwestern grip, position the bottom-hand base knuckle of the index finger bevel on 2 and the heel pad of the palm on bevels 1 and 2. The top-hand base knuckle of the index finger is placed on bevel 6, with the heel pad of the palm on bevel 6.

To reinforce the dominant role the top hand plays, I have my students practice hitting with one hand, the top hand, in a semiwestern grip, teaching them to use the top hand to drive the racket head forward. Martina Hingis and both Williams sisters do this exercise every day, as did Andre Agassi. The key is exaggerated racket-head speed on contact, following through the ball above the nonhitting shoulder with the palm of the hand to the outside.

Conclusion

We discussed grips that have proved to be successful for the majority of players. Keep in mind, however, that age, strength, and level of play all influence the grips used. Some of the very best players have unorthodox grips. They are able to be successful with them because they play all of the time and have learned to make the necessary adjustments to overcome the deficiencies of their unorthodox grips.

The next chapter will discuss forehands. You will notice that the modern grips will vary from eastern to full western. If I were pinned down and had to choose just one forehand grip for most students to use, I would have to choose the semiwestern.

Chapter 3

Forehands

An aggressive forehand is a lethal weapon in a player's strategic arsenal that will win points outright and give you defensive replies. It is a huge part of today's game, executed from every inch of the tennis court.

Over the past five decades, our staff at IMG Academy have trained thousands of players. Among these players are numerous world champions, collegiate champions, everyday warriors, and some of the future's brightest young stars. We are mainly responsible for the aggressive forehand that started with Jimmy Arias at the Colony Beach Tennis Resort in the early 1980s. We have established a trademark that our players possess huge Bollettieri forehand weapons.

Perhaps my greatest assets are the ability to inspire and motivate our students to improve and the ability to instill in them the confidence they need to succeed. Our formula for developing new technique and building it into habit involves progressive steps. This is the process our IMG Academy coaches apply each and every day. My method is a duplicate of Mr. Agassi's: Hit it—don't worry about where it goes—and then work on techniques and consistency.

Step 1: Just Hit It

As Andre Agassi's father said to him when he was young, "This is the way you refine your swing and improve your power. For now, don't worry so much about accuracy and consistency. Just relax, groove the swing, and hit big."

59

An aggressive forehand cannot come about by just getting the ball back in play. No way. I can still close my eyes and almost hear myself yelling at Agassi, Seles, Courier, Arias, Krickstein, Venus and Serena, Sharapova, and so on: "Are you a baby? Hit the ball!" Every night when you end your practice, have your coach or hitting partner feed you 50 balls that you can go for broke with.

Step 2: Target Training

Once you have established your stroke and improved your skill, you should build and test that skill under pressure conditions in practice. Use target zones and drills that test your accuracy and consistency. (Remember, it may take months of practicing step 1 before you progress to step 2.)

Step 3: Become Match Tough

The final stage is to test your skill under match-pressure conditions to see if the habits maintain effectiveness. To be successful, you must believe in your skill. Never fear making a mistake, and always execute with a full follow-through under pressure.

What Is an Aggressive Forehand?

An aggressive forehand is a lethal weapon in a player's strategic arsenal. All other forehands in a specific rally must be forceful and dynamic, controlling the center of the court until the aggressive forehand either ends the point or forces a weak return for you to attack and volley. Not all forehands are hit with the aggressive mentality. You must create the situation while keeping your opponent always under the threat of the aggressive shot. Players today are hitting their forehands from positions far into the backhand side of the court.

The ingredients of the aggressive forehand call for refined and efficient movement skills. The idea is to get into position to hit the aggressive forehand. Use a variety of shots to set up your power game and keep your opponent guessing. The goal is to put yourself in a situation where you know you will hit your aggressive forehand on your next shot before you even hit your shot.

A baseball pitcher may have a good fastball, but it will be the variety and disguise of his other pitches (e.g., curve, change-up) that maintain the effectiveness of his fastball. This is the balance of touch and power that world-class tennis players possess on their aggressive forehands.

Choose the Correct Grip

To be effective with your forehand, you have to be able to hit balls in all parts of the strike zone, so how you choose to hold the racket as a habit has great effect on the stroke itself (see chapter 14 for more information about grips). The eastern and semiwestern are the most common, versatile, and powerful options overall, and if I were to start you as a beginner today, I would most likely encourage you to use an extreme eastern or semiwestern grip. There are several forehand grips you can use:

- *Continental grip (palm faces down)*—It is difficult to achieve aggressive-forehand power with this grip, although there are a few exceptions. Personally, I prefer to work with grips that offer a higher percentage of success. This grip is seldom used today except for drop shots, forehand slices, and forehand volleys. See figure 3.1*a* for an example of this grip.

- *Eastern grip (palm faces forward)*—This grip provides good leverage and power, works well with both higher and lower balls in the strike zone, and enables the production of spins and power. See figure 3.1*b* for an example of this grip.

- *Semiwestern grip (palm faces forward and upward)*—Common in today's pro game, the semiwestern grip offers great power and spin options, especially higher in the strike zone. See figure 3.1*c* for an example of this grip.

- *Extreme western grip (palm faces upward)*—This grip is capable of good power and spin on balls higher in the zone, but low balls are difficult to work with. This grip requires lower body strength and exaggerated racket-head speed. No one applies this grip better that Rafa Nadal. See figure 3.1*d* for an example of this grip.

Remember, don't hold the racket too tightly. The grip is not a climbing rope that needs to be held as tightly as possible. In fact, tightly holding the grip will take away flexibility, reduce racket-head speed, and increase arm fatigue. Also, remember to develop one primary grip and practice it with your forehand. A lot of practice is required to ingrain the habit and make it reliable. Muscle memory can be created only by hitting thousands of balls until the grip comes naturally without thinking. One of the best ways to develop this muscle memory is to practice against "the undefeated champ of the world": the backboard.

Establish a Strong Athletic Foundation

One thing that helps everyday players the most is a strong athletic foundation. A strong athletic foundation is a must, especially in a sport that demands split-second athletic movements. Without it, your entire body, from your feet to your head, cannot react in balance or quickly. A player who stands straight up with the feet close together will have no chance in a quick reaction sport like tennis.

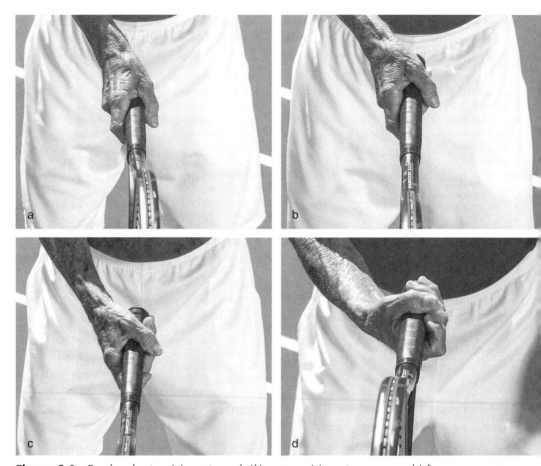

Figure 3.1   Forehand grips: (*a*) continental, (*b*) eastern, (*c*) semiwestern, and (*d*) extreme western.

Athletes can be defined by the body position of a strong foundation. Examples include Rafa Nadal, Novak Djokovic, Andy Murray, Kei Nishikori, David Ferrer, Li Na, Serena Williams. As you learned in chapter 2, an athletic foundation includes several elements:

- Wide base of support
- Low center of gravity
- Balance on the balls of the feet
- Reinforced back posture

Assume a Hitting Stance

Stances for the forehand will vary depending on the speed, height, spin, and position of the oncoming ball. Today, forehands are hit from every inch of the court. The more time a player has, the more options he will have in terms of stances. Returning a 135-mile-per-hour (215 km/h) serve will almost always require an open stance. Keep in mind that an open stance too often on a volley will not give the player much of a chance for a successful shot.

There are three main stances—open, neutral, and closed. For further details on stances, please refer to chapter 2.

- The *open stance* is like one used by a batter stepping into the batter's box with only the back foot and offers all the shot options. Under pressure of a hard-hit ball, you will usually be forced to hit in an open stance. Avoid transferring your weight off the back foot, pulling your body off the shot, in this stance.

- You reach the *neutral stance* by starting from an open stance, driving your weight forward, and pointing the front toe toward the net. You will often use this stance, along with the open stance, for the aggressive forehand. The neutral stance has both feet in the batter's box.

- Using the *closed stance* is a common problem that should be corrected through early and correct racket preparation. The closed stance reduces power, diminishes control and balance, and offers limited shot options.

Pull the Trigger

This concept allows you to maximize racket speed and power. You should pull the racket out of a backswing, driving the butt of the racket toward the ball and then through the ball toward the target. This action allows you to use your racket as a tool and apply leverage. As you pull forward, keeping your arm flexible and swinging out across your body, the racket head will meet the ball with maximum force (see figure 3.2, *a-b*, for a correct example of pulling the trigger). Power and consistency are not the result of snapping the wrist but of accelerating the tip of the racket when meeting the ball and then extending the butt of the racket to the target area. Too many people snap the wrist and have no follow-through.

Nick's Tip

You should not accelerate the racket by snapping the wrist and slapping at the ball or by throwing your body into it. Developing the swing line will achieve acceleration.

Figure 3.2   "Pulling the trigger" on a forehand shot.

Establish a Contact Zone

Contact points are the points at which the racket hits the ball. Contact zones are the areas of the court where the ball hits the racket. Contact points have a major influence on where the ball is directed. The lower the contact point, the more difficult the shot because the position of the wrist is awkward. Very low balls will force you to adjust your swing. The preferred contact zones for grips are as follows:

- *Continental*: lower
- *Eastern*: middle
- *Semiwestern*: middle to higher
- *Western*: higher

Use the Opposite Arm

So few books talk about the nonhitting hand on the forehand. A huge percentage of all players are guilty of not using the nonhitting hand. Why is it important? Look at a skier going down the mountain and how he uses his hands and arms for balance and movement. Look at a sprinter and how both arms work together. Baseball pitchers and football quarterbacks are also examples of how both arms are used together for balance. The very same principles apply to tennis players. The nonhitting hand does the following:

1. Holds the racket in the ready position (see figure 3.3*a*)
2. Holds the racket as the player pivots into the swing pattern (see figure 3.3*b*)
3. Points out toward the oncoming ball (see figure 3.3*c*)
4. Stays out in front as the player hits the ball through the contact point and keeps going out to the target area (see figure 3.3*d*)

To generate aggressive-forehand power in an offensive situation, the opposite arm works like the glove arm of a pitcher that stretches the chest

Figure 3.3 Using the opposite arm on a forehand shot: (*a*) holding racket in ready position; (*b*) holding racket during pivot; (*c*) pointing toward ball; and (*d*) staying out in front when hitting.

Nick's Tip

Beginners typically don't use the opposite arm for any benefit. Often it stays limp and at the side. Your opposite arm can add balance and power to your stroke. When you are wide in the court, the opposite arm adds balance and has an anchoring effect, acting as the balance pole does for a high-wire aerialist to keep the shoulders level.

muscles into the stroke. This sweeping action makes for a longer lever that is capable of generating more power while maintaining swing balance.

When you ski or surf, the hands working together help maintain balance. Your nonhitting hand is also a vital part of your tennis game. The extension of the left hand (if you are a righty) will help you hit through the contact point and to the contact zone. By catching the racket it can also help you recover and help if the next ball is a backhand (changing the grip more easily). If the hand is out and the ball gets behind you, the left-hand extension will also help you get through a late contact point by not stopping but continuing out more.

Load the Hips

Loading the hips involves centering your body weight into the back of the stance and down. As this happens, the body coils like a spring, allowing you to uncoil into the shot (see figure 3.4, *a-b*). Practicing your stroke while maintaining your balance on the back foot throughout will help you develop the feel for this power source. Kei Nishikori, a longtime student ours at IMG Academy, gets his power and balance by loading the hips. P.S.: He is only 5 foot 10 (178 cm).

Average players take the racket back without shifting their body weight back and coiling to prepare the racket. The perfect hip load has you preparing and turning as one unit, as Novak Djokovic does. Even on the run, players like Nadal use hip load for power and disguise.

Recover Quickly

The recovery position may vary, especially if you prefer hitting more offensive weapons, including the aggressive forehand. Roger Federer, Rafa Nadal, Maria Sharapova, and Serena Williams often recover to a position that would give them the best chance of hitting a big forehand. Your play-

Figure 3.4   Loading the hips for a forehand shot.

ing style and your opponent's returns may affect your recovery position. The mentality must be "I will get back into position after every shot." In few sports do you concede open court or field position to your opponent.

When a player runs around a forehand and exposes a large part of the tennis court, the recovery must be immediate, and the forehand hit from that exposed position must be totally offensive. Some players like Novak Djokovic, Andy Murray, and Kei Nishikori actually start their recovery the instant they hit the ball. That's why they can cover so much open court.

Follow Through to the Target

A full extension of the hitting arm on your follow-through will help you maintain a good swing line. In terms of the follow-through, a few major factors are a must for all levels of play. First, when you start going forward on your ground strokes, serves, or swinging volleys, complete the stroke with a deliberate follow-through to the target area. Second, accelerate the racket head just before contact with the ball (i.e., do not stop). Let the racket head continue well through contact and continue to where you are hitting the ball (see figure 3.5, *a-b*). So many players slow down before contact, trying to guide the ball.

Figure 3.5   Following through to the target after hitting a forehand shot.

Forehand Training Drills

Following are training drills for developing muscle memory and perfecting the forehand.

Backboard Drill

Developing a muscle memory habit requires ball after ball, and then more balls. There is no better practice partner than the backboard. Your coach can even stand right next to you, observing and making adjustments to the grip as needed. At times the coach can say "stop" or "freeze" and check your grip. The coach can also feed balls from the teaching basket.

Athletic Foundation Drill

Focus on maintaining good posture while lowering your playing height 6 to 12 inches (15 to 30 cm) below your standing height. As you practice your movement, try to be smooth in your footwork, keeping your head as still as possible. Work on a level, gliding effect.

First-Step Drill

Spread your feet one and a half to two shoulder widths apart as part of your strong athletic foundation position. Mark the position of your feet and then execute a first-step reaction technique as discussed in chapter 2, using an explosive first step.

Ball-Hit Reaction Drill

This drill is great for establishing good timing and rhythm. Audibly saying "ball" at the moment your opponent makes contact forces you to react simultaneously. You will consistently get a better jump on the ball. Then, saying "hit" when you make contact helps you establish a rhythm for the rally. With this exercise, you will also realize how quickly you need to recover your court position before the ball is returned. You must read, react, and recover to stay up with the pace and timing of the points. You can add "recover" to the drill as well, so it's "ball, hit, recover."

Resistance Rope Drill

To achieve quick acceleration, you must use first-gear footwork, pumping the feet quickly and powerfully. To practice this, use resistance training to mimic a dog pulling a sled. You can do this in several ways. It's as simple as tying a rope around your waist and having someone hold on and resist your movement. With resistance, you will naturally shorten your stride lengths. You should do several repetitions with each footwork pattern every day. Eventually you will develop the quick, fluid footwork necessary to cover the court effectively.

Footwork Patterns Drill

The coach should closely observe your pattern of movement in this drill. You hit only forehands as the coach feeds a ball into the backhand side of the court and then into the forehand side of the court.

Anticipation Drill

From your shots you can often anticipate the area where the opponent's ball will go. You might also pick up clues from your opponent if he or she has certain tendencies with ball placement. For early preparation, get in the habit of establishing your backswing before the ball reaches your side of the court. This means preparing as you move to the ball. For correct preparation, the butt end of the racket must be slightly behind and below and pointing at the incoming ball. The low-to-high movement with the racket to the ball will create the spin needed to make the ball fall into the court. Correct preparation also keeps the racket on the right side and ahead of the body if you are right-handed or on the left side and ahead of the body if you are left-handed. If the racket extends to the opposite side of the body, you are getting in the danger zone. I use this standard to rate players on their preparation skills:

- Average—as the ball bounces on your side
- Good—as the ball comes over the net
- Better—as the opponent hits the ball
- Best—before the opponent makes contact

Take-Back Drill

When hitting, yell out "take the racket back" as soon as you recognize whether the ball is coming to your forehand or backhand. This will show the coach when you recognize the oncoming ball and make you aware of how early you should be taking your racket back.

Baseball Glove Drill

A good way to get a feel for how your feet work together with your hands in preparation is to practice the baseball glove drill. Imitate the movements involved in catching a baseball and preparing to throw it. As you position to catch the ball, you will see how your feet set up automatically into the open stance. This drill also establishes the proper alignment to the ball flight with your preparation.

Towel Drill

Use a towel to create a feel for the arm speed and swing line. When drilling, try using a practice swing before you hit each ball by swinging without actually hitting a ball. Doing this can help you increase your swing speed.

Balance Drill

From an open stance, you should practice hitting while maintaining your balance on the back foot throughout the stroke. Slowly work on lowering your position and shifting deep into the back of the stance. You should feel your hips and body coil in preparation and uncoil into the ball as your weight stays centered over the back foot. Avoid launching upward through the stroke. The coach is to stand close to the student, feed the ball, and then see if the student maintains weight on the back foot. Have the student freeze (stay put) to actually see the weight control.

Conclusion

No matter what we think about weapons or aggressive strokes, for most people, the forehand is the weapon of choice. There are many different styles, grips, take-backs, and swings that are used. I encourage students to use what is natural to them and integrate the fundamentals that will make their stroke technically sound. Now let's take a look at the backhand.

Chapter 4

Backhands

Many of the top ATP and WTA players have backhands with the flexibility to be both offensive and defensive.

The game of tennis is constantly evolving with the influx of bigger, stronger, better-conditioned athletes who compete with the latest equipment. Athletes today are more talented and have few, if any, flaws to attack. The bottom line is that years ago you could overcome your weaknesses by focusing on your strengths. You could run around most of your backhands and pound your forehand weapon on a regular basis. But today's players possess more balanced weaponry throughout their games; it is much harder to disguise a weakness. They have developed their ground strokes to near, if not equal, strength, and a number of top players possess truly "Boll-istic" backhands.

Key Elements of the Backhand

A versatile backhand is key in reacting to all variations of shots including aggressive and defensive shots. The versatile backhand includes the following:

- Maximizing power, accuracy, and consistency with your backhand
- Being able to vary the spin and trajectory on the ball
- Understanding how to integrate these skills into a game plan that's effective for your style of play

A Strong Athletic Foundation

The challenge is not about generating speed on your shots. That's the easy part. The true test is in the foundation. If your body position and footwork provide control for your swing, you have a weapon!

To develop a versatile backhand, start at ground level and work your way up. You must realize that the stroke itself is nothing more than an extension of your foundation. Without a strong foundation, you will find it more difficult to achieve any type of shot variation. As we explained in chapter 2, athletic foundation is a body position that involves lowering the overall height of your body by as much as a foot (30 cm).

Body Positioning

You now have a better knowledge of the importance of body position, referred to as the athletic foundation, and how it contributes to both movement and stroke. The lower half of your body is responsible for providing stability to the stroke through either a balanced hitting stance or the correct footwork to hit on the run. Through weight transfer the lower body also generates power to the pivoting action of the body.

The torso region of the body, through strong back posture, works to maintain level shoulders through the stroke and add stability to upper body mechanics. With the foundation being sturdy yet flexible, we are ready to build stroke mechanics. The shoulders, arms, hands, and racket will work in harmony with the foundation to generate power in the swing. To maximize your power and minimize your effort, you must learn to create leverage in your stroke.

Leverage

A general definition of leverage is "the action of using a lever, such as a metal bar, pivoting against a fixed fulcrum to gain mechanical advantage." It refers to your arms, hands, and racket working efficiently.

An example is the action of a hammer. To drive a nail into a piece of wood, the hammer, positioned at a 90-degree angle with the forearm, becomes a lever. The downward action begins by driving the butt of the hammer toward the nail. The head of the hammer follows. As the butt of the hammer drives downward, the energy of the action transfers up to the hammerhead and on to the nail. We call this downward-leverage action.

With this example in mind, think of striking a tennis ball as forward-leverage action. In the backswing, the butt of the racket is positioned to drive forward toward contact. The energy generated by driving the butt of the racket forward accelerates the racket head through the contact zone. Similar to the action used with a hammer, the action of the racket creates leverage.

Movement

Movement and positioning are both instrumental to developing a versatile backhand. You should know the direction and speed of your shots, which strongly affect your ability to move into recovery position in time. If a point averages three or four shots, then close to 80 percent of the time you are hitting to continue the point. Only one time out of four does your shot result in the end of the point. If you are unable to maintain effective court position, your opponent ends up with open-court opportunities. Recovery of your court position is critical nearly all of the time, so you must make it a habit 100 percent of the time. As you learn about the art of movement, keep in mind the importance of maintaining good position through an understanding of timing and correct positioning for each shot selection.

Timing and Rhythm

A good analogy for understanding timing and rhythm is to look at how we dance to music. When we hear a good dance tune, many of us will automatically start the body into movement. The timing of the music beat, the rhythm of the instruments, and the style of the song seem to engulf good dancers as they synchronize their movement with the music. The beat of a tennis match is established by the speed at which two players rally. The quicker the exchange of the ball, the quicker each player must respond and move to keep pace with the beat. Like great dancers, tennis athletes move to the beat with fluid grace as they run everything down and then recover.

We can break the process into five stages of action as the ball travels from one player to the other and back. To stay up with the timing, you need speed (or more important, quickness), and you must choose shots that allow you the opportunity to recover at least 80 percent of the time. At the highest level of play, you must be extremely efficient to maintain the pace. Let's look at each stage of the movement process.

Stage 1: Ready to React
As the ball is starting up off the bounce to your opponent during a baseline rally, you prepare for your initial reaction to his shot. Even if you haven't

fully recovered court position from your previous shot, you should hold your ground so that as your opponent makes contact you can read the direction and depth of the shot and move toward it. This is when you set into your ready position, your athletic foundation, with your Ferrari ready to race.

Stage 2: Read and React

As your opponent begins to stroke, you should be looking for any indication of where the ball will be going so you can begin to anticipate your next move. At the moment of contact, read your opponent's shot and start

Nick's Tip

You must recognize the following before the ball crosses the net: direction of the ball, speed of the ball, height of the ball, and spin on the ball.

into motion. Because the ball travels the length of the court in only one to two seconds, you have to react quickly.

Stage 3: Footwork and Preparation

You have reacted sharply to your opponent's shot and are tracking down the ball. Your footwork should be quick and fluid as you maintain your low athletic height. Immediate preparation and correct positioning of the racket are critical to your footwork for the stroke. By the time the ball bounces on your side, you have prepared your racket and adjusted your feet to execute.

Stage 4: Set Up and Execute

When you have time, you'll load into a hitting stance and be ready to fire, able to make any last-second adjustments for the bounce. In situations when you must hit on the run, your feet will adjust according to your racket preparation as you prepare to execute at the location of contact.

Stage 5: Recover

Great athletes learn to recover as part of the natural follow-through of the stroke. As they stroke, they have already begun to recover, especially when they are on the run and have to change direction on recovery. You have only the time it takes for your shot to reach your opponent to recover your court position. This means that the harder you strike the ball, the less time you have to reposition. The position on the court for recovery varies according to the direction you hit the ball. You should make every effort to recover fully after every shot. Otherwise, you leave the court open for your opponent. By the time the ball has bounced on the opponent's side, you should be back into position and ready to start the process again.

The objective on recovery is for you to position yourself halfway between your opponent's best possible shots. You must eliminate open-court opportunities for your opponent by keeping yourself in reach of any shot he might hit. As you learn more about your opponent and become more skilled at anticipating his shots, you can start to hedge your position.

Strokes

Over the past 10 years the top-ranked ATP player has been a one-hand backhand player four times and a two-hand backhand player six times. Over the same period of the top 10 ranked players, there averaged two or three one-hand players and seven or eight two-hand players. On the WTA tour, all the number one players in the past 10 years have been two-hand backhand players. Over the same period of the top 10 ranked players, there averaged fewer than one player with a one-hand backhand. Let's look at the ingredients of a good backhand and the advantages and disadvantages of each technique.

▶ One-Hand Backhand

With the backhand grip intact, the one-hand backhand begins with the backswing position. The key elements are as follows:

- Position the butt of the racket to drive forward to start the forward swing. Various styles are used to take the racket back, and often the arm is bent in the backswing.

- As the stroke begins the forward action, the arm extends fully and becomes a lever. Extended, but not locked at the elbow completely, the arm is firm yet flexible. "Boll-istic" power is generated when the hitting arm (lever) incorporates the rib cage as a support fulcrum.

- The racket head accelerates rapidly into the contact zone as it follows the swing line of the butt end.

- As the arm continues to fully reach in the direction of the target on the follow-through, the racket head will have passed through a contact zone that provides a great margin of error and directional control for the various shot selections. How the racket head finishes at the end of the stroke will depend on the amount of spin versus driving flat power that was applied in the stroke.

The role of the foundation in the one-hand backhand is to resist the tendency of the body to rotate open. The pivoting action of the body stops completely as the forward action of the racket begins. By stopping the pivoting action, the energy from the foundation is transferred into the power of the stroke. The opposite arm counterbalances the shoulders, keeping them level through the stroke and preventing them from rotating as the stroke begins.

The one-hand backhand operates most effectively from a neutral hitting stance that allows the power of the weight transfer to work in the same direction as the stroke. One-handers, however, have the luxury of being effective from the closed stance as well. The open stance is slightly more difficult for one-handers, although they can use it for returns and in other situations when time is limited. You must develop the ability to execute from all these hitting stances. See figure 4.1, *a* through *d*, for an example of the one-hand backhand.

Nick's Tip

Versatile backhands, whether one-handed or two, operate within a game plan with a constant objective of setting up the weapon in mind. Players must give a strong message that their backhand is capable of doing what has to be done, including consistent deep strokes, slices and drop shots, down-the-line drives, and lobs.

You must establish a threat in the mind of your opponent that at any given moment your backhand could end the point. Still, most of the time you are working at various rally speeds with variations of trajectory and spin to establish more margin for error in your game plan. Over the course of a match, you wear your opponent down with consistent, accurate placements. By using your put-aways sparingly, you will have a more effective result in your game plan. Remember, when you decide to pull the trigger you can't second-guess yourself and become tentative. Always maintain positive expectations and a confident outlook.

Following is an overview of the fundamentals of the one-hand backhand.

Figure 4.1 One-hand backhand.

Grip

The most critical aspects in the construction of the one-hand backhand are the grip and the position of leverage in the wrist. The semiwestern backhand grip (see figure 4.2a) provides the strongest position of support in the wrist, which prevents the stroke from breaking down at contact. The full eastern backhand grip (see figure 4.2b) is used in today's game for slices and drop shots and by many club-level players.

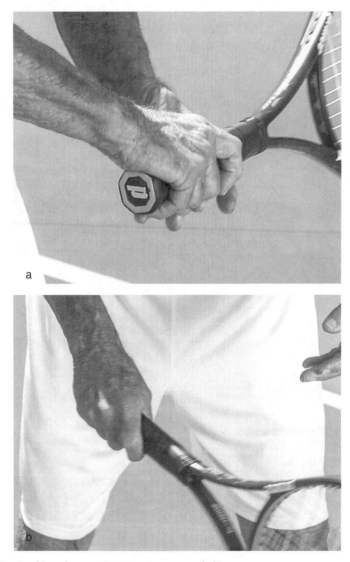

a

b

Figure 4.2   Backhand grips: (a) semiwestern and (b) eastern.

Athletic Foundation

The ready position, as described in detail in chapter 2, determines a player's readiness to react quickly to the ball as the opponent makes contact. Here are the key elements of the ready position:

- The upper body is slightly leaning forward to position the body weight more on the balls of the feet.
- The feet should be spread approximately one and a half to two shoulder widths apart, with the knees bent and flexed.

In this position, the player achieves an athletic reaction height approximately 6 to 9 inches (15 to 23 cm) below normal standing height. Players should be at a heightened intensity level anticipating reaction and ready to explode from at rest into motion as sharply as possible. Maintaining this ready position throughout the duration of a point provides power, control, quickness, and stability to the strokes and movement. Strengthening the structural integrity of your athletic foundation enables you to resist being forced into errors.

First-Step Reaction

Before reaction, pros build up to a heightened intensity level, expecting to have to make a powerful move to explode from at rest into motion, timed as sharply as possible to the contact point of the opponent. The traditional hip and shoulder unit turn is an effective response for balls well within reach. However, for more difficult balls farther away, the pros focus first on establishing upper body momentum in the direction of movement. In doing so, the foot nearest to the intended direction of movement will often tuck underneath the torso, while the opposite foot shifts the upper body in the direction of movement. Shifting the upper body over the inside foot provides weighted traction for an explosive drive off the inside foot, as the opposite leg crosses over. For lesser distances, a shuffle step on the first move will often suffice. To ensure they set up correctly, pro players have the racket prepared ahead of the body as they move to the ball. This helps them adjust their feet for the stance or to hit on the run.

Butt-End Alignment

Whether they have a straight or circular backswing, pro players achieve what's referred to as the lock-in position—a wrist position at nearly a 90-degree angle in relation to the racket. The butt end of the racket is positioned nearly in line and pointing at the incoming ball, beneath the height of contact.

Contact Point

One advantage of the one-hand backhand is that the stance can be open, neutral, or closed. For neutral and closed stances, it's best if the body weight shifts forward to the front foot well before contact. The hitting arm should reach full extension, with no bend in the elbow, as early in the forward swing as possible. The contact point should be aligned with the center of the chest, out in front of the body. The opposite arm should work as a counterbalance to ensure the shoulders don't pivot open before contact.

Follow-Through

On the follow-through, the hitting arm should be fully extended toward the target before continuing on to the finish. This will maximize the length of the contact zone for optimal control. Pro players learn to incorporate a variety of built-in recovery maneuvers into their follow-through of the swing to reduce recovery time back toward center.

▶ One-Hand Backhand (Knifing) Slice

An aggressive stroke with underspin, the one-hand knifing slice serves as the strategic counterpart to the blast. Even most two-hand players learn to develop a more biting action by using just one hand. In the most difficult forcing situations, the knifing slice is often the only option you'll have. It is a versatile tool capable of offering disguise in both preparation and execution because you are able to attack both deep and short. Used effectively and set up well, the stroke leaves the opponent on the heels every time you drop-shot. The slice can be used to change the tempo of rallies or as a defensive shot to buy time when you are out of position. See figure 4.3, *a* through *d*, for an example of the one-hand backhand slice.

On approach shots, the slice enables you to attack deep and occasionally short. You can move through the stroke with your footwork more readily and have more time to position yourself. Finally, a well-executed slice gives the opponent less to work with because the ball skids low off the bounce. The key elements are as follows:

- With the proper backhand grip intact, in the backswing you want to prepare the butt of the racket behind the incoming ball, beneath the intended contact point. The racket head is tilted back, making an L-shaped position with the arm and racket.

- The shoulders rotate to a position perpendicular to the net and level. For the forward movement, the hitting shoulder starts to rotate open as the butt of the racket drives forward toward the contact point. The opposite shoulder, working as a counterbalance, prevents rotation, maintaining the perpendicular relationship of the shoulders to the net. This anchoring function of the opposite arm and shoulder provides the pulling action of the hitting arm with more power and helps maintain the swing line.

- The butt end starts forward and then arcs across the body, sending the racket head up into contact. The racket head then follows the path of the butt end. The arm should remain flexible as it extends in the backswing. The hitting arm works with the rib cage to create power and support for the stroke.

- As the stroke passes through the contact zone, the arm separates from the rib cage to a full reach toward the target on the follow-through.

Figure 4.3 One-hand backhand slice.

The foundation of the body works to restrict full rotation of the hips and shoulders. Your shoulders, level and perpendicular to the net, lean toward the net ahead of your stance. You might think of how a football player, using the shoulders to block, leans forward for momentum.

To understand the benefits of having a slice in your game plan, think of how a pitcher in baseball uses a variety of pitches—curveballs, change-ups, sliders, and so on—to provide contrast to the fastball. By mixing up the pace, placement, and spin on the ball, the pitcher doesn't permit the batter to become too comfortable anticipating the next pitch.

Your slice adds similar variety to your game plan and has the same effect on your opponent. In addition, the disguise in preparation opens up more opportunity for use of the drop shot and other specialty shots. Steffi Graf, perhaps one of the greatest players in history, had a devastating slice back-hand and rarely hit over the ball. For most players, however, learning to mix the slice into the game in contrast to the blast will prove to be most effective.

Nick's Tip

Having only a slice backhand in today's professional game will severely limit your chances of winning tournaments and majors.

Grip

The preferred grip for the one-hand slice is the full continental or eastern grip. This grip allows a perfect balance of underspin and driving power in the stroke while offering great control and feel on touch shots.

Backswing

For the best results when hitting a knifing slice that doesn't have excess spin, the arm needs to reach full extension before the forward swing. With a bent arm, you end up chopping from the elbow, which forces the wrist to chop into contact, creating uncontrollable spin and less penetration. You need to position the butt of the racket below the height of contact in the backswing and have the butt end pointing a little more above contact.

Forward Stroke to Contact

We prefer to see a 90-degree angle created between the fully extended hitting arm and the racket. This angle should be maintained from start to finish in the stroke.

If the result of your slice is a high floating ball that lacks underspin, you need to focus on getting the racket head to flatten up on contact. When the hitting arm gets away from the body and the handle gets too far under the ball, it causes the ball to rise and float.

It is a big challenge, especially with players with two-hand backhands, to get the body weight positioned on the front foot early enough. As soon as possible, you want your weight forward and balanced on the front foot to provide adequate support for the front shoulder as the stroke begins. Two distinct characteristics of most pro strokes are strong upright back posture and level shoulders throughout the stroke. You want to improve your back posture and try to work with level shoulders. This is particularly crucial for the one-hand slice.

Although we encourage quick recovery, be careful not to push back off the front leg before contact. Instead, keep your weight forward and work on a front-toe pivot recovery on follow-through. Another challenge for the two-hand backhand players is to prohibit the pivoting open of the shoulders on the slice. You need to learn to use your opposite arm to counterbalance the forward swing and resist the tendency to open the shoulders. Make sure your hitting arm is reaching full extension for the forward swing. A bent arm in the forward swing will cause you to rotate open into contact as well.

Follow-Through

One of the great benefits of a slice backhand is the disguise it sets up for the use of drop shots. You want the follow-through to extend fully through contact to lengthen the depth of the shot. When attacking short with a drop shot, be sure to disguise it as a deep attack by showing the opponent a full follow-through. The most important part of the disguise is the take-back.

When you hit from neutral and closed stances, you should be building in a recovery step as part of the natural flow in the follow-through of the stroke. Just be sure not to begin recovery by backing away from the front foot before contact.

▶ Two-Hand Backhand

The two-hand backhand functions quite differently from the one-hand backhand relative to the foundation and the importance of the hitting stances. Whereas the one-hand stroke works more efficiently without full rotation of the body, the two-hand stroke creates its power through an aggressive hitting stance that must allow the body to rotate fully through the stroke.

The grips for the two-hand stroke determine the look and the function of the stroke and the hands. Depending on the grips, the stroke will become left-hand dominant (in right-handers), have a balance of dominance, or become more right-arm dominant. The grip position of the bottom hand determines the support factor for the stroke. We encourage players to choose a grip set that suits their natural abilities and body type. If the player is likely to become very tall, we would select a grip set that enables the player to extend both arms for a lower strike zone. If the player does not possess natural ambidextrous qualities, we would shy away from grip sets that feature the nondominant arm or even consider a possible switch to a one-hand backhand. Generally, most players today use a continental grip on the bottom hand and either a semiwestern or eastern grip for the top hand. The key elements are as follows:

- Whether they have a straight or circular backswing, pro players achieve what's referred to as the lock-in position, where the butt end of the racket is positioned nearly in line and pointing at the incoming ball (like Novak Djokovic and Serena Williams), starting beneath the height of contact in the backswing. For most backhands, the lock-in angle of leverage relative to the racket will occur in the wrist of the top hand on the grip. However, this depends on the grip set. The lock-in refers to the wrist position at nearly a 90-degree angle in relation to the racket.

- The forward swing begins with the hips and shoulders pivoting forward to begin the motion. At the same time, the hands are working together to generate racket-head speed as the stroke approaches the contact zone.

- The contact point should be aligned with the center of the chest out in front of the body, ideally at hip level. Contact height will vary relative to the grips and also to your position when hitting the ball, especially when you are in a defensive position. When players are hitting from a neutral stance they make every effort to shift the body weight forward and make contact out in front of the body.

- On the follow-through, the hitting arm should be fully extended toward the target before continuing on to the finish. Remember that the finish will be different depending on your grip. This will maximize the length of the contact zone for optimal control. Pro players learn to save time and eliminate unnecessary footwork by incorporating a variety of built-in recovery maneuvers that occur simultaneously with the stroke follow-through. This allows them to cover and defend the court more effectively.

See figure 4.4, *a* through *c*, for an example of the two-hand backhand. Following is an overview of the fundamentals of the two-hand backhand.

Figure 4.4 Two-hand backhand.

Backhand Drills

The following drills are designed to help improve your backhand technique and effectiveness. Similar to the forehand, repetition is key to developing the muscle memory that is necessary to improve consistency. The backhand is one of the most difficult shots to perfect as it typically involves moving in a manner that feels unnatural. A reliable backhand is a critical weapon for any player, and as you complete the drills you'll notice that the swing pattern will gradually feel more natural, and this muscle memory will result in increased accuracy on your shots.

Tug-of-War Drill

Grab a friend and a length of rope. Face each other and stand a few feet apart. Work at pulling your friend off balance. You will notice that by widening your base and lowering your center of gravity, you can stay balanced and powerful. Continue the tug-of-war, alternating between the open, neutral, and closed stances. Have your friend take the same stance, and then alternate between different stances.

Backhand Towel Drill

Grab a towel, set up in a neutral stance, and position your wrist in a backhand grip. Have a friend hold the towel behind you close to your hands. Now pull the towel out of your partner's hands and swing forward as though you were hitting a ball. Repeat several times to feel the swing line and shape that your arm and wrist create. The harder you pull, the more racket-head speed you generate.

Backhand Backboard Drill

Gaining feel and racket awareness on your backhand is the first step to improving your consistency. Find a partner or use a ball machine or backboard. Start slow and work your way up to 20-ball rallies on both crosscourt and down the line.

Bounce-Hit Drill

All players will benefit from this drill. No doubt you have seen it before, but it's a classic! During the drill, say outloud either "Bounce-hit" or "Ball-bounce-hit." There is no better way to improve your timing than to use all your senses—auditory, visual, and kinesthetic. Yes, the drill is simple, but we at the academy consider it a fundamental drill.

Spin It, Place It, Hit It Drill

Once the player has a feel for the swing and the contact point with the ball, the next progressions are to be able to add spin, placement, and power to the shot. You can develop the skills for this drill as follows:

Spin It

Begin to vary the spin. Be creative, using underspin and topspin on your shots. If you find your consistency dropping, back off the power until you find the right blend of speed and spin on your shots.

Place It

Now that you have a feel for your backhand, add targets to take your game to another level. Vary the size and placement of targets for both crosscourt and down-the-line backhand patterns. Challenge yourself to hit 20 or more balls consecutively to each target. It's not easy!

Hit It

Finally, add the power component to your backhand. Resist the temptation to go for it right away. Remember, power without consistency or placement is power you don't need! Gain control over your swing and the ball—then turn up the heat!

Conclusion

Whether you have a two handed or one handed backhand, the key to success is a foundation that is balanced and supports whatever shot you select to hit. Power without consistency loses. Every point begins with the serve. If you don't get it in the box with the right pace and placement, your chances of success are slim.

Chapter 5

Serves

Serves are exceeding 140 miles per hour (225 km/h), but returners have also improved their returns. The most effective servers must have variations that include change of pace, slices, kick serves, and jamming the returner.

The sonic serve is an aggressive serve with the power to keep the returner on the defensive. In addition to sheer pace, however, its variations keep the returner off balance and guessing the type, speed, and placement of the serve she must defend against. Like the game itself, the service motion has evolved to levels of power and control never imagined decades ago. With bigger, stronger athletes; more powerful rackets; and total precision timing with their body mechanics, there are WTA players breaking the 130-mile-per-hour (210 km/h) barrier and ATP players breaking the 150-mile-per-hour (240 km/h) barrier. Backing up that powerful serve, top players have the support weapons of the wicked slice and kick serves as well as off-speed change-ups. Mixing the rotation in the first-serve position while using variations of placement in the attack, the artful server has the opportunity to play "king of the mountain," allowing no one to rule his turf. Holding serve becomes an easier task against most players, allowing the aggressive server to focus on achieving the one break of serve needed to take the set.

In recent years, professionals such as Milos Raonic, Andy Roddick, Ivo Karlovic, Ryan Harrison, and Feliciano Lopez have all eclipsed the 150-mile-per-hour mark. Many more like John Isner, Jerzy Janowicz, Ernests Gulbis, Dmitry Tursunov, Jo-Wilfried Tsonga, and Gael Monfils serve regularly in the high 140s. An up and coming Australian player, Samuel Groth, has the fastest serve on record at 163.4 miles per hour (263 km/h), according to *Guinness World Records.*

But there is more to holding serve than just the serve itself. In the era of Pete Sampras, it was more common to see players who predominantly played serve and volley to best capitalize on their serve weapons. With the majority of players possessing weapons on the return, the pure serve-and-volley player is a rare find today. Then you have players like Federer and Nadal who are both very effective at holding serve and rarely serve above 140 miles per hour. Some of their most effective tactics are to attack placements with slice and kick serves, then look to play their second ball to the open court. This two-ball combination ploy is a mainstay of both their first- and second-serve strategies. That's how Federer in 2013 was able to maintain an astonishing 60 percent in the category of second-serve points won.

▶ Serve Fundamentals

Fundamentals are elements of technique that can be found in common among the majority of all great examples. *Style* represents elements that are unique to an individual and not necessarily in common with other examples. Coaches tend to focus on developing fundamentals and disregard style unless it is adversely affecting the fundamentals.

Players develop personal styles built on preferences that feel most comfortable to them without coaching. Although players may share the vital fundamental components, there are acceptable variations of technique style that can also produce aggressive serve results. In any deviations you make as you create your signature of style, just make sure you do not sacrifice any of the key elements.

Nick's Tip

Be careful—the more unorthodox your style, the greater the likelihood of inconsistency and even injury. There are, however, servers with unorthodox styles that have great success and without injury. Coaches, be open to styles that are unorthodox.

A player's technique is often most influenced by role models and the attempt to emulate the same "look." For most players trying to learn by watching other players, elements of style stand out and catch their eye more than the fundamentals. This often results in what looks to be a bad impression of a top player's motion that lacks the functionality. Be careful with trying to copy segments of another player's style or technique. Be yourself and do what is natural for you.

The serve is like a baseball pitch—or is it? The best analogy for many years in teaching the service motion was the comparison to the pitch in baseball. To pitch the baseball, the arm and shoulder mechanics produce what is called a kinetic chain, which is a sequence of movements that begins out of the windup, with the glove arm driving the shoulder rotation and causing the chest muscles to stretch, passing energy into the throwing arm to propel the release of the ball.

Flexibility throughout the arms and chest muscles allows the energy to build in this sequence of movement, stretching and releasing in a transfer of energy like the crack of a whip. This also occurs in the serve, sending energy up to the racket head for contact.

However, with the exception of the throwing mechanics, there are significant differences in the overall technique of the serve and the pitch (see table 5.1). We see distinct differences in the motions because the throwing actions are directed at different targets. The pitch uses mechanical characteristics that create power toward a forward target, the catcher's glove. The aggressive serve has the characteristics required to direct power toward an upward target, the point of contact. The best way to describe the aggressive serve mechanics would be "an upward pitch."

The serve is a classic example of what would be considered a counterintuitive exercise. That means logically thinking people will often make the wrong assumptions. If you have the wrong concept in your mind about the action of serving, it creates a skewed mental blueprint from which

Table 5.1   Differences Between a Pitch and Serve

Pitch	Serve
The front foot takes a big forward stride.	No step is taken with the front foot.
The shoulders maintain a level plane in line with the catcher's mitt (target).	The shoulders tilt to a position that aligns to the contact point.
The throwing elbow follows a forward track through the motion.	The hitting elbow follows an upward track on line with the point of contact.
The throwing arm releases the ball with the arm bent.	The hitting arm straightens into contact.

your technique gets built. It is extremely important to have great clarity about what you are trying to do in the serve motion so that you develop a correct blueprint from which to build. Most players develop their serve technique believing the objective is to drive the ball from the point of contact into the service box. The problem is, players who see that as the objective end up with most of their power generated after contact in the follow-through. The real objective in producing an aggressive serve is to see the challenge as driving your racket-head speed up to the ball rather than down to the court. To be able to hit down on the ball, a player must be at least 6 feet 10 inches (208 cm) tall. Very few of us have that luxury.

Nick's Tip

Players who believe the objective is to drive the ball from the point of contact into the service box end up with most of their power generated after contact in the follow-through. The real objective in delivering an aggressive serve is to see the challenge as driving your racket-head speed up to the ball rather than down to the court.

I want to be sure that my readers and coaches understand the following. There are so many swing motions used by amateurs and professional players and ach person must find the motion she feels comfortable with. With that said, the toss, hitting up, the wrist snap, and acceleration on contact must be a part of your serve. When throwing upward toward the point of contact, the hitting arm straightens, creating a forearm rotation and wrist snap that takes the ball down into the service box. So to develop an aggressive serve, you must focus on the upward pitch technique as follows.

Grip

It is extremely important that you position the racket in your hand correctly. If you have a forehand grip, the wrist action and forearm rotation required for unrestricted release of the racket-head energy onto the ball can be restricted and eventually lead to injury.

To ensure proper wrist action through contact, you must develop the habit of serving with a continental grip. You must place the heel of your hand on the top edge of the grip. This grip will allow you to produce the action required to execute the aggressive serve.

To create more spin, you have the option to shift your grip slightly toward the backhand side, which alters the angle of the racket head. You can become creative with different spin actions by shifting in varying degrees from the continental grip toward the backhand side. However, avoid shifting to the forehand side of the grip.

Nick's Tip

When teaching the serve, especially in the early stages, take into consideration the age of your students and do not get too technical. Start with a simple eastern forehand grip and tell them to hit the front of the ball, concentrating on the toss and hitting up on the ball. Do not talk about the legs, hip and shoulder rotation, and so on. Do not make it too complicated for them.

Toss

The preferred contact point for the various flat and spin serves is different for each type of serve. Although you toss well into the court for your biggest aggressive booms, the preferred position of contact for the kick serve is much closer to the baseline, barely inside the court. This means you must have command over the placement of your toss to execute all types of serves.

The toss itself is a major key to all serves and a rather simple part of the motion. Nevertheless, players struggle with it, especially under pressure. If you eliminate some of the moving parts, you can gain better control. If you extend the toss arm to a straight position and firm up the wrist position, your arm will work as one unit in a lever action. Lifting from the shoulders with just enough power to achieve the desired height, you release the ball at eye level as the toss arm continues upward until it lines up with the point of contact. Do not release the ball until your tossing hand and arm are almost fully extended, just past eye level. With the ball positioned within the fingers and thumb, the hand opens up at eye level, releasing the ball, preferably with little spin. If you allow your wrist to snap on the release of the toss, your fingers will create spin on the ball, often flipping it back over your head. See figure 5.1, *a* and *b*, for an example of a correct toss.

The tossing motion should lift the ball into the air to approximately 12 inches (30 cm) above the desired point of contact, allowing the ball to drop into the point of contact as your racket head extends to full reach. The desired height of your toss will vary based on the tempo and rhythm of your motion. This is your toss–hit rhythm. There are different opinions about the height of the toss. I do not teach that there is only one toss height for all. When you get a little nervous, I suggest a lower toss.

Toss–Hit Rhythm

Your toss–hit rhythm is the measure of time between the release of your toss and the point of contact. If your toss is rather high and you are slow in

Figure 5.1 Toss for a serve.

creating the set-to-launch position, you will likely prefer a more extended toss–hit rhythm. If you prefer a lower toss and can quickly establish the set-to-launch position as you toss, you can work with a much tighter toss–hit rhythm. When you are serving well, you are usually in a groove, maintaining a consistent toss–hit rhythm.

When you begin to struggle with your toss placement or the motion in general, your timing can get thrown off, causing your serve to fail. Become familiar with the toss–hit rhythm that works best for your motion, and do everything possible to maintain that timing for every serve. When your serve seems to leave you in a match, go back to the toss–hit rhythm that works best as the first course of remedy.

To establish your optimal toss–hit rhythm, use the verbal cues of saying "toss" as you release the ball and "hit" on contact. Repeat this until you begin to find the timing that works best for you. Rather than always searching for the perfect toss to hit and often starting over, try to maintain your rhythm as the top priority. When you tell yourself that you're going to be on time no matter where the toss positions the ball, it seems to improve your toss while keeping your timing intact.

Serving Position

To prevent the dreaded foot fault, you must be able to position your front foot without stepping on or inside the baseline before making contact with the ball. Although players use many stance variations, the primary contributions of the stance are to provide balance throughout the motion and maximum reach at contact. The starting stance we recommend has the front foot pointed in the direction of the net post. The back foot positions perpendicularly to the front foot, lined up with the heel of the front foot. With this starting stance, your body can stretch inside the court and maintain the best lower body support and balance. As the body shifts forward into the set-to-launch position, the back foot will slide forward next to the front foot for some players, while others choose to keep their feet in their starting stance. See figure 5.2 for an example of a correct serving position.

There is no one stance for every player. Players should use what's comfortable for them. Pete Sampras and Roger Federer keep the rear foot back. Andy Roddick and Gael Monfils draw the back foot up to the front foot. I suggest that players 10 and under keep the foot back, but I like to see what they do without my telling them. It is also common to see players line up sideways to the baseline, à la John McEnroe. This stance can prevent full rotation of the body in the motion unless your feet leave the ground and you are highly skilled at rotating your hips and shoulders in the launch to contact. Maintaining your balance in this stance is difficult because your front knee is unable to extend inside the baseline to support and balance the body. You can make it work, but we don't recommend it. Once again, coaches should see what the student does. If your student lines up sideways, tell him to go forward as if he is serving and volleying. This will help him get the rear foot to go into the court.

Figure 5.2   A well-balanced serving position.

When your opponent uses this McEnroe-style stance but does not seem to have the entire motion mastered, she will likely have difficulty serving to certain targets. For a right-handed server with a closed stance, the best serve will be down the T in the deuce box and out wide on the ad court. Serves to these locations are likely to be your opponent's choice under pressure.

The real test will be when you change court position on the return, taking away the preferred target, forcing your opponent to go for the wide target in the deuce court and down the T in the ad court. You may find that your opponent has difficulty reaching those targets, allowing you to cheat on your return position for better coverage of serves that your opponent can hit.

Nick's Tip

Try to establish a serve stance that will provide the best control of your balance and allow you to access all the targets in both the deuce and ad courts without being limited by the mechanics of your motion.

Set-to-Launch Position

To create the set-to-launch position, set up in a stance so that your front foot points toward the net post in front of you. Your back foot should be a comfortable distance behind the heel of the front foot. Extend your arms at shoulder level to create a straight line from hand to hand. Now turn your shoulders sideways until the tossing hand is over the toes of your front foot. You are now set to stretch your body over the front toes, under the point of contact. The best way to stretch the hips forward is over the toes of the front foot. Rather than stretching the rear end inside the baseline, you want to stretch the front side from the front knee up to the front shoulder. If you were to put a ball in your pocket in line with your kneecap and at hip-socket level, that would be the ideal stretch point. As you stretch, the ball in your pocket should shift straight forward over the toes of the front foot.

The set-to-launch position is a critical factor in producing the aggressive serve. It is the "energy in" phase that sets the stage for the "energy out" launch to contact. With the body in a flexible yet controlled state, the hips stretch forward under the toss as the shoulders tilt and align with the point of contact, enabling the body to simulate the bending action of the pole-vaulter's pole. The body stretches and bends in preparation to snap the throwing mechanics toward the point of contact. See figure 5.3 for an example of the correct set-to-launch position.

It may take some time to discover the set-to-launch position, a position of balance centered on the front foot. You will need to relax and release the muscles and tendons along the front side of your hip region and across the chest and arms to enable yourself to become more flexible.

Launch Position

Equipped with a long flexible pole, a pole-vaulter sprints down a runway, plants the end of the pole into a fixed base, and uses the energy of forward momentum to bend the pole. As the vaulter positions for the upward lift, the pole releases that energy to thrust the athlete nearly 20 feet (6 m) in the air and over the bar.

Figure 5.3 Set-to-launch position for a serve.

The human body can learn to function like the pole-vaulter's pole to snap energy to the throwing mechanics for the upward throw. By stretching the hips in the set-to-launch position of the serve while tilting your shoulders back, you can achieve a launch position with the potential energy of the pole-vaulter's pole. The hips work to straighten the body just before contact on a lean over the court. This action often generates enough hip-snap energy to lift the body off the ground.

At the same time as the hip snap, the toss arm begins the shoulder rotation, initiating the pitching mechanics. The toss arm works as if pulling the upper body toward contact, tucking and starting the upward rotation of the shoulders. As the shoulders rotate to a position perpendicular to the ground at contact, the hitting elbow follows in sequence on a straight upward track in line with the point of contact. Once the body and arm straighten together before contact, all the energy from the motion passes into the racket head, sending it over the top into contact and then leading the way back down on the follow-through. With the hitting arm flexible and relaxed throughout this motion, the arm straightens to create the wrist snap and pronation. Direct your power toward contact, extend your arm fully into impact, and the rest will take care of itself if you use the continental grip correctly positioned in the hand. Caution: Attempting to add power by forcing the wrist snap will only slow down the energy created in the sequence of movement, so work to maintain a passive wrist throughout.

Launch-to-Contact Position

You have stretched all the energy into your hip position in the set to launch, and you are aimed and ready to fire toward the point of contact. The key to the hip snap upward is to maintain your hips inside the court. When you force your hips to stay fixed in position, the energy of the upward snap will drive the upper body toward contact, achieving a straight position leaning over the court before contact. On the follow-through you will find yourself inside the baseline, with forward momentum pulling you toward the net. You can create enough power in your upward snap to lift your feet off the ground, enabling you to reach higher contact points. When you leave the ground using this technique style on the serve, the action is not a jump with the legs and a hit. The snap of the hip is what creates the liftoff. The sequence of this serving routine should come about in segments. Coaches should not start beginners with more than a simple routine stressing rhythm with the toss and swing motion. See figure 5.4 for an example of a correct launch-to-contact position.

Figure 5.4   Launch-to-contact position for a serve.

Types of Serves

For many years only one technique was taught for the serve. Set your feet shoulder-width apart, point your front foot toward the target, put your racket hand and ball-tossing hand in front of you at waist height, start with your racket hand and ball-tossing hand going down together and up together, and do not move your back foot until you make contact with the ball and step into the court. Wow, times have changed.

There are still classic service motions such as those used by Roger Federer and Pete Sampras, but many others used today are just as effective. There is the half motion where the racket does not go down but starts immediately upward, and there's also the abbreviated motion where the racket is set above the shoulder before the toss is made.

Elements of the Aggressive Serve

An aggressive serve can have different variations and if delivered properly will provide the server with an outright winner, an error by the returner, or a defensive reply by the returner. Here are the important elements of the aggressive serve.

Grip

It is acceptable for very young and basic beginners to learn to serve with the forehand grip they have become comfortable with. We make this exception in order to ensure that young players experience more success in the beginning. As they begin to progress and become open to adjustments to improve, it's time to introduce them to serving in a full continental grip. It is an essential fundamental to serving at higher levels of play.

Starting Position

Most players start with the ball and racket together. For the stance, the feet are approximately shoulder-width apart, preferably with the front foot pointed toward the net post. It is quite common for the pros to start with their body weight forward in the stance for the start position, then shift the weight to the back foot as they start the motion, then shift forward to toss and hit. It's all a matter of what you feel comfortable with. Coaches should look at the student's natural style and then determine what will be the best for him. See figure 5.5 for an example of a correct starting position for the serve.

Take-Back

There are several predominant styles of take-back. There's over the shoulder, used by Andy Roddick and Venus Williams. Then you have the classic Federer pendulum down swing that takes the racket up into position. There are other abbreviated take-backs as well. Regardless of which style you prefer, what's most important is that the hitting arm and racket are positioned properly and on time in the set-to-launch position. The take-back should be in sync with the timing of the toss action to ensure consistent toss–hit rhythm on the serve. See figure 5.6 for an example of a correct take-back for the serve.

Figure 5.5   Starting position for a serve.

Figure 5.6   Take-back for a serve.

Toss Action

To be precise with the toss, most pros keep the toss arm fully extended throughout the toss motion. The ball is released from the hand at approximately eye level. The toss arm continues upward until the palm of the toss hand faces toward the sky. As the toss arm starts going up, the body weight is shifting forward in the stance for the release of the ball to produce a straighter up and down ball path. The height of the toss varies based on the serve, but the ball should reach a height at least 12 inches (30 cm) higher than the top of the racket at contact. Players vary the ball position for the various types of serves, but as a general rule, you want your toss to remain inside the baseline and to the hitting-arm side of the body. See figure 5.7, *a* and *b*, for an example of a correct tossing action for the serve.

Figure 5.7 Tossing action for a serve.

Set to Launch: Platform and Pinpoint Stance

The platform stance describes the technique of those players who maintain the same starting stance throughout the motion. Platform servers such as Federer and Djokovic shift their weight forward for the set-to-launch position. As they bend their knees, the hips shift forward toward the toes of both feet as the chest angles upward toward the contact point. This chest angle aimed at the contact point is a crucial fundamental for developing a powerful and healthy serve motion. The shoulders tilt as the chest aims upward so that the tilted shoulders and arms establish a straight line with the contact point. The heels of the feet are elevated, indicating the weight is into the toes of both feet for the launch.

The pinpoint stance describes the technique of those players who bring the back foot forward to a position near the front foot for the set-to-launch. Many pros shift the front side of their hips forward over their toes to create a position similar to the look of a pole-vaulter's pole stretched back and bent into an arc shape. This stretched position enables the player to create an upward snap from the hip to launch the racket head up toward contact. With the body weight primarily on the front foot, the chest angle aims upward at the contact point, which is a crucial fundamental for developing a powerful and healthy serve motion. The shoulders tilt as the chest aims upward so that the shoulders and arms create a straight line with the contact point.

Launch to Contact:
Platform and Pinpoint Stance

To start the launch to contact from the platform stance, the legs begin driving up primarily from the front leg as the toss arm drives the rotation of the shoulders up toward contact. As the shoulder rotation progresses through an upward pitching motion, the butt of the racket aims up toward contact along the way. As the shoulders quickly rotate, the racket head sweeps through the back-scratch position as the player's chest drives up toward contact, enabling the player to direct the power of the swing upward. The launch to contact should function on a consistent timing relative to the height of the ball toss and the rhythm of the player's technique in order to achieve a full extension of the body on contact each time.

For the launch to contact using the pinpoint stance, with the hips fully extended forward inside the baseline for the launch to contact, the player starts an upward snap action from the front of the hips, similar to a pole-vault pole, as the toss arm begins the rotation of the shoulders up toward contact. As the shoulder rotation progresses through an upward pitching motion, the butt of the racket aims up toward contact along the way. As the shoulders quickly rotate, the racket head sweeps through the back-scratch position as the player's chest points up toward contact, enabling the player to direct the power of the swing upward. It's important that the hips maintain their stretched position out in the court upon launch to keep the hips from jackknifing backward before contact. The launch to contact should function on a consistent timing. The serve's toss–hit rhythm will depend on the height of the ball toss and technique style. The objective is to find the timing that achieves a full extension of the body on contact each time.

Contact

The desired position of contact varies based on the type of serve. For flat serves, the contact point should be inside the baseline at least a foot or so, and even farther for taller players at higher skill levels. For a stance with the front foot pointed toward the net post, the toss placement should be generally in line with the toes of the front foot. Your toss should be reasonably reachable but challenging enough to have the body fully extended,

Figure 5.8   Contact position for a serve.

elevated off the ground on contact, and leaning into the court. See figure 5.8 for a correct example of contact position for the serve.

Finish

On the finish, the body weight should land inside the baseline. If you have a big serve weapon, you can land and split inside the baseline in preparation for the return. If it is a second serve or it's a weaker serve, you must be prepared to quickly recover back behind the baseline to react to the opponent's return. See figure 5.9 for a correct example of the finish for the serve.

At the IMG Academy Bollettieri Tennis Program, we recommend that you practice a shadow return every time you practice your serve. Be sure you end up in the court no matter what serve you are hitting or whether you are serving and volleying. As soon as you land in the court, prepare for the return.

Figure 5.9   Finish for a serve.

The Wicked Slice Serve

No one did the wide sliding serve (nicknamed the wicked slice serve) better than John McEnroe. He even told the returner exactly what to expect, and most of the time they still were not able to return it. Remember, John was a lefty and his wicked slice to the ad court took the returner well outside the doubles alley, leaving an empty court open for John. This sliding slice serve does not come close to the speed of the sonic serve, but it can be more effective - Just ask Roger Federer, Rafa Nadal, or Pete Sampras.

The biggest factor in learning the wicked slice is to forget about trying to make logical sense of it. Focus solely on the action you are applying to the ball and nothing else. From the depth of your set-to-launch position, think only about brushing up across the outer side of the ball, leading with the edge of the frame, and throwing in the right direction. Everything else will take care of itself. If you can maintain your swing direction and racket-face angle, the harder you swing the more it adds spin to the ball and the better the ball bites down into the court. As soon as you understand that spin adds control and the actions you create work opposite to the result, you will own the wicked slice.

Adjust Your Grip

If you use a continental grip, or worse yet anything toward the forehand side of the grip, you want to shift slightly beyond the continental toward the backhand side of the grip for better natural spin production. This makes it easier to throw the edge of the racket in a cutting action to apply spin to the ball. In golf, it is the difference between a one iron and a wedge. The wedge has an ability to create spin on the ball that you can't achieve with a one iron. Adjusting the grip makes the racket perform more like a wedge. This does not apply to children just learning the serve. Teaching pros should use discretion when starting their students close to an eastern backhand grip needed for the slice.

Align Your Toss Arm

Toss position is critical for being able to brush the outer side of the ball and create the angle on the placement. For right-handers to slice the ball to the sideline of the deuce court, the toss arm should start in line with the right net post or even between the net post and center strap. The toss arm should travel straight upward and release the ball on that line. No matter what toss position you select, do not release the ball before reaching eye level, and then continue going up, with the fingers pointing toward the ball.

Control the Direction of Your Throwing Motion

You must learn to control the direction of your throwing motion and get comfortable throwing on an angle up and away from your intended placement. You must be able to apply spin and provide room for the spin to work. Aim your throw on the same line as your toss arm, and throw high toward the ball. It is like throwing a curveball in baseball. You can't aim and throw straight at the catcher when throwing a curveball. The pitcher has to trust the spin and aim to the right of the catcher's glove to provide room for the curve to break left.

Lead With the Edge of the Racket Head

Rather than leading with the racket face into contact as you would to hit flat, you must lead with the edge of the racket to slice. Most players tend to lead too much with the racket face, reducing spin production and directional control. If you find you are blading the ball off the edge of the frame, avoid snapping forward too much from your hip. You want your hip snap to take your racket head up to the ball to slice, not forward into the court.

Create Racket-Head Speed

To maximize spin production you need racket-head speed. That means the head of the racket should travel much faster than the handle. Like throwing a hatchet where the blade leads as the head flips end over end, keep your wrist relaxed so that as you throw the edge of the racket head upward and brush across the ball, the head reaches maximum speed into contact.

Spin the Ball Up on a Diagonal

Most players make the mistake of trying to carve the slice and spin the ball toward the court. The spin you create should send the ball spinning up on a diagonal high above the net post, as opposed to spinning the ball forward toward the intended placement. The spin action you're looking for is halfway between true topspin and true sidespin. You create just enough sidespin to make the ball break to the left and enough topspin to bring it down into the court.

Contact the Outer Side of the Ball

Make sure your body fully extends to make contact on your slice. You want the ball to be reachable but challenging. Most players brush too much up the backside of the ball when trying to slice, resulting in more of a kick effect. Remember, the key is to brush up on the outer side of the ball to create the spin action and angle of placement.

Follow Through High Above the Net Post

Again, the key is to not try to carve the slice toward the intended target and follow through in that direction. You have to control the swing direction all the way to follow-through and trust the spin will take the ball toward your intended target. You should finish with your feet inside the baseline if all goes well.

Second Serve

Very few parts of the game indicate to me the type of player you are more than your second serve. A competitive player who is interested in getting better is willing to go for it on the second serve. In my mind, that is the difference in determining if a player has the confidence and belief to get to higher levels of play. To play the game at almost any level, you must have an aggressive second serve. To have the aggressive mind-set for your second serve, you must not be afraid to hit your second serve and go for it. True, you will miss some second serves by being more aggressive, but in time they will start falling in and your serve will get better.

Serve Drills

These are the drills we use at the IMG Academy Bollettieri Tennis Program to teach and practice serving skills. Use these drills to improve your serve technique for all types of serves.

Whoosh Drill

Simply listening to the sound of your swing will help you understand whether you are directing your throwing action and power in the right direction. Without using a ball, go through your normal serve motion, swinging at full speed. Listen to the sound of the racket and try to determine where the whoosh sound is the loudest. If the swing is loudest in front of your face, past where the contact would occur, you are directing your throwing action and power forward, not up.

If you direct your power up toward the point of contact, the whoosh sound will be above your head through the contact zone. As you practice your serve, do what is necessary to move the whoosh sound before contact.

Toss and Catch Drill

If your throwing motion needs some work, you should practice playing toss and catch with a partner on a daily basis. Start close to each other and then slowly extend the distance until you are able to throw from baseline to baseline with some accuracy.

You will improve your throwing speed and distance if you learn to use shoulder rotation and both arms to accelerate the throwing action. Begin with your arms and shoulders level and your opposite arm lined up with your partner, the target. Use your opposite arm to drive the shoulder rotation, stretching the chest muscles in the sequence of movement. Your chest will rotate and face your target as you release the throw. Try to spread your elbows to increase the stretching of the chest in the action. As you develop your throwing skill, you can progress to the next challenge, the upward pitch.

You Can't Reach Me Drill

Simulating the full aggressive serve motion, work on creating the set-to-launch position by throwing toward a target where the point of contact would be on your serve. Work on improving your hip snap as part of the motion. Try to see how high you can throw the ball. If you do it correctly, the ball will come down in the service box area on the bounce.

Midair Collision Drill

This drill requires two balls, one for each hand. Toss the first ball into the air to the desired height of your serve. In the timing and toss–hit rhythm of your serve, throw the second ball toward the point of contact and attempt to make the two balls collide. You must not let the tossed ball drop below the height of contact for the serve.

Balance Until the Bounce Drill

The test of your set to launch is whether you can maintain total control of your balance. As you create the position of potential energy for the upward snap, you need to be in command of your balance so that you can direct your power and energy up toward contact without losing control of your motion. You must have enough flexibility to stretch and snap with your body but not be so loose that your movement becomes sloppy. You must develop a precise habit that you can duplicate. The set-to-launch position is something you can practice off court as well, in front of a mirror. On court you can use videotape or your shadow to check for the qualities you should see. You need to become familiar with your technique. Learning the look and associated feel of this position is integral to the development process. Your ball toss in the right area for the serve will help you control your balance throughout the entire serve motion.

In the drill, keep your arms and shoulders in line with the front foot as you tilt upward in the toss action. Without a ball or racket, begin in alignment with the toss hand over the front foot. Tilt the shoulder line until it is almost perpendicular to the ground as you shift the ball in your pocket over the front foot. You should find a balanced position, with the weight of your stretch behind the ball in your pocket. If your front knee is quivering to support your weight as you stretch, you don't have the position set correctly. Straighten the front knee more and focus on even more stretch in the hips until you feel the weight of the stretch in your hip area, not down by the knee.

When you think you have it, try the balance-until-bounce test. Using a racket and ball, go through the motion and freeze in the set-to-launch position. Toss to the desired height of your serve, and see if you can freeze on balance until the tossed ball bounces on the ground. Practice this until you can balance totally under control. Check a video of yourself to see if you are stretching your hips enough and to see if your shoulders reach a line with contact. All your body weight should be on the front foot as you set.

Crossing-the-Line Drill

On the follow-through of the serve, you should find yourself completely inside the baseline. If you create enough upward snap, your feet will leave the ground. If your hips work properly, you will land in a forward-momentum position with your upper body. Like the body of a sprinter crossing the finish line, your body should be leaning forward on the finish, making the serve and volley a natural progression of the follow-through. I tell my students to pretend to serve and volley every time. This forces them to land inside the court.

Conclusion

I want to make it very clear that the majority of this chapter applies to advanced tennis players and not to beginners. Whether working by yourself or with a coach, you must be realistic with much of the chapter to capture and then apply the important elements to your game. To be most success-ful in this process I recommend help from a professional tennis teacher.

Chapter 6

Returns

Just as the serve is a key part of the game and can be the difference between winning and losing, the return of serve is a crucial element of your game.

When you are facing an opponent who is launching a full-scale aerial assault, you have the choice to either run for cover or hang in there and blast right back. Every point starts with the serve and the return of serve. Yes, the power serve has a huge advantage, but you can offset the serve with a reliable return of serve and a mind-set that says "I will find a way to return serve and get it right back atcha." Sonic servers may have an advantage, but the returners today such as Rafael Nadal, Novak Djokovic, Andy Murray, Serena Williams, and Maria Sharapova have more of a chance to break serve.

The return of serve has come a long way over the past several years, especially because of the slower courts, slower balls, and the new developments with racket and string technologies that allow players to hit powerful returns with just the flick of the wrist.

Even if you had the exceptional athletic skills of Rafa Nadal, you would need more than just quick reflexes to be an effective returner. You need powers of intuition to anticipate the action before it happens. You need to learn the techniques for gaining more control of each situation and the indicators that can help you detect the server's intent.

You must have a game plan for breaking serve and the mind-set and discipline to execute it. With less than a half second to read, react, and execute, you should have a target for the return in mind before the serve is struck.

There are different opinions about the return of serve: Some players prefer to get the ball in play by hitting it crosscourt so that the ball crosses the lowest part of the net and travels the longest distance, while other players go for broke. After a few games, Andre Agassi seemed to zone in and wrestle the edge away from the server, something Serena Williams does as well. Coaches and players spend considerable time trying to pick up little tips indicating where a server will serve (e.g., by watching the toss, body motion, and so on).

Return Fundamentals

Highly skilled returners are capable of hacking through the security codes and essentially cracking the safe to gain access to the server's classified strategic documents. Within the first few games of a match, the artful returner establishes her timing and rhythm as she zeros in on the server's routine and patterns. Like a computer, the returner logs the data of the previous points played, tracking trends or tendencies that may be predictable. Like a highly skilled card player, the intuitive returner searches for "tells," the telltale signs of what will happen next. By the time the first set comes to a close, returners like Djokovic and Nadal have figured out the server's "go to" serves in both courts and the decisions he will tend to make under pressure. They also become aware of the placements the server has difficulty with and uses that to their advantage. The proactive returner will add pressure to the situation, using court position and setup to manipulate the server's thought process.

You too can become adept at delivering returns by leaving no stone unturned and by understanding that the battle of overcoming the serve is often won before it is ever fought. From the moment you step on the court, you should feel as if you are on the hunt, stalking your prey, looking for signs of weakness and moments of vulnerability that allow you to strike. Your intensity must build up to the moment you react, letting nothing distract you from the task of returning the ball back in play. Convince yourself that returning serve is a challenge you love. You expect—you want—every serve to be in. You need that mind-set to be fully prepared for the return.

Nick's Tip

One of the most productive ways of adding to your chances of breaking serve is to hold your own serve. The pressure on the server will increase every time you hold your serve.

Understanding Serve Strategy

To improve your anticipation skills as a returner, you need to understand the server's thought process. Within the first few service games, you should have a good idea of what you are up against. You cannot allow yourself to become frustrated if you do not break serve early in the match. You need to keep your spirits up and give yourself an opportunity to establish your timing and your feel for the serves as you gather information to help you break serve later in the set. After all, it's rather unrealistic to expect to break serve every time. If you can hold serve regularly, all you need is one break of serve to win the set.

Level 1: Living on Second Serves
The first level of serve strategy has little thought behind it. Thinking they have two shots at getting the ball in, players blast the first serve and see if it goes in and then use a "push" second serve. Players who use this strategy do not have a lot of confidence in their serve and have no idea how to use it strategically.

Typically, the majority of these first-serve blasts are faults, and the first-serve percentage falls off the charts. If these players survive the battle, they will be using their second serves to do it.

Servers with methodical serve routines are easy to break because you have so many second serves to work with. Be careful not to get too carried away on the easy sitter second serves or you may give away too many points on errors. If you add a little more pressure to the situation by standing closer to the service line on occasion, you can dramatically increase the likelihood of double faults.

Level 2: Attacking the Weakness
The next progression of serve mentality recognizes the value of attacking weakness. Rather than just getting it in, such servers will place their serves. Servers will often assume that your backhand is the weaker side, so with great predictability they focus most of their serves toward the returner's backhand. Unless you prove to them otherwise, they will continue to play to your backhand most of the time. You can alter your starting court position left or right to create the perception of opportunity and influence the server to change the serve placement.

Level 3: Rotation of Placements
Still working with the hard first serves and spin second serves, level 3 evolves from predictably attacking a weakness to making a more calculated change of placement. Your return timing should be easy to establish because the serve speed is still not changing much; only the placement varies. These players will begin to challenge your range and reach on the return as they work you side to side.

Level 4: Full Rotation of Speed, Spin, and Placement

"Say hello to my little friend. . . ." You are up against a serve weapon! If the server can maintain a high percentage between 60 and 70 percent of first serves in play while varying the speed, spin, and placement, you will have to overcome a complete serve arsenal and a server who knows how to use it. But don't throw in the white towel and just go for big returns and pray. You still have your serve.

The server's ability to work the variation of placements keeps the returner uncertain of which side to prepare for. The variation of speed and spin on the first serve toys with the returner's timing. When the server can sense that the returner is expecting the big flat serve, he can effectively mix in the off-speed spinner.

The server who has an effective and reliable second serve is likely to be more aggressive with the first serve. A very important category for a server is second-serve points won. If you can win more than half the points you start on your second serve, you can afford to take more risk on the first serve to achieve a higher first-serve points won. But the server should understand that living on the second serve too much is flirting with disaster. On first serves, the pressure is on the returner, who is preparing in a defensive mind-set. On second serves, the pressure shifts to the server. Like a baseball pitcher with a 3-2 count, the server has no room for error. The returner can begin to assume a more offensive role when facing a second serve.

When sonic serve weapons clash with right-back-atcha returns, be ready for a rumble. Like two boxers staring each other down at the weigh-in, the game of intimidation begins long before the ball is even in play. With no fear on their faces, the two gunslingers stand off, neither backing down to the other's threat.

The server begins a routine of rituals that she methodically performs before every serve, bouncing the ball several times to prepare for battle. The server takes one last look to make sure the returner is ready and then makes the final decision about what to do with the serve. Meanwhile, the returner studies the server's every move and prepares with similar rituals. In a rocking side-to-side motion and a bounce in her step, the returner prepares to react quickly when the server strikes the ball. As the toss goes up in the air, the returner starts moving forward and is elevated at contact of the serve, ready to hit the ground running.

To add a little punch to the block returns, the returner wants her body to have a little forward momentum on the split step and reaction. Before the serve is in play, the returner has predetermined her actions. When the serve is struck, all the returner has to do is read and react according to plan.

You can answer several questions before playing the point:

- Considering whether it is a first or second serve, will I block, chip, or drive the ball back into play?
- Is the server likely to attack the net behind the serve?
- In what direction will I attempt to execute—down the line, to the middle, or crosscourt?
- Do I plan to attack or stay back after the return?
- Will I attempt to pressure and influence serve selection?
- What can I anticipate happening off my return shot?

Going into points with the answers to these questions in place will better prepare you to make the right decisions in the reaction mode and may allow you to anticipate the action before it happens. Do not overthink!

Assuming the Server's Perspective

As the server takes one last look at the returner before sending the toss into the air, he is looking to see if the returner is ready to play. The server is also determining whether the returner's court position will affect the type of serve and placement he should use.

During the first few games, the server is collecting information about the returner and logging the data. Once the returner establishes a starting position in both the deuce and ad boxes, the server adjusts his visual perspective to those positions.

Where you typically position yourself side to side and up and back in the deuce and ad boxes is your neutral position. You are neutral because you are at the midpoint between the two extreme placements on the serve. Your position gives you a range of coverage that matches nearly all serve possibilities. The server quickly becomes familiar and comfortable with your neutral court position. Each time you take that neutral position, the server feels a little less pressure in selecting the serve, and you'll play an increasingly smaller role in his choice. When you use your court position to alter the server's perspective, you can become part of the decision, manipulating the server into thinking that an opportunity is available for exploitation. As you become more proactive by sporadically varying your court position, you can affect the serve, narrowing the possible options and allowing you to anticipate the serve with greater accuracy.

As in a game of poker, when another player has revealed his hand and shown you every weapon available, you might find that your opponent has difficulty with particular serve placements. You may be able to predict the serve a split second before it is hit by picking up on certain indicators—how the server stands to serve, how the server adjusts the toss, or how the server positions differently on particular serves.

When your opponent shows limited use of the service boxes, neglects certain targets, or provides you the indicators you need to anticipate the serve, you have more control. You may need to adjust your neutral court position to create better opportunities for your returns. Suppose the server is clearly struggling on the wide serves, hitting most of them into the net. Most of the time, the server is serving down the T and coming to the net, a pattern that has been working well for him. Your adjusted neutral court position favoring the T placements will give you a better opportunity to return the strongest serves while challenging your opponent to go for the wider placements he is struggling with.

Nick's Tip

Returners play with a server's mind by changing their ready and waiting position as the server starts the serve motion. Many times this will cause the server to change where he is going to serve the ball. Boris Becker never looked at the returner once he decided where he was going to serve.

Bait and Switch

To throw off the server's perspective, you use a different starting position this time. In taking that last look before the toss, the server notices that your position seems to be favoring one side. The server feels that you are looking for the down-the-T placement, offering a challenge to go for the wide ace. But as the server looks away from you to watch the toss, you shift your position back to true neutral with a good idea of where the serve might be going. Even if the server doesn't take the bait and serves down the T, you are reacting from the neutral position, so you give the server nothing open down the T, either.

When you shift your starting position right or left of neutral, the server tends to choose the part of the court you leave open—that is, until she becomes wise to your tricks. When you position farther back from neutral, deep in the court, you challenge the server to go for more angle and spins to beat you, lessening the effect of a powerful first serve. If you position a step or two closer to the service line, inside of neutral, you challenge the server to overpower you. To force the server to double-fault or use a second serve, you can close in tighter to make the service box seem much smaller to the server.

You Make the Call

Unless you are a regular on the professional tour, it is a rare occasion when you have the luxury of an umpire to call the lines for you. You must be able to determine whether a serve is in or out without losing focus on executing your return. You will improve this skill with experience.

When you see that a serve is out, be quick and decisive, making sure the server is aware of your call. You can gesture with your arm, raise your index finger, or make the call verbally, but you do not want the server to think you are indecisive. If you seem unsure, your opponent will challenge you and often convince himself that you are playing unfairly. Sometimes it can be difficult to make a clear judgment, which can occasionally lead to making a bad call unintentionally. If you are hoping the ball is out, under pressure you can convince yourself it went out, even when it hit the line.

For one reason or another, some players are so obsessed with winning that they cheat on line calls. You do not want to have the notorious reputation of lacking character as a competitor. Nobody has ever cheated their way to becoming a true champion in any sport. Good players can often tell if their ball went in or out by the feel of the shot at contact. When the server makes contact he can feel as well as see whether the ball is in. If you repeatedly make bad line calls, you can be sure your opponent is aware of it. Once you establish a pattern of making bad line calls, you can expect your opponent to do the same. It is a no-win situation for both players and an ugly match from that point on.

In the end, you are much better off playing it straight. If you believe you are getting hooked, call an umpire. Even professionals who challenge calls using the hawk eye only tend to get calls reversed around a third of the time. Ultimately, the last thing you want to do is to reward anyone who may be cheating by playing poorly and giving the victory to him. So, if you typically go on to play much worse once you've come to the conclusion you are playing someone who is making some bad calls, then for your own sake, give the opponent the benefit of the doubt.

Neutral Then Commit

Against the biggest servers, at times you have to rely on an educated guess to get you through. They have seen all the tricks and do not fall for them easily. Your best chance is to figure out the pattern of attack. When you have a good sense of what is coming, especially in a second-serve situation, you can play it neutral until the server looks up with the toss. You then commit yourself to run around what would be a backhand and play it as a forehand return. Because you are committing yourself, however, you run a risk of being burned if you do not guess correctly. To break serve you must take risks at times.

Work sparingly with your court-position tactics and make your adjustments more subtle. If you adjust too often, you will fail to affect the server. You do not want the server to be aware that you are baiting the serve selection to increase your control of the situation. Save these tactics for the most crucial points, and do not expect them to work all the time, especially against servers who know better.

Nick's Tip

I always make sure my students pay attention to the ball and do not allow themselves to be distracted from watching the ball by watching the opponent. Even though you have to watch the server to pick up clues about where the ball is going, remember to play the ball, not the opponent.

Reading Serve Technique

The server's stance to start the motion, the toss of the ball, an adjustment to the swing, or even a change of position on the baseline are possible indicators of the server's limitations or intent on the serve:

- If the starting stance has the server turned sideways with the front foot parallel to the baseline, you should look to see if the feet leave the ground on the serve.

- See if the server's body rotates completely and faces the net on the finish. If the server does not launch up off the ground and completely rotate, she will have trouble with certain placements.

- A right-handed player serving into the deuce box will always struggle to reach the wide and up-the-sideline placements unless she leaves the ground and rotates well in the motion. This server's best and favorite serve is likely to be down the T in the deuce box. In the ad box the same server will favor the wide serve to the right-handed returner's backhand and will have more difficulty down the T.

- Left-handed servers with this stance limitation will have the opposite occur—strong wide and weak down the T in the deuce box, strong down the T and weak wide in the ad box.

- When the server is facing the net with the front foot pointing more toward the net post, you cannot assume by the stance any patterns of strong versus weak placements.

So, what can you learn from watching the server's toss? Unless you are up against a highly skilled server who knows how to adjust the toss for the slice, kick, and flat serves under complete disguise, you can often predict the serve by the toss placement.

If you know the look of the toss for the server's biggest hard, flat serve, you can use that as a guide. If the right-handed server tosses the ball over the head, from the returner's perspective that toss would be *right* of where the server tosses on the flat serve. You can expect to see the kick serve, probably to your backhand side if you are right-handed. If you see the toss to the left of the hard, flat toss, you can expect a slice serve, likely into your body or to the forehand side much of the time. Do not expect the better servers to telegraph their toss adjustments this way, but if the opportunity arises, take advantage of it.

Also, at times you will see players position wider than normal behind the baseline. Agassi would at times position out by the doubles alley when serving to the ad court to give him a better angle, pulling the returner off the court. Any time you see the server in a wider position, be ready for the wide serve because there is a good chance you will see one.

Nick's Tip

The most successful servers have very little variation in the location of their toss. Even their kicker serve toss is placed slightly to the left but more behind them, as this is more difficult to read.

Establish Neutral Ground

When facing a server you have never played before, you will have to learn about the serve strengths and weaknesses in the first few games. You will have to defend against all potential serve placements until you learn otherwise. Find a position that locates you at the midpoint of the server's best possible serves. You should be one step and a full reach from covering the down-the-T placement and the same distance from covering the wide serve. Make sure you factor in the spin effect of the right-handed server versus a left-handed server. The power potential of the server will often determine how close or far back from the service line you should be. Once you establish that center point, your neutral position, you are ready to go.

If the server is neglecting certain areas of the service boxes, he may not be able to reach all the targets in both boxes. If the server focuses most of the serve placements to one side or the other, you can shift your court position accordingly. There is no sense in positioning to cover parts of the service box that are never used. Now you can narrow the possibilities and give yourself a better chance of covering the parts of the court your opponent is using. At the same time, you challenge the opponent to go for difficult placements. Early in the match you are better off giving yourself a little more time to react against first serves by taking a position a little deeper in the court. As you begin to zone in on the return and establish your confidence, you can take a more aggressive position a few steps closer to the service line.

The problem with closing in too tight in the return position is that you limit the time available for reaction to the power serve. Positioning very deep in the court opens the opportunity for angle spins, which pull you even wider off the court on the return and allow the serve and volleyer to move in closer. You need quick feet to play deep behind the baseline on the return because you have more ground to cover. So find a middle ground that works for you, and be willing to vary your court position as part of your attack.

The rituals and routines leading up to executing the return have an important role in your readiness to react and your ability to execute. Although routines will differ from player to player based on style and preference, you must include some key elements if you want accurate and successful returns.

▶ Assume the Correct Stance

Your neutral position is the location you normally take before the server's toss is in the air. Your position to react to the serve may or may not be the same as your neutral position. This position involves a split step timed to elevate and land just after contact on the serve, creating a wide base of support with your feet nearly two shoulder widths apart, so you are down and ready to react quickly to either the forehand or backhand side. The key to having better reach and range of coverage begins with a wider split step, precisely timed to the server's routine. See figure 6.1 for an example of correctly assuming your stance for return of serve.

Some players make a habit of starting in a neutral position well inside the baseline. As the server puts the toss in the air, the returner backs up a few steps before creating the split step. This routine is fine as long as you are able to position quickly and get your body weight forward as you split. If the server catches you leaning backward, you will have problems controlling the return. This position is unforgiving. Be careful.

Most players are better off in a neutral position a few steps back from where they want to split-step. As the toss goes into the air, they move forward to make the split, giving more punch to the defensive return. You will find other players who start in a neutral position and never move forward or back. Your routine may change from first- to second-serve situations and

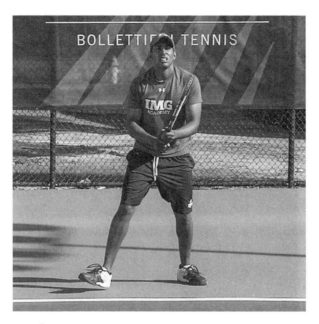

Figure 6.1   Return-of-serve stance.

as you work court-position tactics. Whichever routine you choose, make sure you include a well-timed wide split-step.

Make Controlled and Aggressive Returns

Although the serve can be a player's biggest offensive threat, the return should be a player's biggest defensive threat. The server is providing the power for you and is hitting the ball in your general direction. All you have to do is get the ball back into play. Of course, against the bigger servers this is a task easier said than done. Your goal is to neutralize the opponent's weapon and get the server into the point. You may wonder why the players with the most powerful serves aren't always winning all the tournaments. Well, it takes more than a big serve to win. All too often, the big servers struggle to come up with enough breaks of serve because they are deficient in other aspects of the game. So if you can just get past the serve and return the ball back into play, you may find those big servers much easier to beat out of the rally. Thinking offensively and always going for return winners on first serves will lead to errors in starting the point. That is not the correct strategic mind-set!

Thinking defensively naturally puts you into a reflex-reaction mode, simplifying your ground strokes for quickness and permitting better timing on the return. You begin to see the value of blocking, chipping, and slicing as well as compact driving returns. You should feel like a backboard, setting up a wall of defense like the one that a volleyer creates at the net.

You are defending your territory against an aerial assault, using a shield to deflect the incoming serves back into play. Any way you can, you seek to neutralize the server's strength, get the point started, and gain offensive control before the point ends.

If you can lure the server into going for more aggressive placements and more powerful serves to overcome your tenacious defensive stand, you will likely see more faults on the first serve. The second-serve opportunities are your best chance for capitalizing. Now you have the option to be more aggressive and think more offensively, depending on the strength of the second serve. You can become more active in adjusting your court position by pressuring and baiting the server. You can think about driving the ball rather than just blocking it back. On occasion, you might attack the net off the return, forcing the server to try to pass you on the second shot. What you do not want to do is squander opportunities by always going for too much. The return must get points started in your mind. When you try to end points with the return, your percentage of errors to winners favors the opponent.

Types of Returns

Different types of returns are appropriate in different situations. Here we'll discuss the technique and strategy for each of them.

▶ Sonic Return

The aggressive, or sonic, serve is best described as a lethal weapon that is almost impossible to return (in fact at times you cannot even touch the ball). At other times the serve is so aggressive that your return options are very limited. Andre Agassi would go for big returns from the server's first serve. He felt confident that this strategy would be successful for him even though it might take him a few games to establish it.

Grip

The preferred starting grip for the return of serve is the forehand grip on the bottom hand. This enables players with two-hand backhands to immediately separate the top hand to react to the forehand side, without having to first change the grip and then react. To react to the backhand side, players learn to use the top hand to position the racket as the bottom hand shifts to the backhand grip. There are a few players with western forehand grips who do the opposite. They spin the top hand into position on the grip for the backhand as the bottom hand positions the racket. When circumstances require, however, some players such as Roger Federer, Kei Nishikori, and Stan Wawrinka use a continental or eastern grip to chip their forehand return back into play.

Footwork and Reaction

The starting depth of court position will depend on the potential threat of the serve. Big servers will force you to position farther back, unless you have very strong reaction and return skills. Given less than a second to read, react, and make contact when returning a big first serve, it is essential to simplify the preparation of the racket on reaction as follows:

- Most players prefer to start back a step or two from where they react to make contact. Starting back allows them to create some forward movement before the toss and have momentum forward as they move diagonally to cut off the serve.

- Players work with a full body turn toward contact and typically maintain an open stance unless forced to lunge wide for the ball.

- On the forehand side, the body turns toward contact and the hitting arm extends to get out toward the ball flight; the palm of the hitting hand should point toward the contact point and no farther back than that (see figure 6.2, *a-c*). It is not necessary to achieve full butt end pointing toward contact when blocking back a powerful serve.

Figure 6.2   Preparation and reaction for a return of serve on the forehand side.

- On the backhand side, the same limited take-back should occur as with the forehand, and the palm of the top hand points toward contact (see figure 6.3, *a* and b). The racket preparation can be a little more similar to a ground stroke when facing a second serve.

Figure 6.3 Preparation and reaction for a return of serve on the backhand side.

Contact

The limited racket preparation on reaction enables a player to make late adjustments for the bounce and still meet the ball out in front with the racket aligned to the center of the chest at contact. To maintain high percentages of returns in play, players should remember that the return is intended to start points, not end them. A well-placed return can be the front end of a combination of shots that ends the point. See figure 6.4 for an example of proper contact for the return.

Figure 6.4   Racket and ball contact for the return.

Nick's Tip

Simplify the preparation of the racket to save time on the return. Most players will want to start back a step or two from where they want to make contact and move forward to meet the ball.

Follow-Through and Recovery

When driving a return, there should be a full extension of the hitting arm on follow-through. The more time you have gives you more follow-through. The recovery movement begins with a crossover step or two followed by shuffle steps to get back into position for the next shot. See figure 6.5 for a correct example of the follow-through on the return.

Return Against Serve and Volley

Big servers will often establish a pattern of regularly attacking the net behind every first serve and not so often behind the second. Breaking this offensive can be challenging unless you know how to adjust on your returns. Preplanning the point before your return is especially important against the serve-and-volley player because your returns have to work as passing shots. To overcome the serve-and-volley attack, you must make several adjustments.

Adjust Shot Selection

Rather than using deep crosscourt returns to get a rally started, you should have as your primary targets the feet of the incoming server, down the line, and angle crosscourt. The key to returning a serve when the server is coming in almost all of the time is to make the server volley. Try to dip the return with spin.

Figure 6.5 Follow-through on the return.

Adjust Stroke Selection

Rather than blasting the topspin drives that are high clearing over the net, work with slicing, chipping, and blocking on the returns to give the server less to work with on the first volley. If you can force your opponent to volley with the ball at the feet, control of the point often shifts to you.

Vary Court Position

The serve-and-volley player relies on a specific timing of the serve, moves in as close to the net as she can, and when the returner starts the backswing, makes her split step and moves to the volley position. As the returner, if you change the distance between you and the server by adjusting up and back, you will make it difficult for the server to establish consistent timing for the attack.

Rather than maintaining the same neutral court position for each serve, move in a step or two for some points and move back a step or two at other times. If you don't permit the server to become comfortable with the depth of your court position, she will have more trouble getting into a strong groove.

Think Two

If you feel immense pressure to hit passing-shot winners off every return, you are likely to end up making many errors. Get yourself into the point on the return, and go for the pass on the second or third shot you hit. The longer the point extends, the more the odds favor the returner at the baseline. If you neutralize the first serve and keep the return low or difficult to reach, you can take control of the point and then close on the following shots.

> **Nick's Tip**
>
> If I were coaching John Isner or Milos Raonic, I would have them coming in almost all of the time. The fear factor of a big server will cause their opponent to tighten up and give away points. When the big server stays back, the fear factor is lost.

Return Against Baseliner

When you are not under pressure of serve and volley, you want to maintain the primary objective of getting the ball into play a high percentage of the time. The single most important strength for Nadal and Djokovic that enables them to break serve so often lies in the intent to use their returns as great defensive weapons that get points started. You have to be disciplined in your game plan to overcome wanting to do too much with the returns, which will lead to unnecessary errors. Unless one player comes to the net behind either the serve or return, the point will progress into a rally off the return ball. If both players are right-handed on the deuce side, and if the server pulls you off the court with a wide serve, a return crosscourt will allow you to recover for the next shot and will likely create the forehand-to-forehand crosscourt rally pattern. A return of the wide serve to the deep midcourt will give the server the option of hitting to either corner.

A return down the line puts you at risk unless it is an outright winner or an approach that you follow in and to the net. Down the line is considered a low-percentage play based on recovering your baseline court position and will likely lead to a crosscourt shot that could easily catch you out of position. Wide serves in the ad box work much the same way. If you return crosscourt you will likely establish a crosscourt backhand-to-backhand rally. Serves to the T placement in both boxes present the option of hitting to either corner depending on which rally pattern you wish to establish. Keep in mind that players must know the level of their opponent. If the opposing player is better than you are, you must gamble a bit when you have opportunities to go for it.

▶ Defensive Returns

Most ground strokes are hit offensively with bigger strokes to generate power. On the return, you must adjust your forehand and backhand ground strokes for a more defensive application. The serve speed generally provides plenty of power, so you will not need big offensive swings.

You need to work with compact, abbreviated versions of your ground strokes using the existing power on the ball to create your shots. You should use relatively no backswing and a focus on the contact point and follow-through. When using the block return, you do not have much backswing or follow-through. See figure 6.6 for an example of a defensive return.

Nick's Tip

If you try to adjust your feet quickly into a more comfortable neutral stance, you will often be too late to execute. Avoid becoming wrong-footed. Minimize the footwork involved, and develop your skills in working with an open stance.

Figure 6.6   Defensive return.

Against powerful serve weapons, you barely have time to get your racket on the ball, let alone set up the perfect stance. You need to learn to execute from the open stance and be able to lunge transfer from the open stance on both the forehand and backhand sides. When the power serve is placed well within your reach, all you have to do is rotate your hips and shoulders, never moving your feet out of the split step. If the ball is one step away, you will still set up in the open stance to execute.

The ultimate test for a returner is having to move and reach to execute the returns. Most players have far more success with their returns on serves hit very near to them compared with serves that make them move. If your hitting stance changes from open to closed, your options on the return become much more limited and predictable. Unless you are hitting a one-hand backhand return, the closed hitting stances will cause problems. The open and neutral stances are the ones to use in all circumstances to keep your return options open.

To return a ball that is within reach is one thing, but to be able to stretch, reach, and lunge for a return and still do damage is the mark of a skilled returner. Some of the most spectacular returns occur when the player has to lunge and reach. Players such as Jimmy Connors and Andre Agassi in the past, and now, Rafa Nadal, David Ferrer, Novak Djokovic, Serena Williams, and Andy Murray, are very dangerous on full-reach returns. Most players break down significantly when you test their reach and range of coverage on the return. They experience a lack of control and a total loss of power in that situation. The reason for most of their problems has to do with stroke technique. The best returners do not take a backswing and then stroke out to make contact. The technique used by all the greatest returners is different from the approach the average player uses.

As if trying to catch the ball with a baseball glove, outstanding returners first react by extending the racket out to get behind the incoming ball. As they reach out to get the hitting hand behind and beneath the ball, their feet automatically adjust to support the stroke. Driving out of an open stance, they lunge on a diagonal toward the point of contact and generate a powerful pulling action across the body. They reach out and then pull the stroke back across the body, producing a powerful result on contact. This action is very different from that of the average returner, who reaches back into a backswing and then strokes out to reach the ball. If you work on the advanced technique for full-reach returns, you will strengthen your range of coverage and frustrate your opponents with your titanium wall of defense. See figure 6.7, *a* and *b*, for an example of reacting to the ball using a lunge.

Figure 6.7   Lunging for the return.

Return Drills

These are the drills we use at the IMG Academy Bollettieri Tennis Program to teach and practice returning skills. Use these drills to improve your serve technique for your returns.

Backboard Drill

Go to the backboard. Start out 20-30 feet from the wall. Rally against the wall. Then move in a few steps, then a few more steps while rallying against the wall. As you get closer to the wall, you have to shorten your backswing and revert to a more and more open stance. In the same way, in order to return serve effectively, you must be able to shorten your backswing and hit from an open or semi open stances.

Return-of-Serve Drill

I had Andre Agassi do a return-of-serve drill every day to increase his reaction time and ability to prepare quickly for big serves. Andre (the returner) and the server would each start out at the baseline hitting serves and returns. I would then have them each move in closer to the service line step by step, serving and returning closer and closer to one another. Finally, each player ended up just behind the service line serving and returning. Each time the players got closer and closer to each other, because of the lack of reaction time, the returner was required to use shorter and shorter swing patterns and stance adjustments. If you don't have a partner or coach to practice this drill with you, you can use the backboard. Start back and then gradually move in closer and closer to reduce the time you have to react for the return of serve.

Conclusion

For most players, making the mental adjustment from thinking offensively on the return to thinking defensively will boost success on the return. Opening your senses and becoming more aware of the patterns and tendencies throughout point play will help you anticipate the action before it happens.

Getting into the habit of preplanning the start of the point will help you make better decisions in the reflex mode. Take control as a returner, and don't allow yourself to fall into a victim mind-set. Finally, learning to love the challenge of returning the big serves will put you in the mind-set for creating positive results. Before you know it, you will be making right-back-atcha returns.

You can do it! You must believe you can return serve and look forward to breaking down your opponent with a consistent return of serve that can be executed in offensive and defensive situations. Do not become predictable or your opponent will gain the advantage. Skip around and keep the server guessing where your next return will be.

Chapter 7

Net Play

Tennis will always have changes, but the future is becoming very clear about two things: You cannot have a weakness, and you must be able to play from every inch of the court, including the net.

This chapter offers insight into the mentality of being offensive even when on the defense and building toward closing combinations. You will learn the tools of the trade and how they work together within the flow of building a point toward your desired outcome. Building a game plan around the right objectives takes the pressure off hitting individual shots. You use the power of shot combinations to do the work. Making the right decisions in match play determines whether you are gambling against the casino or you are the casino! With statistics on your side and an understanding of how to stage the end of points, you can beat the house even against players of greater skill.

Court-Position Considerations for Net Play

A player's position on the court will have a big impact on the shot selection of their volley, which may range from deep to short angle volleys.

Rally Positioning

The recovery position to the center hash mark after the majority of your shots has changed in many ways. You are positioned wide in the court in a rally if you hit the ball crosscourt to shot selection 1. This is the highest-percentage shot because it allows you to recover fully. You would recover behind the center hash mark only if you were to choose shot selection 2. Otherwise, the recovery position shifts as you hit to different targets. These recovery positions allow you to cover the sharp angles as well as down the line, putting you halfway in between.

The problem is that you have less than two seconds to reach these positions. When you drive the ball for an attempted winner to shot selection 3, you must hope to end the point on that shot. Unable to recover in time, you will leave the crosscourt open for the opponent. To preserve adequate recovery time, players maintain crosscourt rallies as they build points. If their intent is to hit down the line within a rally to force a change in the rally pattern, they do so with underspin or high loopers to give themselves enough time to recover.

Positioning When Attacking the Net

When advancing to the net, you have even less time to reach proper position, and you must avoid leaving high-percentage openings for passing shots. The shot direction that provides the shortest distance for improving your net position is down the line. When you are approaching off balls in the midcourt, straight down the middle is the highest-percentage shot.

To become more tenacious at the net, you must realize that your positioning at the net is more important than your power! Regardless of the strength of your net game, your ability to achieve position poses a great threat to the opponent. Without the skills to defend the net effectively, however, your threatening position there will lose its influence. The approach shot determines not only your ability to position but also the difficulty you will face in volleying.

Your ability to force your opponent will depend on many factors, including the quality of your opponent. When you think of a forcing shot, you probably think of a deep shot to the baseline, penetrating and powerful. A drop shot set up with disguise and used correctly is a forcing shot as

Nick's Tip

A variety of shot selections will break down your opponents. Do not develop a pattern of play when coming to the net.

well. An opponent who positions deep behind the baseline in the rally is much more difficult to force on deep balls than an opponent who positions right on the baseline.

Many players who excel at attacking the net use a variety of shots on the approach. Besides driving with topspin, they will use the slice and chip approaches, which allow them to adjust the depth of their shots from deep shots to drop shots.

Working with a slice or chip allows you a little added time to reach better net position. Mixing up the attack and using a variety of shots on the down-the-line approach will keep the opponent confused about how deep in the court to play. Also note that opponents playing deep behind the baseline are very vulnerable to the sharp spin angles that take them off the court.

Also, when in net position you need quick and compact preparation for all volleys, especially the reflex volley, so you need to be sharp in your ready position. Make it a habit to keep the racket head up in front of you so that you can react quickly to both sides. Exaggerate your normal athletic ready position for net play. If you are to favor one side over the other in your ready position, remember that your backhand volley can go across your body whereas the forehand gets jammed. When in doubt, react with the backhand volley by sliding your racket across your body, but be sure to have a firm wrist. Most players volley with their arms. I want you to volley with your feet.

Closing Position

When you work your way into closing net position, you need to establish a position that enables you to defend against the down-the-line pass, sharp-angle pass, and lob. Generally speaking, this means the ideal position would have you within one step and a full reach of the racket from the sideline, within one step and a full reach of the angle pass, and within range of still covering the lob. As you begin to learn about the opponent and what he can and can't do well, you can adjust this position accordingly. When you approach down the center, your net position is in the center, forcing your opponent to create angles to pass you. The closer you get to the net, the better you can cover the angle pass but the more vulnerable you are to the lob. If you hang back to cover the lob, you leave the angle open, so you must develop a sense of when you can close in tight by considering the strengths and weaknesses of the opponent.

The majority of players who range from 2.5 to 4.0 do not come in close enough. No matter what level of play you are, I recommend closing into the net, and if necessary, giving the lob away. In time, you will be able to make your approaches more effective causing the opponent to hit defensive lobs and giving you time to move back and hit an overhead or swinging volley.

This pattern of play (to protect against the lob) will be counterproductive to their game. Most fear that if they move in closer, their opponent will lob them. Yes, when you attack you will be susceptible to the lob, but in time your approach shot will get better and better, forcing your opponent to hit a defensive lob and enabling you to hit an overhead. Being close to the net forces your opponent to gamble with shot selection and makes your volley much easier.

Approaching Effectiveness

A lot of players ask, "If I always follow the percentage rules of maintaining crosscourt patterns in rallies and approaching down the line, won't I be too predictable?"

Being predictable is not always bad if you maintain the patterns that provide little opportunity for the opponent to capitalize. Although percentage rules may dictate the direction of your shots, you can create variety by varying the depth of your shots without changing the direction. What is important is that you understand how it affects you when you decide to deviate from the percentage rules.

If you are playing someone with a huge forehand but no backhand threat, you may be able to justify attacking on a low-percentage crosscourt approach into that weak backhand, even though you leave much wider passing lanes. If that tactic proves to be a risk that is not paying off, however, you may need to stick to the high-percentage play.

The last thing you want to do on the approach is provide the opponent with the type of shot she loves to work with for hitting passing shots. Most players prefer an approach shot hit with some power, with a little topspin, and that bounces within a few feet of the baseline right up into their preferred height of contact. All too often, players approach repeatedly on this type of shot and then wonder why the opponent is having a field day passing them.

The use of variety on the approach is about giving the opponent less to work with on the pass. Varying spin, speed, and depth on the attack will force opponents to work outside their comfort zone and generate their own pace to earn every pass. If you want to improve the conditions of play at the net and increase your effectiveness on the attack, then don't feed the giant!

Nick's Tip

An opponent has a huge forehand and a defensive backhand. To get to his backhand, first hit deep and wide to his strength (forehand) and then hit to his weakness (backhand). Don't always start out hitting to his weakness (backhand).

Net-Position Objectives

Your objective at the net is to position yourself at the midpoint of your opponent's possible shots. The three shots you must be able to reach are the down-the-line pass, the crosscourt pass, and the lob. When you approach the net you are challenging your opponent to beat you with one of these shots.

Nick's Tip

When Tommy Haas was 10 years old he asked me, Nick, when do I go to the net? I told him to go in all the time and you will discover the answer.

The shot direction that works best for your court position is down the line because it provides the shortest distance to good position at the net (see figure 7.1).

When you work with a short ball near the middle of the court, hitting the approach straight down the center allows you to move into position and limit the angles on your opponent's passing shots. When you have an opportunity to attack the net, it is important to understand the shot pattern that allows you to establish good position behind your approach shots. When you attack from inside the baseline, your ball will take even less time to reach the opponent, thus giving you less time to move into the correct recovery position.

Approaching crosscourt requires you to run farther to establish net position while leaving an open court for your opponent to pass. But the crosscourt approach that delivers the ball to an opponent's weaker forehand or backhand can prove successful. This is a strategic choice you must make on a case-by-case basis (see figure 7.2). Note that the player must travel farther to the correct position to cover the opponent's passing shot or lob.

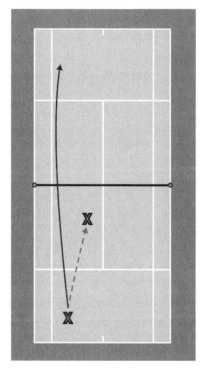

Figure 7.1 Optimal position when approaching down the line. This position allows you to cover a down-the-line pass, crosscourt pass, and lob with the least travel time.

The situation created in the rally can also influence your decision on where to approach. When you have your opponent in trouble, you have more options because you are close to ending the point with your approach. In this instance, position becomes less important in determining the direction for approach. The crosscourt approach thus becomes a more attractive option, but you must still cover the return by proper positioning, always anticipating the ball to come back (see figure 7.3).

Sometimes you will be faced with a first volley but not be in position to end the point. Your objective should be to use the first volley to position yourself better to end the point on the next ball. In this case, think of a first volley as nothing more than another approach shot. Use the shot patterns that you applied to your approach shots. Down-the-line or straight-ahead volleys will allow you to improve your court position for a second volley or overhead to end the point. For a point-ending volley or overhead, hit primarily to the open court. Remember that if you don't hit this volley with enough force to end the point, you'll have to move farther to establish good positioning at the net. Hitting behind an opponent occasionally will prevent an opponent from anticipating your patterns.

Don't underestimate the value of being in good position at the net. By being in good position, you will put pressure on your opponent to hit better shots, often resulting in errors. Penetrating approaches and firm first volleys also produce forced errors. Good position at the net should place you one step and a reach from a down-the-line pass, close

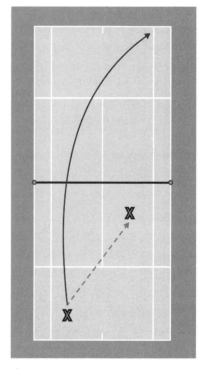

Figure 7.2 Position when approaching crosscourt.

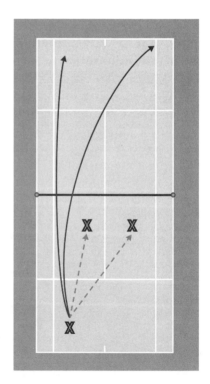

Figure 7.3 The player must travel farther to establish correct position at the net when approaching crosscourt rather than down the line.

enough to the net to reach an angle pass, and still able to guard against the lob. As you learn more about your opponent's strengths, weaknesses, and tendency to hit certain shots, you can adjust your position accordingly. In general, when you are in good position you will be approximately 6 to 8 feet (2 to 2.5 m) from the net.

Types of Net-Play Shots

There are many shot sequences that can occur at the net. Here, we've identified some of them and described the correct execution of the shots.

Approach Shots

An approach shot is a shot you select to hit and then continue moving forward to volley the opponent's reply. Many times an effective approach shot will result in an unforced or forced error by the opponent as they try to hit a passing shot or lob you when you're at the net. Keep in mind that there are several options available for approach shots. Do not overhit your approach shot! The position on the court and the level of play must be considered when hitting the approach shot. A few other considerations are as follows:

- Have continuous movement to the net. This will get you a step closer for your volley and put more pressure on your opponent.
- Do not try to anticipate what your opponent will do.
- Don't try to hit your approach shot on the line. Give yourself a margin for error.

Your objective on approach shots will be determined by what you have to do according to the ability of your opponent. It's not necessary to go for a winner on the approach if your volleys are strengths; the idea is to put pressure on the opponent to pass in this case and to minimize mistakes on the approach shot. The more powerful the approach, the less time you give yourself to establish position at the net. So, it is essential to move through the approach shot with your footwork without losing time. The underspin approaches are easier to move through than the flat drives. The footwork patterns commonly used for the approach shots are the cross-behind step, in which the back foot crosses behind the front, and the kick step. For the flatter drives, you may find the open stance more suitable. Remember to be careful of hitting too many underspin approach shots. Why? Many players have a tendency to stop moving to the ball and then hitting slices because the ball has dropped so low. I discouraged Andre Agassi from hitting any sliced approach shots for the entire first year he was with me. I had him get to the ball and go for it.

First Volley

The first volley is often the determining factor in who wins the point. Yes, you want your first volley to go over the net, but it must also put your opponent into a defensive position.

Move in as much as you can behind your approach for your first volley, but when your opponent is about to make contact, you have to split-step to play the next shot without coming to a complete stop. Work to get both feet to the ground, and try to maintain your forward momentum while directing it toward the incoming ball. You want your body to have a light feel so that you can react quickly. You just want your feet to touch briefly so that you can make your next move.

No matter where you are for the volleys, especially the first, come to a split-step (stop) movement as the opponent starts his backswing. Then when he's hit the ball and it is approaching you, move to the ball with your feet. Do not think it's ok to lunge to hit the volley or to stretch out your arms to hit the volley. Max Mirnyi, a top ATP doubles player from the academy, always says to move to the ball with your feet, trying to make contact with the ball at its highest level above the net. A low first volley will require you to open the face of the racket, applying underspin for control and usually requiring depth. The closer you get to the net for your first and second volleys, the more court you will have to volley into.

If your first volley is below the level of the net, you will likely need a second volley to close the point. In this case, use the first volley like an approach, going down the line to protect your court position as you close farther in to the net. On the second volley you will have a better opportunity to angle the ball away. Remember to use your position to pressure the opponent and create a wall of defense that the opponent cannot easily penetrate.

Nick's Tip

For the underspin approaches, all volleys, and your overhead, you should consider using the continental grip so that you will not be caught between grip changes in reflex situations. The continental grip can be equally effective on both the forehand and backhand sides and be right for touch volleys.

▶ Forehand Volley

To develop quick and compact volley technique, you have to overcome the urge to add power. Your first reaction to the volley should be to prepare as you would to catch the ball. On the forehand side, if you had a baseball glove instead of a racket in your hand, your natural reaction would be to reach forward to catch. You would not react by moving the elbow back. The same should occur on the volley. Your hitting elbow reacts in the first move by going forward to meet the ball out in front of you as you pivot your hips and shoulders to face the contact point. Use your opponent's power, and direct the ball back.

For the forehand volley (see figure 7.4, *a* and *b,* for an example), get into a strong ready position with your arms and racket extended in front of you. Simply turn your hips and shoulders. This motion will automatically take your racket back, producing a short, compact backswing perfect for the

Figure 7.4   Forehand volley.

volley. This hip and shoulder turn will place the racket head in a position where you can see it in your peripheral vision when your eyes are facing totally forward.

Overhead Smash

When the contact point is much higher than shoulder level, you should prepare for the overhead smash (see figure 7.5, *a-d*, for an example). To react to the overhead, point your hitting elbow toward the back fence, keeping it with the shoulders and parallel to the ground. Use your footwork to position the contact point in front of you whenever possible. The overhead is like a half-serve motion, compact and easy to time. The hitting arm should be relaxed and the back posture straight throughout the motion. Here are three tips for the overhead smash:

- Point the nonhitting hand toward the ball. This keeps the shoulders up.
- Do not set your feet in the hitting position until the racket starts going up. Wind and spin will vary the ball in flight.
- You must also copy your serve motion to go up to hit the ball.

▶ Backhand Volley

You should react to the backhand volley with the hitting elbow, again moving forward to meet the ball (see figure 7.6, *a* and *b*, for an example). React with a hip and shoulder turn to face the point of contact as you position the racket for contact. Make sure your racket head does not cut across your body. To offset this, make sure the racket head extends past your hitting hand at the end of the volley.

▶ Backhand Overhead Volley

This shot is and always will be in the category of very difficult to execute. Why? Lack of strength when the ball and the racket are above your head on your weaker side. Following is how you can offset this:

1. Try to run around and hit the ball from the forehand side. (You must make this move immediately.)
2. With a one-hand backhand, your grip selection will be the key to your success. You must have your hand behind the racket in order to snap and accelerate the racket head to bring the ball down.

Nick's Tip

The higher your non hitting hand goes up and stays up, the better the chances are that your hitting arm will be fully extended when making contact with the ball.

Figure 7.5 Overhead smash.

Figure 7.6 Backhand volley.

3. With the two-hand backhand, you first must accept that you will not be able to reach up to the ball as high as with the one-hand backhand smash, but two hands give you much more strength. You will have two choices:

   a. Reach up to the ball with two hands on the racket and when contacting the ball; accelerate the top hand as you do with a two-hand backhand ground stroke.

   b. Reach up to the ball with two hands on the racket. Do not try to bring the ball down, but hit it back up to a neutral position on the court.

4. Some players make contact with two hands and then release the top hand.

Nick's Tip

The longer you keep your non hitting hand on the racquet, the more support and strength you will give to the hitting hand.

To execute the backhand overhead (see figure 7.7, *a-c*, for an example), you prepare by turning your back to the net as you move into position under the ball. The elbow of the hitting arm will point upward toward contact. This will position the butt of the racket to point straight up toward the point of contact. Then, in a pulling motion upward, the butt of the racket drives up, straightening the arm into contact and sending the racket head over the top. It is like a service motion, only in reverse.

Figure 7.7   Backhand overhead volley.

The lower you let the ball drop, the more strength and options you will have including the two-hand swing volley. To
execute this you must move your feet.

▶ Drop Volley

When you find your opponent comfortably deep in the backcourt, it is a
perfect time for a drop volley (see figure 7.8, *a-d,* for an example). The
occasional drop volley forces the opponent to pay attention to the short
court and play closer to the baseline. Then when you volley deep, you have
a better chance to force the opponent. You want to keep the opponent
thinking the volley could be left or right, deep or short.

To drop-volley effectively, your arm and racket must work together as
a unit to absorb the impact of the incoming ball. Your preparation looks
identical to the deep block volley, so the opponent never expects it. Like
a shock absorber, you want to absorb the shock of impact. Avoid trying
to make the drop volley too good or you'll likely hit into the net. Think
of it as a short attack that the opponent will struggle to reach. By merely
forcing your opponent with a drop volley, you will often win the point
on the next shot. It is helpful when learning this skill to use the softer
10-and-under balls to get the feel of how the ball cushions into the strings.
I suggest you use the same grip as you use for your volleys, in a continental
or weak eastern position.

▶ Swinging Volley

In the late 1980s, even though I had coached Brian Gottfried, Paul Annacone, and other students with great volleys, there was gossip in the tennis
community that my students never volleyed. I took this as a compliment
and told Agassi, Courier, and Seles to swing at the volleys. This shot today
is a major weapon on the tour and even at lower levels. It's the swinging
volley.

The swinging volley (see figure 7.9, *a-d*, for an example) is nothing
more than a regular ground stroke without letting the ball bounce—same
grip, same level swing, same footwork. Adding some topspin to this shot
will add more control. You can use the swinging volley on a surprise
attack out of the rally when you see that your shot is very penetrating
and has your opponent in deep trouble. Move in early and look for the
swinging volley. You can also use it to thwart the high looping balls that

Figure 7.8   Drop volley.

players can get into a pattern of hitting. Once the opponent settles in after one or two high loopers, move in early when you sense another one is on the way and look to strike with a swinging volley. Treat it like an approach shot and follow it in to the net. This is a very common shot in doubles play.

Figure 7.9   Swinging volley.

The keys to an effective swinging volley are as follows:

1. The grip used is the same as for your ground strokes. I recommend a strong semiwestern.
2. Make contact with the ball at shoulder height.
3. Swing level, as when hitting a flat-drive forehand. The shoulders should stay level with no upper body movement.
4. Have your left hand extended (nonhitting hand) and catch the racket at the end of the swing. For lefties, it's just the opposite.
5. Accelerate the racket head on contact, and go out to the nonhitting hand.
6. Move forward to anticipate a defensive reply.

Conclusion

There are numerous variations of shots, but keep in mind that versatility is effective if you don't give the shot away with different swings for different shots. It's all about disguise! Please don't try all the option shots at once. Concentrate on a few and make them work for you. Too many cooks can spoil the broth.

Chapter 8

Specialty Shots

Because of the power in today's game, adding "touch" and the specialty shots is as important as ever before. Power, power, and more power is not a guarantee of winning tennis matches. Power with variety will, however, increase your chances greatly.

The majority of tennis players at all levels of play say, "Wow, look how hard the pros are hitting the ball. I want to hit it like them." Power without control and variation will not pay the bills. Home runs are not the key to winning.

Deep, penetrating power shots drive opponents back to positions deeper behind the baseline. This opens up opportunities to attack the short court with drop shots, which sets up the lob as a perfect closing combination. Use slice to set up the drop shot, the drop shot to set up the lob—it's about connecting shots together to take the opponent down. Use a sharp angle to pull your opponent in and wide off the court, followed by a closing shot deep to the opposite corner. It's a balance of power and touch that makes the best players so tough to beat. Anytime the opponent is expecting a deep, powerful shot, she is vulnerable to the "touch" attack.

Drop Shot

I can promise you that after reading this section you will have newfound respect for the potential of the drop shot. Characteristic of classical players

153

in the early years of tennis, the drop shot was a cleverly disguised weapon built around a game of attacking with the use of underspin. The deep-slice ground stroke and the chip-and-slice approach are examples of shots that combine well in a one-two punch with the drop shot.

It is not enough to work your opponent side to side to create open-court opportunities. Learning to work with deep and short shot combinations can add another dimension to your game. Keep your opponent guessing what you will do, and make him defend the whole court. That is the key to winning.

What Is the Drop Shot?

An effective drop shot crosses the net with a margin for error and bounces twice before the opponent's service line, bouncing no higher than the height of the net. The drop shot has often been referred to as a low-percentage shot, and it can be when not used correctly and when there is very little margin for error. When players resort to a drop shot that has not been set up, they are often looking to bail out of a point. When the drop shot is used this way, it is often hit with no margin for error, resulting in an error in the net. Thus, it is a low-percentage play. By setting up the drop shot through combinations and disguise, it becomes a very valuable weapon and a high-percentage play. In other words, you need not put pressure on yourself to hit the perfect drop shot. Set it up and give yourself margin for error.

The drop shot is the key element of many combinations of shots that use disguise to create deep and short opportunities in the court. Power players are effective at moving their opponents left and right, keeping them positioned deep in the back of the court. Touch players use deep slices and chips together with the drop shot to create opportunities and manipulate their opponent's court position (yes, they will also slip in a few driving-deep ground strokes to keep their opponents guessing).

Having a balance of touch and power allows you to keep your opponent guessing about what you are going to do. Once that happens, you have the advantage. When your opponent is deep in the court, you beat them short. This will force the opponent to pay attention to the potential of your attacking short by positioning closer to the baseline as they defend. Now, any deep, penetrating shots you hit have a better chance to force

Nick's Tip

Combinations with a drop shot add a new dimension to a power game by making your game plan more diverse and effective.

errors. When you pull your opponent off the court to the left, you attack the open court to her right.

Many players use the drop shot at the wrong time and without setting it up. For example, in a long rally from the baseline, you may become anxious about the length of the point and want to end it with a winning drop shot. You might occasionally be successful in this scenario, but more often than not you'll lose the point because you didn't set up the drop shot with a combination. Your opponent is able to get an early read on your drop shot, run it down, and put it away.

Once you have established the use of chips and deep slices, you have conditioned your opponent to associate your drop-shot preparation with your hitting the ball deep. An opponent in that mind-set is vulnerable to your drop shot.

Other variables that affect the use of the drop shot are your ability to disguise it, the weather, and the playing surface. How often you use the drop shot during a match depends on several factors. As a rule, you should use it sparingly, just often enough to affect your opponent's positioning and anticipation. On windy days or on days when the ball becomes heavy because of humidity, you might use the drop shot more frequently. If the opponent's weaknesses, fitness, or an injury makes her particularly vulnerable, use the drop shot more often. Clay and grass surfaces are more conducive to successful drop shots than hard courts are. However, Nadal and Djokovic commonly incorporate the drop shot into their attack, even on hard courts. In addition, you must cater to the conditions and your opponent to determine how frequently you use the drop shot. You need to open your senses to what is around you and take everything into consideration—where the sun is, which way the wind is blowing, and what works against your opponent.

Disguising the Drop Shot

When hitting your ground strokes, you must look exactly the same with your preparation from A to Z and just before contact with the ball change to your drop-shot grip. The key to a winning drop shot is disguise. The whole concept of disguise is to get the opponent to believe he is seeing one thing while you deliver the opposite. For example, when you appear to have hit a deep-slice backhand, your opponent begins to lean and step back, waiting for the ball to come back deep. As the ball begins to cross the net, your opponent realizes that you have really hit a drop shot, but by then, it is too late to react in time. Your drop shot is therefore only as good as the shots you use to set it up. If you don't have deep, penetrating slices and ground strokes, your drop shot will not be very successful.

It is also possible to set up effective drop shots that look as if you are setting up to drive your ground strokes, but this takes some practice. You can still have adequate disguise in your drop shot, especially in the backswing and body motions you apply on your ground stroke. Remember, drop shots usually require grip changes. This can be a giveaway. Try to delay your grip change until the last second or on the forward swing.

Elements of disguise include setup, preparation, swing and execution, footwork, direction, and height.

Setup

You need to show your opponent the use of underspin deep on occasion to disarm him with the setup of what looks to be a drop shot, but it must be done at the right time.

Preparation

Players anticipate the shot that you will hit based largely on how you prepare. If your backswing loops back and down, they will expect a drive or topspin. If the racket stays up in the backswing, they will expect underspin deep or short. The preparation of the drop shot should look the same as the preparation of your deep ground strokes, no matter what type of swing patterns you have.

Swing and Execution

The disguise you establish in preparation extends to the swing. The swing path on the drop shot can look like a deep shot with a slight adjustment in the angle of the racket face to create more spin and less power and depth. Adding a follow-through adds to the disguise as well. What opponents see is a deep swing. What they get is a drop shot.

Footwork

When using the drop approach, it is especially important that your footwork and body language "sell" the disguise. Try to maintain identical footwork for your deep and short shots, with only slight adjustments.

Direction

Experts say the human eye can accurately judge depth only up to a distance of 15 to 20 feet (4.5 to 6 m). You can therefore use the direction you hit the ball to further the disguise. Let's look at two scenarios:

1. Suppose a car is some distance away and traveling toward you in a straight line. How close must it get to you before you can estimate its speed?
2. In the same situation, if you were to change your position to the side of the road, could you better judge the speed of the car?

Scenario 2 provides the best perspective for your depth perception and for determining the car's speed, correct? Let's apply this to disguising a drop shot. If you hit the drop shot away from your opponent, the flight of the ball will alert the opponent to respond because of the direction of the ball. But if the situation has your opponent out of position, deep in the backcourt, you've created a great opportunity to hit the drop shot away from her.

A drop shot hit straight toward your opponent usually best disguises the shot using depth perception limitations to your advantage. For example, if you regularly mix a deep-slice backhand into your ground-stroke rally, you're in a crosscourt pattern when you drop-shot. If your pattern is down the line to approach, you would mix in the drop approach down the line.

Height

Deep slices and chips can themselves be penetrating and offensive weapons. When you use them to set up a drop shot, you need to hit with more height (or trajectory) over the net. Likewise, you want the same trajectory on your drop shot as on your deep shots. So to disguise your drop shots effectively, you should increase the height of your deep balls and avoid popping the drop shot up in the air too much.

Developing the Drop Shot

The major technical aspects involved in executing the drop shot are grip, preparation and swing, and balance and foundation.

Grip

Players will vary their grips when hitting the drop shot, including the regular grip they use on ground strokes. Most will adjust to a continental grip. The more extreme your grips are with your ground strokes, the bigger adjustments you must have. Because of this you must wait until the last second to make the grip change.

Preparation and Swing

Again, for disguise, you should use the same backswing for the deep slice and the drop shot. The stroke is the same, although for the drop you may use less follow-through because you are applying less power and more spin. Avoid bunting the ball with your swing. Use the swing pattern that brings success to you.

Balance and Foundation

As with all shots, your balance and foundation often determine the success of the shot. To establish consistency with the drop shot, you need a delicate touch, which requires full control of your balance and foundation. Establish a strong foundation and relax your front knee as you step forward. Maintaining the same look of the strong foundation you would apply to a powerful shot adds further disguise for the drop shot. You cannot cheat with your foundation and balance in hitting the drop shot and even other touch shots.

Drop-Shot Combinations

Serve and volley is an example of a combination in which the serve creates the opportunity for you to advance to the net for a point-ending volley or overhead. If you are serving and volleying, you want to get your first serve in play.

If you try to ace your opponent with the serve, you are not thinking of the combination, and your serve percentage will be low. The same idea applies to the drop shot. By trying to hit the drop shot as an outright winner, you put pressure on yourself to make the shot better than it needs to be. Your success will be limited. Used in combination, however, the drop shot offers a new dimension to your strategy.

Forehand Loop and Drop Shot

The strategy is to push your opponent progressively to a position deeper into the backcourt, where she becomes vulnerable to a drop shot.

Backhand Loop and Drop Shot

Using the same strategy, you can use the deep looping ball with spin to force the opponent back. From this position you can expect several defensive short returns. You can then move forward and apply the drop shot, the killer forehand (see chapter 3), or an offensive placement that allows you to move in and end the point with a volley or by an unforced error.

Backhand Deep Slice and Drop Shot

Like bread and butter, these two shots were made to go together. Use this combination to bring to the net someone who likes to be there, though not on your terms. By using the deep slice in the rally, you set up the constant threat of your drop shot. Your opponent should see your drop shot only often enough to know that you will hit it when the opportunity arises.

Forehand Deep Chip and Drop Shot

Only a handful of players use a chip forehand from the backcourt. However, as demonstrated by Jimmy Connors and Chris Evert, and now Roger Federer and Novak Djokovic, it can be a very effective tool. Like the backhand slice and drop shot, this combination poses a deep, short threat to your opponent in the crosscourt rally. The Williams sisters and Martina Hingis apply the chip forehand.

Backhand Slice Approach and Drop Shot

Attacking the net on underspin gives you the flexibility to adjust depth effectively while still hitting down the line to position yourself at the net. Most of the time, you can knife the ball deep to attack. But bringing the opponent closer to the baseline in fear of your drop shot will make your deep balls more forcing. As your opponent starts playing back more, you mix in the drop approach or other options, including the angle.

Forehand Chip Approach and Drop Shot

Martina Hingis uses the chip approach from the era of traditional tennis with great success. Younger players like Roger Federer and Novak Djokovic are two of the players who use it regularly today; they can attack you deep and short. The deep chip often has a sidespin–underspin that makes it difficult to pass with. Try it!

Drop Shot and Lob

Here you can use a three-ball combination to end the point. Your opponent can often recover a well-executed drop shot, but only with a defensive return. With your opponent's weight coming forward, the lob is the perfect win–win situation. To position yourself for the opponent's weak return of your drop shot, move inside to guard against a possible drop shot. You may wind up using a lob volley on occasion as well.

Drop Shot and Pass

When your drop shot puts the opponent in a vulnerable position, you can use an average-quality passing shot to the open court. Players who execute the drop shot effectively will often move in a step or two to guard against a short return.

Because the drop shot so closely resembles the look of deep slices and chips, you should be able to execute the deep counterparts to the drop shot. If, for instance, your slice backhand is unreliable, your drop shot will be less effective and vice versa. Hopefully you've learned to respect the use of deep underspin enough to work on these strokes. If you want to realize the full potential of the drop shot, you need to be skilled at the deep counterparts to it.

Through developing these skills, you will begin to get a sense of how you can hinder your opponent's ability to anticipate both the direction and depth of your shots. Formidable competition, however, will require you to be crafty in how and when you employ your combinations. You'll need keen senses to tell you how often you can incorporate your drop-shot strategy. Weak movement opens the door to specialty shots, especially the drop shot.

A perfect drill to gain confidence with your drop shot and also the slice is to play the mini tennis game within the service boxes with the 10 and under green and yellow ball. Once you get the feel for the shots, switch to using the regular ball.

Lob

Like the drop shot, the lob is misunderstood and underused in both singles and doubles. The lob can be hit in various ways to accomplish both offensive and defensive objectives. This section explains the many facets of the lob and shows you how to integrate it more successfully into your game.

What Is a Lob?

A lob can be an offensive or defensive shot. It is a ball that is hit with height and depth and crosses the net with a very high trajectory. Lobs can be hit with topspin, underspin, or no spin.

An intelligent doubles team uses angles, drop shots, and lobs to create opportunities to close out points. The lob is invaluable in doubles for backing a team off the net and creating openings for you to pass. You will see the lob used much more frequently in doubles than in singles, ranging from lob returns of serves to topspin lob winners. Successful doubles teams of all levels apply the lob to their game strategy.

The lob tends to get a bad rap. Many power players think of it as a sissy shot. The most dominant players in the world, however, understand that the lob and its variations are important ingredients of a complete game. The lob is a specialty shot like the angle, drop shot, and high looper.

The lob can be a good choice in the following circumstances:

As a Defensive Weapon
In a match you will occasionally be caught in a defensive situation and have few options. The lob can be the answer to keep you in the point, allowing you time to establish better court position and force your opponent to put you away with an overhead. On pressure points, it can be very difficult for opponents to execute aggressively on overheads, and they often choke. Overhead errors on big points can create a swing of momentum in your favor.

Under Adverse Conditions
When the weather begins to play a big role in a match, either through wind, sun position, or intermittent drizzle, your specialty shots can become more effective. A lob into the sun or into a crosswind can create a challenging overhead for your opponent. Make yourself aware of how to use

the elements to your advantage, and note how conditions shift with each changeover. You must consider weather conditions, especially when they change during your match.

Lob Strategy

To have a complete game, you must be able to use both power shots and touch shots. By possessing a combination of power and finesse, you can force your opponent to defend in all four directions—left, right, up, and back. When you draw your opponent in tight to the net, the lob or the lob–volley allows you to attack the open backcourt to win the point. You will need to hit the lob at times, so don't allow hitting it to unnerve you. If you treat it like a regular ground stroke, you'll find more success.

You will often confront opponents who stay back on the baseline and never advance to the net. One of the best strategies you can use against these players is to set up a situation that forces the opponent to come in. Short, defensive ground strokes; dinks; and especially drop shots can pull the opponent out of his comfort zone and in to the net. The opponent's skill level at the net will determine your success with the lob or passing shots. If the opponent is weak at the net, you can exploit his position tirelessly.

Even players who choose to come in and are effective with the volley and overhead should be lobbed on occasion. The lob creates another opportunity to beat your opponent and improve the opportunities for your passing shots. You must use a variety of shots including the lob even if you lose the point. You cannot be predictable like an open book, allowing your opponent to know the complete story.

What ultimately determines when you should lob and when you should pass has much to do with how well positioned your opponent is. If your opponent closes tight to the net as a habit, you can lob until the opponent gains respect for it and adjusts position. Do what you can do most successfully most of the time.

Nick's Tip

When your opponent's approach forces you deeper into the backcourt, it is advisable to lob rather than hit a passing shot. The lob will allow you time to reposition and continue the point. Besides, your passing shots are more susceptible to being picked off because they have to travel an extra 8 to 10 feet (2.5 to 3 m) because of your position in the court.

When you lob occasionally, your opponent will begin to adjust position to prepare for the possibility of the lob. The opponent then becomes vulnerable to your passing shot. Alternating between the crosscourt and the down-the-line pass forces your opponent to move left or right. Using the lob will force her to move back. Using all three shots forces your opponent to adopt a more neutral position at the net, increasing the effectiveness of your pass and lob.

Developing the Lob

The major technical aspects involved in executing the lob are grip, stance, and racket pattern.

Grip

Forehand defensive lobs can be hit with an eastern forehand grip. To hit an offensive forehand lob you need a stronger grip, especially when you apply spin. I suggest the semiwestern. For the backhand offensive lob, use your two-hand grip but apply more acceleration from your top hand. Hit more low to high to add more spin and control.

Table 8.1 shows the grips that have the most success for the lob. But, remember, there are always exceptions.

Stance

You must be able to hit the lob from all stances and all positions, especially when on the run.

Table 8.1   Types of Lobs and Grips

Type of lob	Grip
Defensive forehand lob	• Eastern • Continental
Offensive forehand lob	• Strong eastern • Semiwestern • Western
Defensive one-hand backhand lob	• Eastern
Offensive one-hand backhand lob	• Semiwestern • Western
Defensive and offensive two-hand backhand lob	• Top hand • Strong eastern • Semiwestern • Bottom hand • Continental

Racket Pattern

The simple low-to-high lob is hit relatively flat and is disguised as a regular ground stroke with a slightly open racket face, aiming 10 to 15 feet (3 to 4.5 m) over the net and using less power.

The underspin lob looks more like the slice or chip ground stroke and is the easiest lob to execute when in trouble. The underspin works well in the wind because it hangs in the air, making for a more difficult overhead. The topspin lob is executed with a low-to-high motion together with excessive racket-head speed and a slightly angled racket face to create the height on the shot.

Lob Combinations

The lob can be used in a variety of combinations. It is a must-have shot for all players, both in singles and doubles.

Lob and Volley

The lob–volley is used in doubles and when following your drop shot to the net to get the ball over the head of an opponent who is also at the net with you.

Block, Half Volley, and Lob

The block–half volley–lob is used in doubles and when following your drop shot to the net to get the ball over the head of an opponent who is also at the net with you, but when you are presented with a half volley.

Return-of-Serve Lob

The return-of-serve lob is used when you are placed into a very defensive position when returning serve in order to get the ball back in play.

Drop Shot and Lob

In singles, the simplest combination using the lob is the drop shot–lob. In this combination your drop shot will bring your opponent in. With your opponent's body momentum continuing forward after contact, your lob is the perfect answer. When set up effectively, the drop shot–lob combination can be used sporadically throughout a match with great success. Using this combination will make your opponent respect your drop shot, thereby forcing her into a position closer to the baseline, making your deep shots more forcing in nature.

Passing Shot and Lob

As mentioned earlier, you must be capable of hitting all three shots (drop shot, lob, and slice) and be willing to use them at the right times. You are constantly adjusting the opponent's court position through the shots you've hit previously in points. The opponent who never sees you lob will stop positioning to guard against it. You must use the lob to push the opposition back from the net to open up opportunities for you to pass.

To master the lob, you must be able to hit it in all situations and stances—on your back foot, when off balance, or on the dead run. Developing this versatility takes time and practice, so make a point of practicing the lob under all conditions and circumstances.

The lob, useful at all levels of play, should be part of your game. Even if you have little success with it early in the match, employing the lob sends a message to your opponent that you are able to use it. You then have a better chance of passing because your opponent must always be concerned that your next shot will be a lob.

You may lose some points as the opponent painfully punishes your lob with overheads or a swinging volley. Do not let that discourage you from using the lob when the time is right. The more you practice and use lobs in match play, the more successful you will be at executing the stroke.

Specialty Shot Drills

10-and-Under Ball Drill

Get up to the service line and use the 10-and-under balls. Don't change your grip, just hit groundies within the service line. Then change the grip and do the same drill. For most players, the new grip will automatically open the face when making contact. Next, move back a few steps and hit your regular groundies, mixing in some drop shots.

Cross-Court Drop Shots and Slices Drill

Play one on one in the service boxes with the green and yellow ball hitting cross-courts and only using your drop shots and slices.

Cross-Court and Down-the-Line Drop Shots and Slices Drill

Play one on one in the service boxes with the green and yellow ball hitting cross-courts and down the lines, and only using your drop shots and slices.

Adding the Volley Drill

Do the same drills as the previous drills but also hitting a volley at times.

Conclusion

Swallow your ego and accept that the top pros of the world use the lob and drop shot throughout their matches. The lob used together with your passing shots at different times will keep your opponent guessing what you are going to do next. In the same way, the drop shot forces him to defend the entire court. You must use these tactics when you play practice sets. If you don't practice these shots, chances are that you won't be able to execute them efficiently during a real match when the opportunities present themselves.

Chapter 9

Doubles Techniques

The game of doubles can be exciting and challenging when players know how it should be played.

Throughout my career I focused on developing singles players, but I eventually came to appreciate the game of doubles and how the skills needed for doubles can also help your singles game. Before long, I realized that people continued to play the doubles game long after their singles careers were over. Doubles is a social game that lends itself to recreation as well as business. Paul Annacone, Cyril Suk, Mark Knowles, and Max Mirnyi are just four of my students who went on to develop successful careers as doubles players. This chapter provides insight into the game of doubles for a wide range of players. I hope to help the millions of players who love the camaraderie and recreational interaction that doubles offers. By providing you with imaginative, tried-and-true techniques, I hope to make you a little bit better and perhaps add to your love of the game.

When I think about the doubles game, my mind entertains all kinds of exciting thoughts:

- The start of a car race when the drivers all jockey for position after the green light flashes.

- A battle between two people trying to protect their property.
- A social event in which each person tries to avoid putting any pressure on a partner.

By this you can see that doubles can be anything you can imagine. It boils down to a simple explanation, however, and when players lack a plan and do not communicate, doubles cannot reach the high level of excitement and excellence that is possible with teamwork.

The game of doubles can be exciting and challenging when players know how it should be played. Let it be a challenge and an amusement to learn the strategies of the game. One more thing—if you want to test your relationship with your spouse or significant other, play mixed doubles. You will either break up or stay together forever.

This chapter discusses the science of doubles. It provides fundamental tactics and options that will allow you and your partner to experience personal growth. If you identify techniques that you don't currently employ, be daring and work on some of them. Recognize the techniques in which you excel, and continue to improve them. You must also recognize the techniques you need to work on. The majority of tennis players tend to do what they know they do well. To reach higher levels, you must practice the techniques and strategies you're uncomfortable with.

Singles Versus Doubles

The main difference between doubles and singles is that doubles is a game of court positioning and playing as a team. Singles is more about shot making and the building of points through a combination of shots, and it's only you versus your opponent. In addition, doubles is a game of shot selection, positions, strategy, constant teamwork, and communication. It is simple but can become complex. Doubles can be played by amateur players well after they are not comfortable playing singles. It is truly a game of a lifetime.

Nick's Tip

In watching a game of doubles, note where players get into position, especially the server's partner and the receiving partner. Unless the ball comes directly at them, some players never move from their starting positions. When this happens, for the most part, the game is played by two players who stay at their baselines. They might as well play singles.

Having two players on one side of the court automatically means less open space. Singles will thus have many more variations because open space requires more movement. Variables in the game will always result. Also, in doubles the reduced court space limits creativity and results in specific shots being hit more often. Doubles teams can use different formations to find the most effective way to play against another team. Variety will play on the opponents' minds.

Although the court is basically the same, the addition of the doubles alleys (and the additional players) changes the strategy (see table 9.1).

Perhaps the biggest difference between singles and doubles is that the pressure of singles can often prevent a player from reaching his potential. Doubles players often find that a strong, intelligent partner can pull them through if they have skills, constant communication, and support. The teamwork factor can change self-esteem from negative to positive and may have an impact on an individual's singles play at a later stage.

Coaching doubles is totally different from coaching singles. Why? Singles is a one-versus-one competition, while doubles is a team of two versus a team of two. In doubles, strategies and adjustments are made based on what two players can do to complement each other. The coach must determine which two players fit together and at the same time evaluate their separate skills. In doubles play there is constant communication between the players.

So, why play doubles? Doubles can be played by people who cannot move around the court as well as they need to in order to compete in singles—you need to cover only half the court. In addition, for those who do play singles, doubles is an excellent way to improve singles play. For example, the volley is used extensively in doubles, so you get volleying practice while being required to defend only half the court. Doubles helps you place your return of serve in different locations depending on

Table 9.1   Comparison of Singles and Doubles Strategy

Singles strategy	• Movement and power are key elements.
	• Serve and volley is not mandatory.
	• Points are built through shot combinations.
	• Strategy is based on a player's individual strengths and weaknesses.
Doubles strategy	• You must know your game, maximize the strengths of your partner, and minimize the weaknesses of your partner.
	• Your shot must take into consideration not only where your partner may be but also your opponents' court position.
	• Defensive and tentative shots must be executed more accurately because there are two players on each side.
	• Players must know and accept their roles on every point.

whether the server's partner poaches or not. Doubles can also help your lobs because there are times when both opponents will be at the net and you will be in a position where you will have very little chance of winning the point without hitting a lob. Finally, doubles will also encourage you to serve and volley and give you more confidence to do so since you have to defend only half the court.

Not convinced yet? Here are some more reasons to play doubles:

- You can play your entire life. As you grow older, movement, reflexes, timing, and so forth begin to slow. Doubles requires you to protect only half the space, so you'll be able to prolong your participation in the sport. Many seniors play doubles well into their 80s.
- Players of any level, even those with only modest skills, can enjoy the game and have a physical workout.
- Doubles can be played in leagues as well as at the high school and college level. College scholarships often go to those who can play both singles and doubles.
- The variety of shots and knowledge of team play is enriching.
- Doubles will force you to return at a higher level to prevent the server's partner from poaching.
- Starting positions give the tentative volleyer a chance to be closer to the net when attempting to volley.
- Servers come in behind the serve knowing they have to protect only half the court.
- Levels of play can be uneven because players can make up their partner's shortfalls.
- Doubles is very often included in charity events because all levels of play can have fun, plus there's the option of having celebrities play with top players at your function.

On a much higher level, including college and pro ranks, doubles has come into its own, much as snowboarding has emerged from skiing. Many players seeking a professional career have found the dream of becoming a top singles player out of reach for several reasons:

- They can't endure the pressure of one-on-one competition.
- The modern pro game has reached a level that requires players to have certain dominant shots. With creativity, imagination, and thoughtful selection of a complementary partner, players with less dominant weapons can be successful in doubles.
- To some, team competition is the formula for success.
- Age is less of a factor. Max Mirnyi is now 37 and still playing top-notch doubles. He has been with us at IMG Academy since he was 14 years old.

Working as a Team

It is imperative to find a doubles partner compatible with your personality and style of play. Good communication will make or break a doubles team. A good doubles player will pump up a partner who makes an unforced error. Both must stay positive in the heat of the battle.

Quite often doubles teams clearly indicate an advantage by their lineup. But results will often be negative because of lack of communication. There are four levels of communication in doubles:

1. Constantly blaming a partner
2. Partners never saying a word to each other and playing each point as if they were playing singles
3. Asking the partner for forgiveness after making a mistake
4. Using positive communication about how the partners can protect each other to set up necessary strategies

No matter the level of play, players with certain strengths and weaknesses can complement one another. Here are a few examples:

- A player with a consistent baseline game who does not enjoy the net should find a partner with a good net game.
- A player with a weak serve should identify a partner with a good serve.
- A player with a weak return should look for a partner with a good return to break serve.
- A player lacking power should find a partner with the strength to put the ball away.
- A player with limited movement should find a partner who is active and moves well.
- A player must find a partner that she can get along with and communicate with.

Also, which side you return best from is the most important point in determining your position. If your partner likes to return serve on the same side that you do, the player with the most confidence about switching sides should yield. Remember, you can switch sides after each set if you need to make a change.

Nick's Tip

Consider the strengths and weaknesses of each player before deciding on a particular strategy.

Nick's Tip

Try new tactics no matter what level you are. Be bold, serve and volley, and poach. Talk with your partner and compliment one another. Remember, teamwork will help in many ways. Doubles will give you skills that will also help your singles.

Many coaches think that the best returner should play from the ad court because most of the key points are played from there. Others say it is more important to win the first point, and that the most difficult serve to return is the ball served down the middle, forcing a difficult inside-out backhand crosscourt return. Partners and coaches will have to decide which way to play it.

Communicate with your partner about which side of the court you prefer to return from (deuce or ad) and which formation you prefer. Don't commit to a side until you've spent enough time to make a decision based on results.

I'm Left-Handed; Where Do I Play?

Opinions differ on where the left-hander should play:

- It is natural for the left-hander to hit crosscourt from the ad court on the return of serve, which is the best return.
- The left-handed returner can protect the kicker serve into the alley on key points better than a right-handed player, who must defend with the backhand.
- The left-hander can use more shot variations, making it more difficult for the opposing team.
- Having both forehands in the middle is a great selling point. Here the left-hander plays the deuce court.

Simply put, partners should play where they feel they form the most effective team.

Doubles Positions and Strategies

This section discusses the roles of the different positions in advanced doubles and club-level adult doubles: the server and receiver and their partners.

Advanced Doubles

Advanced doubles is a broad term describing a level of doubles where the player can perform all the skills covered in this section. Typically, this includes top-level junior players, college-level players, and professional players. Advanced doubles players are able to change their strategies during the course of a match according to what is taking place. For example, if the receiver is having difficulty returning the serve, he might tell his partner to move back to the baseline when he is receiving serve (for more examples see table 9.2). Conversely, if the receiver is having no trouble receiving serve, he might tell his partner to move in and poach after the return is made.

Server

The serving team has the first opportunity to strike the ball, giving it the advantage if the serve is aggressive and used correctly. As the server, you must keep the returner off balance by mixing up serves just as a baseball pitcher varies the pitches to a batter. Following are a few key points for a server in advanced doubles:

- Serve the majority of serves down the middle, making it more difficult for the receiver to hit angles. If the receiver's strength is down the middle, however, serve out wide. Serve to the returner's weakness and mix it up. Do not have one general rule but be able to determine what strategy works best for you in any match.
- Spinning the first serve into play will allow you to get closer to the net for the first volley.
- On the first volley, hit the majority crosscourt. But if the net person is always poaching, hit the volley at her.
- Use the I formation to break the rhythm of the receiver. This formation creates havoc for the returner.
- If you elect to serve and stay at the baseline, hit your ground strokes deep to keep your opponent at the baseline. Look for the first short ball and approach the net.
- Variation will confuse the receiver and cause the occasional "boom-boom" first serve to be more productive.

The placement of your serve should keep your opponent off balance and guessing (see table 9.3). If the returner has an obvious weakness, exploit it until the receiver finds a rhythm. But remember, when the receiver focuses on protecting a weakness, you might serve effectively to his strength. It boils down to mixing it up!

As a rule, especially with players with a one-hand backhand, the high bouncing serve to the backhand is very effective, especially if the server's partner poaches. For a left-hander, this applies to the deuce court.

Table 9.2 Advanced Doubles Standard and Optional Responsibilities

	Standard responsibilities	Optional responsibilities
Receiver	• Decide on a formation with your partner. • Use the return to set up the next shot. • Change your position to break the server's concentration. • Attack second serves.	• Follow the return into the net to pressure the server. • Use lobs to take control of the net. • Hit straight at the net player as a surprise tactic. • Hit down the line to keep your opponents off balance.
Server	• Make a high percentage of first serves. • Serve a majority of balls down the middle. • Serve out wide for variety and to attack a weakness. • Spin serve to get closer to the net for the first volley. • Hit the majority of first volleys crosscourt.	• Serve and volley on both first and second serves. • Stay back and rally from the baseline.
Receiver's partner	• Your first responsibility is to cover your half of the court. • Decide on a formation with your partner. • Be ready to move forward to hit the volley. • Be active at the net—poach, fake, cut off floating balls. • Stay focused during the point—don't relax. • Move forward as you volley.	• Move back to the baseline when in a defensive situation. • Move back to the baseline when the receiver is having trouble controlling the return. • Hit overhead or switch sides to cover open court.
Server's partner	• Your first responsibility is to cover your half of the court. • Decide on a formation with your partner. • Know where your partner is serving both serves. • Watch the receiver react to the serve. • Be active at the net—poach, cut off floating balls. • Stay focused during the point—don't relax. • Move forward as you volley.	• Move back to the baseline when in a defensive situation. • Hit overhead or switch sides to cover open court.

Nick's Tip

Don't believe that the deuce side is easier. When hit cross-court, the inside-out backhand return is one of the most difficult shots to master.

Table 9.3   Service Options to the Ad and Deuce Courts

Service options to the deuce court	• Serve to the opponent's weakness.
	• Serve down the middle.
	• Serve into the body (jam the opponent).
	• Use a wide serve to mix it up and keep your opponent honest.
Service options to the ad court	• Serve to obvious weakness.
	• Serve down the middle.
	• Serve into the body.
	• Use a wide, high kicking serve to mix it up and keep your opponent honest.

I have explained where the serves should go based on statistics and probable angle of returns. Now I'll throw everything out the window and give some advice. The strengths and weaknesses of both the serving and returning teams must be considered in doubles. Don't let anyone tell you not to serve out wide. Your opponent's ability to execute the shot will govern your use of this tactic. In simple language, serve wherever it's most effective. Do a little of everything and more of anything to weak positions of both returns and the opponent's entire game. Too many times games are played based solely on form books.

Server's First Volley

The general rule is to volley deep down the center of the court, especially if contact is made near the service line. The deep volley will make it more difficult for your opponent to hit angles.

How close you are to the net will determine the aggressiveness of your first volley. Because of this, the server will vary the first serve with spin and placement to gain more time to close for the first volley. In addition, the height of the return will make a difference as to what the serve and volleyer can do on the first volley.

If you consistently find yourself volleying up on your first volley, your chances of holding serve diminish. The level of play will be determined by the first volley or the poaching ability of the server's partner. Doubles specialists learn their personal preferences through trial and error.

A big issue is whether the server will make an aggressive first volley and, along with her partner, continue to close in, causing the receiving team to hit their best but riskier shot.

Receiver

The doubles return is less forgiving than the return in singles play because the returner has only half the court to hit to, especially if the server's partner volleys effectively and poaches. The receiver's partner is also vulnerable to a formidable poacher. The key for the receiver is to not try to hit outright winners but instead use the return to set up the next shot. Following are a few key points for the receiver in advanced doubles:

- Pick out a target on the return. After you pick your target, do not try to anticipate what the opposition will try to do.
- Don't play your opponent. Focus on the ball.
- Hit most returns inside out or crosscourt. When playing a team that poaches often, however, hit down the line every once in a while to avoid being predictable. Even if you lose the point, you have delivered a message that you can go down the line, thereby keeping the net person honest.

In addition, here are a few other ways to catch the opponent off guard:

- Occasionally hit the return right at the net player as a surprise tactic or if the net player is not comfortable at the net. Beat him up! By this I mean keep going at the net player until he changes his formation. This is not dirty or unsportsmanlike tennis. It's part of the game and what must be done in certain situations.
- An aggressive play is to return serve and immediately follow it to the net. This puts the pressure on the serve and volleyer to make a good first volley. If the opponent pops it up, the point is yours. Quite often, the serve and volleyer will watch you instead of the ball.
- Lob on the return, especially when defending against an aggressive serve and volleyer. This tactic can catch the server's partner off guard, and you can get an error off the overhead or be able to take the net if the net player cannot reach the ball.
- Hit your return directly at the server occasionally.

If you are a receiver returning against a strong serve and volleyer, with the net person ready to pounce on any defensive return, here are a few tips:

- Go for a bigger-than-normal return of serve.
- Try to get the ball to dip as quickly as possible.
- Hit directly at the net person.
- Back up from your regular position and lob.
- Change your partner's position. Move her back to the baseline when you return serve.
- Change position for your return, and try to break the server's concentration.

If you are a receiver in full control of the return, here are a few tips:

- Move in closer for earlier contact, making the server hit the first volley behind the service line.
- Chip and charge.
- Hit directly at the net person with a killer-forehand mentality.
- When you are in control of the return, move your net partner closer than the normal position just inside the service line.
- Your returns should include all shot options—down the middle, to the outside, down the line, at the person, and the lob.
- You must take advantage of tentative serves every time. Consider the advantages you gain from the few choices the server has when tentative:
    - The server must serve and stay back.
    - The server must cut down the power of the first serve because he has little chance to win off the second serve.
- Your partner will gain confidence by being closer to the net, thus able to poach and volley.

Server's Partner

The server's partner is key for all positions at the beginning of each point. The partner has the ability to protect the serve, put fear into the returner about what she will do after the return, and scare the dickens out of the returner's partner, especially by popping that player a few times from the poach.

Following are a few helpful tips for the server's partner in advanced doubles:

- When poaching, always try to move in closer to the net.
- Do not stop poaching after missing a few balls. Even when you miss, the receiver knows that you'll poach, forcing an attempt to make a better return.
- If you are not using signals with your serving partner, the weight shift of the receiver may tell you where the serve is going.

- Both the server and the receiver will determine your ready position. The ability to return can alter your own position.
- Always be in a ready position that will enable you to defend against any type of ball.
- Once the ball is in play, your position will vary during the rally.

Nick's Tip

Tell your partner to keep quiet when you poach and miss. If not, change your partner. Modern-day doubles is all about communicating after each point and also staying confident in your partner.

Receiver's Partner

The receiver's partner is on the back burner by not being in the initial action. But in the end, this position can become valuable for several reasons. First, immediately after the return of serve, the partner's position can put fear into the server's first volley. With a ready position near the service line, the returner's partner can focus on the partner's return and move in closely. This will not only put the returner's partner in better position to receive the server's first volley but will also disrupt the concentration required for the first volley placement. If the volley is anywhere near the returner's partner, he will go for the interception. If the returner controls the return, the returner's partner will move well inside the service line for the ready position. Second, this aggressive movement toward the net creates doubt in the opposition. This is all that the team needs for a chance in the point. And, finally, the partner must have imagination and anticipation and be bold enough to step right into the firing line, no matter what the return of service is.

Communicate with your partner about where you should position yourself—at the net, at the baseline, or at one of these variations:

At the Net

- Net position may vary depending on how comfortable you are with your partner's return and your own volley skills.
- Position yourself closer to the net if your partner has had success returning serve. Back up a few steps if you're unsure.
- Always be ready to move forward to catch the ball at the highest level. This will enable you to hit down at your opponent's feet. Remember, your first responsibility is to cover your half of the court.

- Your first priority is to cover your side of the court, but there are no laws prohibiting you from poaching on other territories. Your partner expects this, knowing that your movement might break the focus of the serve and volleyer.

- The priority to cover half the court does not mean you can't cut off easy floating balls. In fact, your partner expects you to help by moving on easy, as well as difficult, shots.

- Remember that a good fake can fool the returner into hitting right to you at the net. When you are active at the net, the receiver will lose focus.

At the Baseline

- When your opponents have a big first serve or your partner is not having success returning serve, you have the option to move back to the baseline. This happens even at the pro level, but here the receiver's partner will be at the net for the second-serve return.

- If the opponents are in a one up–one back formation, direct your ground strokes to the player at the baseline. Make sure you get good depth to keep the baseline player from advancing. Any time you receive a short ball, hit your approach to the baseline player and come to the net.

Variations

- Well inside the service line (when your partner has displayed good control of the return).

- Between the baseline and the service line (when having difficulty returning the first serve).

- On the baseline (if the serve is sufficiently strong that the server's partner consistently poaches). Note that this positioning will change depending on whether you are returning the first or second serve.

Nick's Tip

The closer you get to the net, the bigger and wider your opponent's court becomes. At the net, you can play aggressively and put pressure on your opponent to hit a good shot or lob. Remember, the team that plays together, supports each other, and knows exactly what the other can do will usually win the match.

Additional Doubles Tips for All Levels of Play

- When crossing sides, always communicate with your partner and determine whether you need to make changes.
- Tell each other what shots you feel most comfortable with. By doing this, your partner can help out. For example, one player may have difficulty going back to hit overheads.
- Try to make all of your moves so that that the team will not split up.
- If you are forced to split court position, you have two options:

    1. Go for a big shot.

    2. Buy time to regroup.

- Don't discourage your partner from poaching, especially if she misses a few easy volleys.
- Don't hide the lob in your racket bag. It is one of the best shots in doubles.
- Try to control the net. Attackers win more matches.
- Establishing sound position is a good strategy in doubles.
- When in doubt, hitting down the middle is the best shot selection.
- The last person to hit a volley or an approach has the best feeling about where the ball will come back. He should be the hitter of this ball.
- The more angles you hit and the less you hit at the players or down the middle, the more you reduce your percentages because you give up more of the court.

Club-Level Adult Doubles

As players get older and their physical skills begin to decline, they gravitate to doubles. Doubles offers many rewards that singles can't provide. It is competitive. It has specific tactics and maneuvers that enhance enjoyment of the game. Many of us have participated in clinics, classes, and leagues and know it should be every player's goal to rush the net to finish the point. But realistically, how often does this happen? At the professional and college level it certainly occurs often, but at the club level it is less likely.

Let's face it, at the club level, the only people at the net are the server's partner and the returner's partner. The server and returner are usually locked in a game of singles, playing crosscourt using half the court. The only time you're involved is when you return or serve. Table 9.4 illustrates standard and optional possibilities for club-level players.

Table 9.4   Club-Level Adult Doubles Standard and Optional Responsibilities

	Standard responsibilities	Optional responsibilities
Receiver	• Decide on a formation with your partner. • Never miss a return wide—always make your opponent play the ball. • Use the return to set up your next shot. • Make contact with the ball in your strike zone for control. • Attack second serves.	• Follow the return into the net to pressure the server.
Server	• Make a high percentage of first serves. • Serve the majority of balls down the middle. • Serve wide for variety and to attack a weakness. • Spin serve in to get closer to the net for first volley. • Hit the majority of first volleys crosscourt.	• Serve and volley on both serves.
Receiver's partner	• Defend your half of the court with your life! • Keep your eyes forward—don't watch your partner hit the ball. • Encourage your partner to come to the net. • Get ready to switch sides if the opposition lobs you. • Be prepared to hit a reflex volley. Hit to the server's partner, who has less time to react. • Although you are not directly involved in the point, stay alert and be ready.	
Server's partner	• Defend your half of the court with your life! • Keep your eyes forward—don't watch your partner hit the ball. • Be ready to switch sides if the opposition lobs you. • Be prepared to hit a reflex volley. Hit to the receiver's partner, who has less time to react. • Although you are not directly involved in the point, stay alert and be ready. • Move back a few steps to cover the opening in the middle when your partner is forced behind the baseline. • If both opponents are at the net, move back and lob.	

Let's look at some tactics that will improve every phase of doubles play at the intermediate club level.

Server

- Don't panic because the returner probably won't come to the net unless you hit it short.
- Try to hit the strokes you're most confident with.
- Try to take something off your first serve to get a higher percentage in.
- If the returner's partner does not move, you can always hit at the player's feet and look for her to panic or hit up on the ball.
- If the opponents lob over your partner, make sure you communicate. Switch sides and get ready to start the point again.
- Try to play inside the baseline as much as possible, especially if you want to hit short to bring your opponent to the net.
- If your opponents have superior strokes, bring your partner back to the baseline with you and offer a steady diet of lobs.
- Be careful if you take a shot that is on your partner's side. This confusion can happen only down the middle. Play the ball crosscourt to avoid hitting your partner. If you can poach to your partner's side and win most of the time, do it.

Server's Partner

- That's your real estate. Defend it with your life! If your partner has an offensive serve you can cover more real estate.
- Try to watch your opponents, not your partner, when the ball goes past you.
- If your partner does not go to the net: Encourage your partner to go to the net. When the ball goes to your partner, pay attention to the receiver's partner after the ball is hit, and get ready to switch sides because they will probably lob over you (especially if you have a consistent partner). If your partner truly has a fear of the net and will not go in, you must alter your position and strategy.
- When you have the opportunity to get a shot, don't panic and take a big swing. Try to hit to the returner's partner, who is closer to you and will have less time to react.
- Be careful if your partner has trouble controlling the direction on the serve. Either move closer to the doubles alley or go back to the baseline with your partner.

- If your partner is forced deep into the backcourt, be ready to move back a few steps to reduce the distance and close off the opening created down the middle of the court.
- Don't become bored if you're not active in the point. Be patient and ready because when you least expect it, one will be coming your way!

Receiver

- Put the ball in play, crosscourt if possible.
- Lob to create confusion.
- Don't worry about the server's partner. He is not going anywhere. Just hit it back to the server until you feel comfortable with a more offensive shot.
- Go at the net person when you get a weak shot.
- Move way up on a second serve. Make your opponents think you are going to attack the serve.
- If you are in control, move inside the baseline and encourage your partner to move forward to the net.
- Don't play back too far. Balls are easier to control when you strike them between the knees and the waist. Vary your position at the baseline. If you make early contact, you will catch the server at the service line for her first volley.
- With an aggressive return, you'll seize the offensive advantage.

Receiver's Partner

- You are not involved in the first phase of the point, so keep your eyes forward and be alert! You can tell where the ball is going by the weight shift of the opponent.
- Don't watch your partner hit the ball.
- Be prepared. If you don't move closer to the net or all the way back to the baseline, your opponents will hit balls at your feet and you'll need a shovel to dig them out.
- If you do get a shot, try to hit to the net person on the other side for a surprise.
- If both opponents come to the net, get the heck out of Dodge and lob, lob, lob.
- If your partner comes to the net, look for your opponents to lob.
- If you are lobbed, don't forget to tell your partner that you are going to switch to the other side.

- If you and your partner are at the baseline together and don't lob, try to hit to the weaker opponent. Don't forget angle shots with spin that dip the ball down to the feet, requiring them to volley up.

In addition, here are a few helpful hints for club-level adult doubles:

- The majority of the time, try to hit to the weaker partner, regardless of whether that person is at the net or on the baseline. By doing this the stronger player leaves her court wide open.

- Always encourage your partner, especially after he makes an error.

- Don't be afraid to both play back, especially if your opponents play one up and one back. Sometimes you can hit a shot between them.

- When you are lobbed, move quickly. Don't wait to see if the ball makes it over your head before you retreat. But if you think you can't read the ball, yell to your partner immediately and move to the other side of the court.

- If your opponents are very aggressive and both play up, load up your lob and start firing!

- Be extremely patient when playing junkers and pushers. Your shot will come.

- Move back on hard serves and move up on easy ones.

- If you choose to go down the line, try a lob. If the net player is not asleep and can get the racket on the ball, he naturally (not instinctively) will hit the ball crosscourt between you and your partner.

- Remember, both up–both back and one up–one back are proper positions if you know what to expect.

Doubles Changes Over the Past 15 Years

First serves and big returns have become essential for success. Most teams now move more aggressively at the net to offset the power of the balls hit from the back of the court.

One of the bigger additions to today's doubles tactics is serving and staying back. This tactic has been a winning formula for most of the top teams in the world, regardless of the surface where the match is played. The amount of topspin these players (baseliners) are able to generate is tremendous. To volley the balls they are hitting is far from fun! These balls are dipping sharply right before your ankles and have so much weight behind them, which puts you on the defensive straight away. Typical doubles shots such as chip returns, chip lobs, and cute passing shots are things of the past. The game in general has become much more powerful.

However, some things are still the same and likely will never change. Doubles teams that are successful will always have great communication. Even if some teams are not noticeably talking, the two players have to be on the same page throughout the whole match in order to win. It comes with the experience of playing together, using hand signals, and wisely spending the 90 seconds of the changeover time to assess the current status of the match and adjust tactics when needed. A lot of studying goes into getting ready for a doubles match to learn your opponents' patterns and tendencies, even more so than in singles because in doubles there is almost no time to react. Things are happening at lightning speed. Unless you know and anticipate your opponents' actions and accordingly have a predetermined play, you will lose most of the time.

When I am asked to identify the most important thing in doubles, without any hesitation I say that two players must make a good team first before anything happens. Do you and your partner share the same goals? Are you both willing to do what it takes to reach those goals? Knowing and understanding each other's strengths and weaknesses will help doubles players come up with the most effective game plan day in and day out. Getting a feel for one another's character and personality will allow two people to understand how to deal best with success and failure during the match and throughout the playing season on and off the court.

Conclusion

The everyday players may look at some of the formations used by the pros today and think they are crazy. However, they should be open to try some of the different formations as they will often confuse the receiver and cause them to take their focus off the ball.

A super game to improve your cross court return of serve is the 1 versus 2 game where the returner plays against two players. This forces the returner to hit cross court or the other team will poach. It also makes the server more confident in serving and volleying because he knows there is no one on the other side of the net who will poach and cut off his volley.

Doubles is a game of strategy and position as a team. The team that has the proper position will win the majority of points. Master player Cyril Suk has won numerous grand slam doubles titles, yet he doesn't possess a major weapon like a big serve or forehand. He knows and understands the game of doubles and is a master at being in the proper position.

Chapter 10

Practice With Purpose

I have often heard athletes as well as people from all walks of life say, "Holy mackerel! Everything went my way." This is not an accident or by chance. It comes about because of the way you practice.

Very rarely do players discover things in match play that they haven't worked out on the practice courts. If you've fully prepared yourself over time leading up to competition, the routines, shot patterns, and skill habits are executed almost without much thought. Let's explore what it takes to practice with purpose to achieve complete preparation for match competition.

Practice and Competition

Practice and competition—they are a team. Practicing skills increases your ability to perform them during a match. Following are a few key points about how to make your practices more competitive.

Add Stress and Pressure to Practice

I hear a lot of players ask, "Why do I play so much better in practice than I do in my matches?" This common phenomenon is typically an indication that there are shortcomings in how you practice.

The accountability and expectations that come with match scoring translate into stress and pressure during performance. Many players don't experience the same stress levels when they practice. When you are less experienced with playing under pressure, it can definitely affect your performance in match play. Those emotions may lessen over time and as you gain experience, but they will never go away completely. You can't do much to change that. What you need to do better is build more accountability, expectation, stress, and pressure into your practice, so you can learn to work through it. Pressure from outsiders, parents, coaches, and peers will alter results.

So, how do you add accountability, pressure, and stress to your practice sessions? There are a number of ways. Rather than just mindlessly hitting ground strokes back and forth with your practice partner, create consistency challenges with goals to achieve. "Let's try to rally forehand crosscourt and reach 100 in a row with no mistakes. Any mistakes, we start over." Think of ways to build in incentive for both players to want to achieve the goal. When competing head to head in practice points, make it competitive, with agreed-upon penalties for the player who fails or rewards for the player who wins. Taking on challenges like this adds competitive pressure and builds confidence as you achieve the goals.

Learn to Concentrate

Five-time Wimbledon and six-time French Open champion Bjorn Borg once gave a motivation speech at the academy. On the subject of concentration he was very clear: "The second you step onto the court, the match begins. Every movement, every contact of the ball, every shot hit must be played with the concentration of match point." If you practice this way, you will improve immediately. You will learn the art of focusing, which in time you will translate into match play.

It's important to remember that most players are unable to concentrate for more than a few minutes. Especially in today's technology-driven, multitasking culture, younger players struggle more than ever to maintain single-minded focus on the task of competing for extended lengths of time. Too often, they are easily distracted and tend to drift in and out mentally over the course of a match. Concentration is a learned art, and with effort, you can develop it. Players like Nadal and Sharapova can maintain intense concentration for a match that lasts as long as three, four, even five hours! It's a remarkable skill but one they developed and honed through intense, high-quality practice every day. For example, in practice, Nadal will often rally nonstop for up to 10 minutes without ever hitting one ball in the net. Building in plenty of net clearance and topspin into every shot in practice, Nadal does not tolerate mistakes in the net. Why? He doesn't practice what he doesn't want to occur in matches.

Reduce Unforced Errors

What is an unforced error? From a match-charting perspective, it is an error that occurs when the player has adequate time to execute. Essentially, the cause of the error cannot be attributed to the incoming ball from the opponent. A forced error occurs when the incoming ball from the opponent reduces time to set up or compromises the balance of the player who commits the error.

Nick's Tip

Don't do it. No one in his right mind would start a point thinking it would be a good idea to make an unforced error, yet unforced errors often occur more often than winners . . . but never by intent. Many unforced errors take place when you stop focusing. Reduce your unforced errors in practice, and you'll reduce them in match play. Focus, focus, focus. The way you practice is the way you will play.

To build new habits you must experiment, find your groove, and then repeat the task over and over again until it happens without thinking. Challenge yourself with targets to improve your precision, consistency goals that build trust in your skills, and any kind of measurability you can incorporate so there's a sense of competing against yourself. The objective is to push yourself to be better today than yesterday.

Practice Aggressive Movement

What happens when you see the ball barely drop over the net and you are positioned in the back of the court? If you pause for even a split second to judge whether you should make an effort to run it down, the opportunity has already passed you by. Accomplished players train themselves to instantaneously react without thought or judgment. Players who assert movement as a primary strength in their game must make an attempt for everything. It sends a strong message to the opponent that you are fit enough and willing to defend every inch of the court. Over time, the opponent will begin to reduce his margin of error, trying to keep the movement specialists from getting to the ball. That's when the errors start stacking up on the opponent. As Richard Williams once said, "Don't play the lines in practice . . . run for every ball whether it's in or out and play everything!" Don't think about whether the ball is in, out, or in the net. This will cost you time. The split second you see the ball coming, move.

Influence Outcome Through Performance

For accomplished players, competition represents a performance, similar to an actor on stage or a musician in concert. Outcome is a completely separate thing. For lesser players, fear of a negative outcome can often adversely affect their process of performing. Many variables can affect a player's performance, but through mental training, accomplished players have the ability to concentrate only on the factors that pertain to the context of the match. They take it one point at a time without dwelling on the past or thinking ahead. Andre Agassi said the most important point in a match is the next point. The last point is over and done. You can only control the next one. Learning to engage mentally in playing each point over the course of a match often leads to the desired outcome you hope to achieve. This is all part of the rehearsal process that creates practice with purpose.

Practice Is a Business

This section gives insight into what we do at IMG Academy and shows you how you can put more purpose into your drilling. I manage my drills to have a positive effect on my students. We don't use mystical drills that no one else does. We never have. What makes us different is the way we run them. Drilling should be fulfilling, exciting, and challenging to both coach and student. It should be an experience that inspires everyone to perform to her highest ability. Our drilling methods have kept us at the forefront of the game for many years.

Nick's Tip

Drilling allows the coach to reinforce the fundamentals of the game, building the foundation for improvement in all aspects of a player's development.

Types of Drills

As far back as I can remember, fed-ball, live-ball, and other types of drills have been used to train tennis players at all levels and offer significant benefits over just playing practice sets. First, drills are specific. They can be tailored to the exact needs of a player and allow the coach to train a variety of skills including technique, consistency, power, spins, hitting to targets, movement, conditioning, recovery, attitude, point development, strategy, and tactics. No one took better advantage of drills than Monica Seles. Monica squeaked and grunted her way to the top of the world by consistent and determined use of the drilling court.

The types of drills are as follows.

Fed-Ball Drills

In a fed-ball drill, the coach feeds the ball to the student. Fed-ball drilling offers many benefits to both coach and student. The coach is able to control the situation when players of varying ability are on court. The coach can observe the students' preparation and movement habits while focusing on repetition of technique. Targets can be introduced to add variety and pressure to the drills. In addition, the coach can test fitness by using endurance drills to push the limits of a student's cardiorespiratory conditioning and see when technique breaks down.

Fed-Ball Drills With Target Scoring

Here a coach feeds the ball, and scoring takes place when the students hit the target with the ball. Target scoring determines the structure and length of the drill and takes players one step closer to true match conditions as the competitive element plays a bigger role. This drilling style allows the coach to control the situation to some degree and measure students under a new level of pressure.

Live-Ball Drills

In live-ball drills, students hit the ball back and forth between themselves. Live-ball drills are most beneficial to players who can consistently control the ball. These drills take players closer to match conditions by having the students drill in head-to-head competition. Students must work together to ensure that the drill is successful and doesn't break down.

Live-Ball Workout

The next progression of live-ball drills is the live-ball workout. This drill promotes consistency and discipline and moves the students even closer to match play by simulating controlled rallies and combinations. For live-ball workouts to be successful, students must use teamwork to prevent chaos.

Match Simulation Drills

Match simulation drills are structured to reinforce better strategic decision making for match play. Some of the match simulation drills enable players to compete within the various stages of the point-building process, while others focus on the outcome of the point.

Drill Safety

Safety must be the single most important aspect for a coach conducting a drill. Coaches must structure the drill so that it does not put either the student or the feeder at risk of being hit by balls and rackets. This is something I am adamant about. I demand that all the balls be cleared from the court after every rally. Here are a few key points:

- You must have the proper equipment. The feeder must have a large basket of balls so that the drill is productive for an extended period. Buckets or smaller baskets should be placed deep in the backcourt of the feeder to provide students a margin of safety when retrieving the balls (see buckets shown in figure 10.1).

- There is no picking up of balls during the drill because it is not safe. When a student misses she must clear the ball on her side of the net. When the feeder's basket is depleted it can be refilled from the bucket or smaller baskets, thus ensuring that no time is wasted in picking up balls.

- You must also have sufficient cones or markers to construct recovery alleys where students can safely recover off court to pick up balls or return to the back of the line (see cones shown in figure 10.1).

- Never have students go to the opposite side of the court during the drill to pick up balls and put them into the feeder's basket. Never ask students to recover near the line of fire.

- Students should not stand too close to each other when in line because they need room to handle a bad feed from the coach. Getting students to shadow swing when in line requires them to be a safe distance from one another. Emphasize this from the outset.

- Students must be taught to clear all balls they hit into the net at the completion of their rotation. Stray balls on the court are the single biggest cause of ankle injuries when drilling. Coaches can continue the drill by hitting balls to the next hitter at a different location, allowing the student to clear the ball.

- Bags and equipment are not to be left on court. The best place for them is outside the fence. Drink bottles and towels should be placed together out of the way. Apart from the safety aspect, having the drink bottles in one place keeps the group together during breaks. This enhances group dynamics enormously because everyone feels a part of the action.

Nick's Tip

Many developing players need to practice but don't have anyone to work out with. Such players can use a backboard or wall to work by themselves on every aspect of the game—ground strokes, half volleys, volleys, overheads, serves, and even playing out points. Adding music can increase the fun.

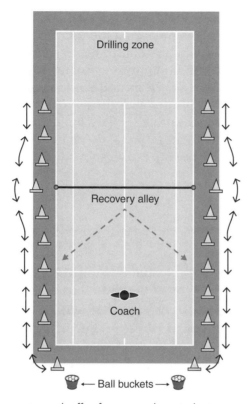

Figure 10.1   Use cones to mark off safe zones when students are performing drills.

Objectives of the Drill

Any drill, no matter how simple, must be appropriate for the level of the group and be run in a manner that accomplishes a specific goal. Each student should understand the goal and how it will benefit the player. Drills can focus on a variety of goals:

- *Technique*—working on specific shots to generate power and to determine if the technique breaks down during a specific sequence of feeds.
- *Hitting to targets*—creating awareness of the court and providing feedback to students about their accuracy, consistency, and placement.
- *Movement*—improving the ABCS (i.e., agility, balance, coordination, and speed).
- *Conditioning*—improving cardiorespiratory fitness, endurance, and overall stamina in the ABCS.
- *Point development*—breaking down points into start (getting the point started), build (building the point), and close (finishing the point).
- *Strategy and tactics*—improving ability to control the center of the court and build points against different styles of play.

Coaches, be aware that a player can't work on all these goals at once. Players, take it one step at a time until the task becomes a habit. A logical progression is to begin with an emphasis on technique; then introduce targets, movement, and conditioning; and finally incorporate the particular stroke into point-development drills and patterns of play for strategy and tactics. This progression ensures that the student learns *how, where,* and *why* to hit. Too often coaches focus solely on technique when drilling. In competition, technique begins to break down because the student has not practiced the other components of the shot.

Drill Introduction

Coaches often fail to provide sufficient explanation of a drill. As a result the drill breaks down. The coach must include several points in the explanation:

- *Set the scene*—Bring the students together, get their attention, and explain the importance of the drill.
- *Explain the purpose and benefit of the drill*—Students need to understand the purpose of the drill and how it relates to their game.
- *Explain the role of each student*—Inform students of their roles to increase the effectiveness of the drill immensely. Those waiting in line can move their feet or shadow swing in time with the hitter, pick up balls, or recover to a certain location on court. An effectively run drill keeps the group together while each player executes the drill.
- *Demonstrate the drill*—A picture is worth a thousand words, so demonstrate the drill visually and verbally and cater to the learning modes of as many students as possible. This is particularly important when you have students from various nations with language differences.

Moods and Attitudes During Drills

Another aspect of effective drilling requires the coach to observe the mood of each student and the groups. Each student reacts in a different way to the tasks and demands you set. Some will withdraw within themselves; others will maintain a constant flow of outbursts and facial expressions during the drill. As a coach, you must be aware of these differences and regulate your feedback accordingly. At times you will have to knock them down, while at other times you will need to build them up. Be attentive and give appropriate feedback to each student as well as to the group. Dealing with the mood of each student correctly will dramatically increase the effectiveness of the drill.

Nick's Tip

Rarely will students within a group be of equal ability. Drilling allows the coach to cater to each student's needs by altering the difficulty of the feed, speed of the drill, target area, and pattern of shots. This is the best way to work specifically on each student's game in a group setting.

Drill Progression

Almost every drill can be progressed to make it more challenging for the group while still emphasizing the needs of the individual. Coaches can progress a drill by

- adding another ball to the sequence;
- increasing the speed of the drill;
- increasing the speed, spin, and height of the ball;
- decreasing the speed of the drill to emphasize technique;
- emphasizing hitting to targets, movement, conditioning, point development, strategy, and tactics; or
- adding games to determine who can win, no matter what!

The list of progressions is endless. The coach must always adjust the drill to match the abilities of the group and student.

Video your drills occasionally and watch them with the group. This is a fantastic way to give students another type of feedback. Review your own level of intensity, enthusiasm, projection, and overall performance. Small changes in the structure of a drill can mean the difference between a good drill and a terrific one. Students often think they perform a drill in a certain way, but review of the videotape convinces them otherwise. Seeing makes believers.

Myth: Great Athletes Are Born, Not Made

It is a popular misconception that athletes are strictly born and not made. Sure, some children are born with exceptional natural athletic qualities and know how to engage their athletic abilities from a very young age. That's the result of good genetics. Then there are other children who have the desire to be a great athlete, but the qualities and skills don't come as naturally. Through hard work and the right training regimen, it is very possible for less naturally athletic people to develop athletic skills and movement techniques and evolve into better athletes over time.

In many respects it's very similar to learning to play a musical instrument. All that's required is effort and time to learn the basics, then quality repetition of the specific skills and techniques to engrain the habits. The more you practice, the quicker you develop.

As a result of genetics, upbringing, environment, and opportunity, some players develop more quickly and excel more than others. Be it sport or music, only a select few will have all the exceptional abilities required to rise to the very top. But that doesn't mean children can't achieve a high level of proficiency with the right training. It's reaching one's personal potential that really matters.

Practice Drills

Following are illustrations of several drills of each type discussed previously.

FED-BALL DRILLS

Warm-Up Drill

Objectives

- Establish an all-business mind-set for a productive practice session.
- Establish early preparation and timing for the contact point.
- Warm up the foundation and focus on good technique repetition.
- Hit to targets with high net clearance to promote depth.

Procedure

- The feeder hits two balls from the service line to alternating sides of the court.
- The student hits both balls down the line to the target area.
- The student rotates to the back of the line.
- All students move their feet.

Variations

- Add more balls to each rotation.
- Hit four, pick up four—the student hits four balls, then picks up four balls.
- Change direction to crosscourt patterns and short angles.
- Move students in to hit approach shots and volleys.

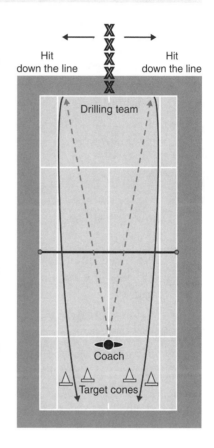

Windshield-Wiper Drill

Objectives

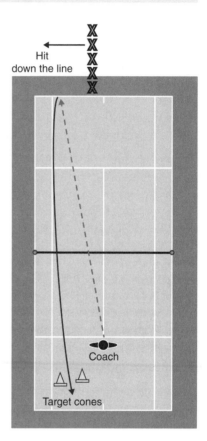

- Bring the group together to establish discipline, focus, and teamwork.
- Work groups of 8 to 12 students, all gaining benefit at once.
- Students warm up and focus on good technique repetition.
- Students hit to targets with high net clearance to promote depth.

Procedure

- The feeder hits two balls from the service line to alternating sides of the court.
- Students form one line at the baseline (curl the line around if there is not room behind the court).
- Students hit down the line to the target area and shadow on the other side.
- Students pick up balls, observe safety procedures, and rotate to the back of the line.
- All students shadow in time with the front two hitters.

Variations

- Add more balls to each rotation.
- Change direction to crosscourt patterns.
- Move students in to hit approach shots and volleys.
- When students hit from in the court, lines can go straight back.

Run-Around Forehand Drill

Objectives

- Develop the mind-set of using a weapon.
- Learn aggressive positioning in the court to take advantage of a big forehand.
- Learn to control the point through aggressive positioning.
- Hit to the target with power and accuracy.

Procedure

- The feeder hits one ball from the service line to the student's backhand side.
- The student is to run around the backhand and hit an inside-out forehand to the target.
- The student rotates to the back of the line.
- The feeder must build the confidence and willingness of students to "just hit the ball."

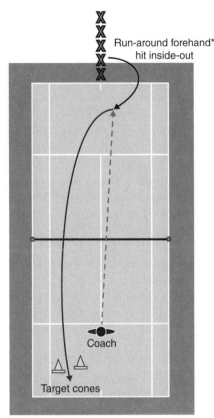

*Feed to opposite side for left-handed players

Variations

- Add a forehand down the line and then position yourself for an inside-out forehand.
- Change direction to an inside-in forehand (down the line).
- Approach the shot and finish with a volley to the other corner.

Run-Around Forehand and Short-Ball Drill

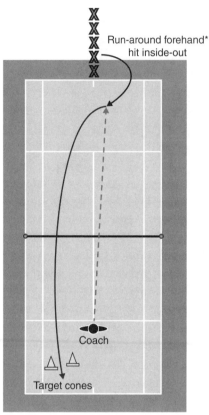

Run-around forehand*
hit inside-out

Hit short ball
down the line

Coach

Coach

Target cones

Target cones

*Feed to opposite side for
left-handed players

a   b

Objectives

- Develop a mind-set of returning every ball.
- Develop shot combinations around the inside-out forehand.
- Learn to close in and continue to attack the short ball.
- Hit to targets with power and accuracy.

Run-Around Forehand and Short-Ball Drill

Procedure

- The feeder hits the first ball from the service line to the student's backhand side.
- The student runs around the backhand and hits an inside-out forehand (see figure a).
- The feeder hits the second ball from the service line to the student's forehand side short.
- The student closes in and hits the approach down the line to finish the point (see figure b).
- The feeder must build confidence and willingness of students to "just hit the ball."

Variations

- Add a volley or overhead to the combination.
- Change direction to inside-in forehand (down the line).
- Students play out the point after the approach.

Short-Ball and Angle Drill

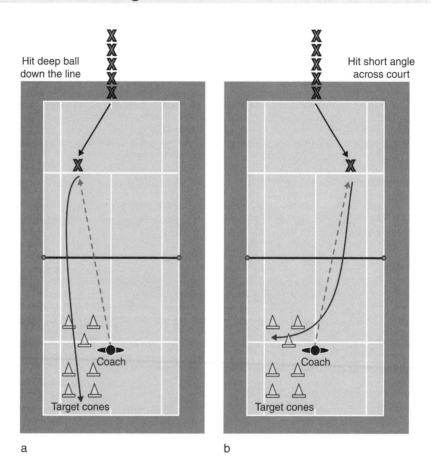

Objectives

- Develop long- and short-angle ground-stroke combinations.
- Develop racket-head speed and acceleration on the angle shot.
- Hit to targets with spin and accuracy.

Procedure

- The feeder hits the first ball from the service line to the student's forehand.
- The student hits a deep forehand down the line with spin (with a margin for error) (see figure a).
- The feeder hits the second ball from the service line to the student's backhand.
- The student hits a short-angle backhand crosscourt with spin to the target (see figure b).
- The student rotates to the back of the line.

Short-Ball and Angle Drill

Variations

- Use backhand down the line and forehand short-angle crosscourt.
- Use forehand crosscourt and backhand short-angle crosscourt.
- Use backhand crosscourt and forehand short-angle crosscourt.
- Students play out the point after the short angle.

Short-Angle, Short-Angle Drill

Objectives

- Develop short-angle, short-angle ground-stroke combinations.
- Develop racket-head speed and acceleration on angle shots.
- Hit to targets with spin and accuracy.

Procedure

- The feeder hits the first ball from the service line to the student's forehand.
- The student hits a short-angle forehand crosscourt with spin to the target.
- The feeder hits the second ball from the service line to the student's forehand.
- The student hits a short-angle backhand crosscourt with spin to the target.

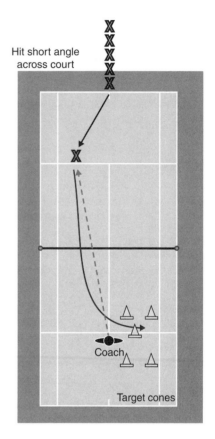

Variations

- Add volley and net exchange after the second short-angle shot.
- Students play out the point after the short angle.

Target Scoring Drill

Objectives

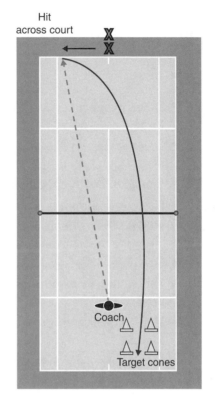

- Develop execution skills—hitting to a target under pressure from a fed ball.
- Simulate match conditions.
- Scoring determines the structure and length of the drill.

Procedure

- The ball is fed to a specific court location.
- The student hits crosscourt to the target.
- Scoring is +1 for in target and −1 for out of target.
- The drill ends when a score of +7 or −7 is achieved.
- Students rotate after each ball.

Variations

- Use ground strokes down the line or short angles.
- Use approach shots, volleys, and overheads.
- Use multiple-ball combinations—two, three, or four balls.
- Score for each target hit.
- Increase difficulty—one point if all targets are hit.

LIVE-BALL DRILLS

Box Target Drill

Objectives

- Develop execution skills—hitting to a target under pressure from a live ball.
- Develop receiving and positioning skills.
- Simulate match conditions.
- Scoring determines the structure and length of the drill.

Procedure

- The hitter starts the drill from the baseline.
- The student hits crosscourt to the target.
- Scoring is +1 for in target and −1 for out of target.
- The drill ends when a score of +5 or −5 is achieved.
- Students rotate when maximum or minimum score is reached.

Variations

- Use ground strokes down the line or short angles.
- Use approach shots, volleys, and overheads.
- Use multiple-ball combinations—two, three, or four balls.
- Score for each target hit.
- Increase difficulty—one point if all targets are hit.

Play to Seven Drill

Objectives

- Develop execution skills hitting to a target under pressure from a live ball.
- Learn to stay with a task until the goal is achieved.
- Simulate match conditions by hitting to the target from all areas of the court.
- Scoring determines structure and length of the drill.

Procedure

- The hitter starts the drill from the baseline.
- The student hits to the target from anywhere on court.
- Scoring is +1 for in target and −1 for out of target.
- The drill ends when a score of +7 or −7 is achieved.
- Students rotate when score is achieved.

Variations

- Play from inside the baseline at all times.
- Use approach shots, volleys, and overheads.

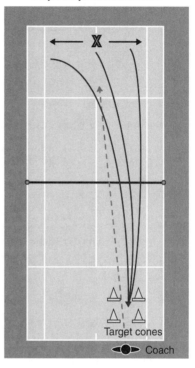

Player stays inside baseline

Target cones

Coach

Alley Drill

Objectives

- Develop concentration skills.
- Develop execution skills hitting to a target under pressure from a live ball.
- Learn to stay with a task until the goal is achieved.
- Simulate match conditions.
- Scoring determines the structure and length of the drill.

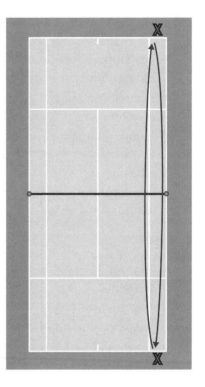

Procedure

- The player starts the drill from the doubles alley on the baseline.
- The partner hits into the doubles alley only.
- Scoring is +1 for in alley and –1 for out of alley.
- The drill ends when a score of +7 or –7 is achieved.

Variations

- Use volley, volley.
- Use ground stroke, volley.
- Restrict players to one shot only (e.g., forehand or backhand).
- Players hit certain spins only (e.g., underspin or topspin).

Controlled-Volley Drill

Objectives

- Develop ball and racket control on volley.
- Develop receiving and positioning skills.
- Follow shot patterns.

Procedure

- Four players are at the net inside the service line.
- Players establish volleying exchange as follows:
  - Up and back with the same partner.
  - Diagonal with the same partner.
  - Across and down.
  - Players hit volleys to continue the drill and control the ball.

Variation

- One player can change the pattern at any time.

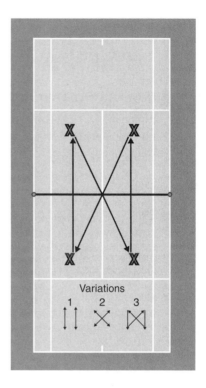

Controlled-Volley Three-on-One Drill

Objectives

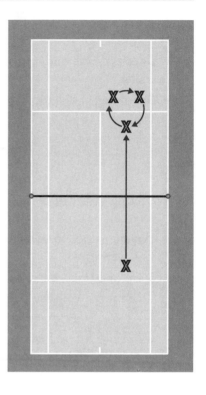

- Develop ball and racket control on volley.
- Develop receiving and positioning skills.
- Follow shot patterns.
- Work as a team.

Procedure

- Three players rotate after one or two volleys.
- Three players must position themselves in and out of the rotation.
- One player on the opposite side controls the ball and keeps the drill going.

Variations

- Use forehand or backhand volleys only.
- Increase number of students (e.g., three on two or three on three).

Two-on-One Drill

Objectives

- Develop movement, reaction, and recovery skills.
- Develop consistency and discipline.
- Define players' rally speed.

Procedure

- Two players hit down the line.
- Solo player hits crosscourt.

Variations

- Solo player hits forehands only.
- All players work within the baseline.
- Solo player uses volleys or over-head-volley combinations.

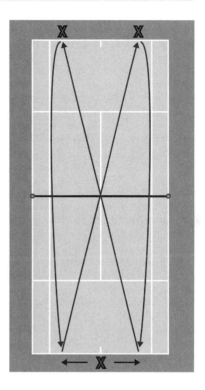

MATCH SIMULATION DRILLS

Serve and Return Drill

Objectives

- Develop skills for starting points.
- Develop first-serve percentage in play.
- Develop return consistency.

Procedure

- Server serves to deuce box.
- Returner returns crosscourt.
- Select target area based on level of players:
  - Serve: service box.
  - Return: half court or half court beyond service line (advanced).
  - Don't play the point beyond serve and return.
  - Alternate sides and change roles after one game.

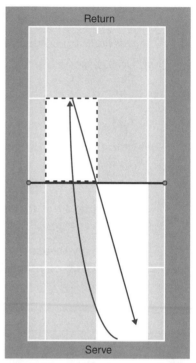

Return

Serve

Scoring

Start at 10-10; end game at 20-0 or on time. Scoring is as follows:

Server		Returner	
First serve in play	+2	Return to target	+2
Second serve in play	+1	Return in play	+1
Double fault	−2	Return error	−1

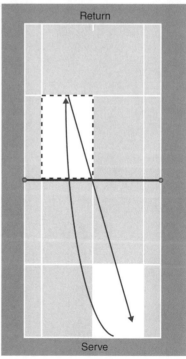

Return

Serve

Serve and Return Accuracy Drill

Objectives

- Develop control and accuracy.
- Develop first-serve percentage and placement.
- Develop return consistency and accuracy.

Procedure

- Server serves to deuce box.
- Returner returns crosscourt.
- Select target area based on level of players:
  - Serve: service box and target area (T and wide).
  - Return: basic target and extreme target.
  - Don't play the point beyond serve and return.
  - Alternate sides and change roles after one game.

Scoring

Start at 10-10; end game at 20-0 or on time. Scoring is as follows:

Server		Returner	
First serve in target	+3	Return to extreme target	+3
First serve in play	+2	Return to basic target	+2
Second serve in target	+1	Return in play	+1
Second serve in play	0	Return error	−1
Double fault	−2		

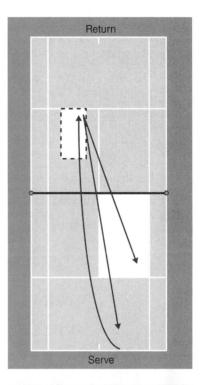

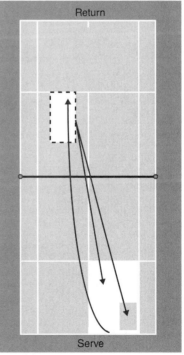

Simplified Serve and Return Accuracy Drill

Objectives

- Develop control and accuracy.
- Develop first-serve percentage and placement.
- Develop return consistency and accuracy.

Procedure

- Server serves to deuce box.
- Returner returns crosscourt.
- Select target area based on level of players:
  - Serve: service box and target area (T and wide).
  - Return: basic target and extreme target.
  - Don't play the point beyond serve and return.
  - Alternate sides and change roles after one game.

Scoring

Start at 10-10; end game at 20-0 or on time. Scoring is as follows:

Server		Returner	
Serve in target	+2	Return to target	+2
Serve in play	+1	Return in play	+1
Serve error	−1	Return error	−1

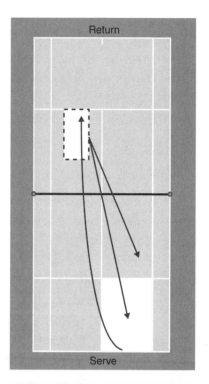

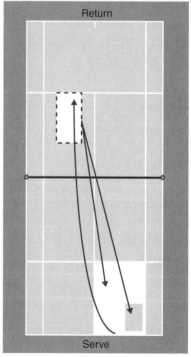

Serve and Volley Drill

Objectives

- Develop serve and volley skills and return against it.
- Develop return consistency and accuracy.

Procedure

- Server serves to deuce box; one serve only.
- Returner returns anywhere.
- Don't play the point beyond third shot in rally (server's volley).
- Alternate sides and change roles after one game.

Scoring

Start at 10-10; end game at 20-0 or on time. Scoring is as follows:

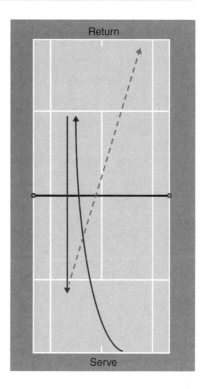

Server		Returner	
Serve in play	+1	Return pass	+2
Volley in play	+1	Return in play	+1
Fault	−1	Return error	−1

Chip and Charge Drill

Objectives

- Develop chip and charge skills and defend against it.
- Develop passing-shot accuracy.

Procedure

- Server serves to deuce box; one serve only.
- Returner returns anywhere.
- Don't play the point beyond fourth shot in rally (returner's volley).
- Alternate sides and change roles after one game.

Scoring

Start at 10-10; end game at 20-0 or on time. Scoring is as follows:

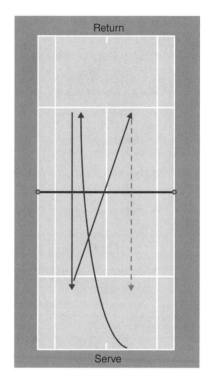

Return

Serve

Server		Returner	
Serve in play	+1	Volley in play	+2
Second shot in play	+1	Return in play	+1
Fault	−1	Return error	−1

Serve and Volley vs. Chip and Charge Drill

Objectives

- Develop combination skills and how to combat them.
- Develop counterpunching skills.

Procedure

- Server hits two serves: must serve and volley on first serve; must stay back on second serve.
- Returner returns anywhere: must stay back on first serve; must chip and charge on second serve.
- Play the point out.
- Alternate sides and change roles after one game.

Scoring

Start at 10-10; end game at 20-0 or on time. Scoring is as follows:

Server		Returner	
Win point	+1	Win point	+1
Volley winner	+1	Volley winner	+1
Double fault	−1	Return error	−1

Depth Drill

Objectives

- Develop ground-stroke consistency of depth.
- Develop ground-stroke control.

Procedure

- Players start on the baseline; feed ball out of the hand, alternating each point.
- Play the full court; target is over the service line for both players.
- Play the point out, and play to win.

Scoring

Start at 10-10; end game at 20-0 or on time. Scoring is as follows:

Winner	+1
Short of service line	−1
Out of play	−1

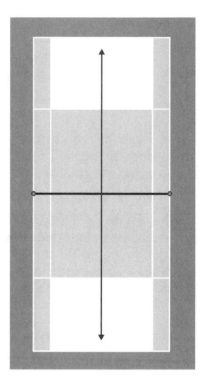

Four Shots and Play It Out Drill

Objectives

- Build longer points.
- Develop consistency and winners.

Procedure

- Players start on the baseline; feed ball out of the hand, alternating each point.
- Feeder counts aloud each shot she hits: 1, 2, 3, 4 (include feed as 1).
- Play the full court.
- Play the point out, and play to win.

Scoring

Start at 10-10; end game at 20-0 or on time. Scoring is as follows:

Win point after four shots	+1			
Win point in four shots or fewer	0			
Error before four shots	−1			
Four shots or fewer		**Five shots**		
Win in four shots or fewer	+1	Fifth shot in play	+1	
Error before fifth shot	−1	Error before fifth shot	−1	

Four Shots or Fewer vs. Five Shots Drill

Objectives

- Contrast players' strategies and styles.
- Accomplish the game plan.

Procedure

- Players start on the baseline.
- Player who has task of five shots feeds ball out of the hand.
- Feeder counts aloud each shot he hits: 1, 2, 3, 4, 5 (include feed as 1).
- Play the full court.
- Play the point out, and play to win.

Scoring

Start at 10-10; end game at 20-0 or on time. Scoring is as follows:

Attacker		Baseliner	
Win point	+1	Win point	+1
Approach error	−1	Feed error	−1

Half-Court Approach and Volley Drill

Objectives

- Defend net and pass and lob.
- Develop one–two combinations.

Procedure

- Attacker starts inside the baseline: must hit a forehand approach from deuce court and backhand approach from ad court (assuming player is right-handed).
- Play half-court singles only (no doubles alley).
- Baseliner feeds ball out of the hand: must land inside the service line.
- Attacker must hit approach and come in.
- Play the point out and play to win.
- Alternate sides and change roles after one game.

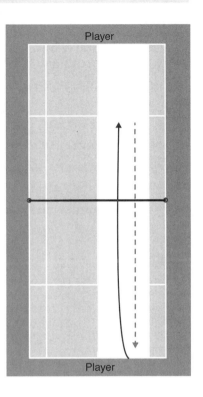

Scoring

Start at 10-10; end game at 20-0 or on time. Scoring is as follows:

Forced errors or closing winners that occur when either player is inside the service line	+2
Other winners	+1
Unforced errors	–1

Force the Finish Drill

Objectives

- Create forced error point outcomes.
- Create forced errors and winners.

Procedure

- Both players start at baseline; game uses the full court.
- Players alternate feeds out of the hand.
- Play the point out and play to win.
- Alternate sides and change roles after one game.

Scoring

Start at 10-10; end game at 20-0 or on time. Scoring is as follows:

Forced errors or closing winners that occur when either player is inside the service line	+2
Other winners	+1
Unforced errors	−1

Force the Finish With Serve and Return Drill

Objectives

- Reward closing winners
- Create forced error point outcomes.

Procedure

- Points begin with serve and return.
- Play the point out and play to win.
- Alternate sides and change roles after one game.

Scoring

Start at 10-10; end game at 20-0 or on time. Scoring is as follows:

Forced errors or closing winners that occur when either player is inside the service line	+2
Other winners	+1
Unforced errors	−1

Momentum Match Play Drill

Objective

Reward maintaining momentum to hold serve while focusing the returner on combating streaks of momentum against the serve.

Procedure

- Play begins with the players spinning to determine who'll serve first.
- Score by winning three consecutive points on your serve.
- Players change sides after every three games scored.

Scoring

Whenever a player loses a point on her serve, she loses the opportunity to serve and the opponent takes over serving, but no games are scored. Again, the only time games are rewarded to a player is when that player wins three points in a row on her serve. The first player to score six games wins the match.

Closing Combos Drill

Objective

Rewards the use of select closing combinations as well as the outcome.

Procedure

- Play begins with the players spinning to determine who'll serve first.
- Players play a set and must earn six points to win a game.
- Players change ends as normal.

Scoring

Points begin as normal with serve and return. Players receive one point for the outcome but can earn an additional point by executing one of the select closing combinations regardless of the outcome of the point. First player to score six games or reach time limit wins. Closing combinations are as follows:

- Serve and volley
- Slice serve wide and opposite corner
- Serve T and corner put-away
- Second return and attack net
- Corner to corner
- Deep down the line and short crosscourt
- Short crosscourt and deep down the line
- Drop shot, lob or pass

Other Drills

Bobby Riggs Self-Imposed Handicapping

In classic gambler style, to level the odds when mismatched players compete against each other, the better player chooses to spot the opponent with some type of advantage to give the weaker player a better chance to win.

Each player in the group is given the same amount of funny money at the start. It is up to the players to find an opponent willing to wager some or all of his money to play a set or 10-point tiebreaker based on handicaps that both players agree on in advance. An example of a handicap is that the lesser player gets 5 points he can take at any time during the set, except on set points. Another type of handicap could be having to play with someone else's racket. At the end of the event, the player who has acquired the most funny money wins. That funny money could be exchanged for assorted prizes.

Regardless of the outcome, the follow-up discussion is to ask the players how they felt while playing from a position of advantage or disadvantage from the start. Coaches can share what they observed in the players as well. When players understand from the start the conditions they agreed to playing under, it creates a different mind-set and emotional state during their performance. If they can perform well under those conditions, they should be able to respond the same way to adversity such as bad calls and cheating under real match conditions. The value of going into matches realizing that unfairness and disadvantage are very likely to arise in competition empowers players to be mentally prepared, know how to react, and perform at their best.

Competitive Mini-Tennis

A fun and extremely beneficial game as an alternative to playing full-court tennis, the competitive version of mini-tennis is a great developmental exercise for players in so many ways. Mini-tennis is a highly condensed action-packed version of full-court tennis. It becomes all-out warfare that will improve many elements of the game, many of which rarely get enough practice. The playing area includes all four service boxes. Once the point is in play, pretty much anything goes including attacking the net, volleying, and hitting overheads. As long as the ball stays within the four service boxes, it is legal. Although the game can be played as doubles, singles is a much greater challenge.

Mini-tennis can be played on any surface, but clay is best for training the most efficient movement techniques. This game will test players' reaction and recovery skills as well as their overall ability to cover the court. On clay, the challenge increases as the ability to slide comes into play.

Use single-point scoring as in ping-pong. Spin to determine who will serve first. Like full-court tennis, the first point is served diagonally on the deuce side, the next point is served to the ad side, and so on. The player serving must stand behind the service line and bounce the ball before striking it. Contact on the serve can be no higher than shoulder height on the server. The serve must land within the intended diagonal service box on the other side or the server loses the point. The server gets only one attempt to serve the ball in play. The server will serve a total of five points before the serve shifts to the other player. Play continues until one player reaches the designated total score, winning by a margin of two points. You can play to a total score of 11, 15, or 21 points, depending on how long you want the game to last.

Players learn quickly that underspin provides better control and touch than does topspin. Those who work strictly with topspin shots often find it difficult to keep the ball in play. A great mini-tennis competitor's arsenal includes chip forehands, slice backhands, sharp angles, drop shots, angle and touch volleys, and a limited use of topspin. For most players, many of these specialty skills are rarely used in their full-court play. Remember, the shot selection decisions made in mini-tennis affect players the same way as in full-court tennis. If you hit the wrong shot for your position in the court, you'll often leave the court open for the opponent to end the point. If you make the right shot selections, your ability to cover the court and reduce open-court opportunities increases. So, mini-tennis teaches the value of choosing the right shots that apply to full-court play.

Hidden Handicaps

Coaches can add an extra dimension to their drills by secretly giving each player a handicap, limitation, or restriction they must deal with as they compete in a 10-point tiebreaker. The purpose of this competitive exercise is to improve players' ability to probe for and identify weaknesses in their opponent as quickly as possible.

Options for Court Position

- Player cannot go inside service line during points.
- Player must position inside the baseline except to serve.
- Player cannot go beyond the singles sidelines during points.
- Player cannot go inside the baseline during points.

Options for Style of Play

- Player must play like the ultimate "pusher."
- Player must serve and volley and chip and charge on every point.
- Player must be super aggressive and offensive on every shot.
- Player must end the point within four shots.

Options for Fair Play

- Player can call balls close to the line out.

Options for Shot Limitations

- Player must play all high-percentage shot directions.
- Player must play all low-percentage shot directions.
- Player cannot intentionally attempt an outright winner.
- Player can return only with the forehand.
- Player can return only with the backhand.

Options for Between Points

- Player must minimize time between points and do no rituals.
- Player must stretch time between points through extended rituals.
- Player must impersonate a pro like Sharapova or Nadal.
- Player must be an "emotional roller coaster."
- Player must be void of emotion.

Unhidden Handicap Options

- Both players must switch rackets.
- Both players must play with no net strap/high net.
- Both players must play with dead balls.
- Player gets choice of side with no end changes.
- Player gets a specific number of serves (e.g., one or three).
- Player gets use of the doubles alleys.
- Player must hit every shot beyond the service line, except serves.
- An unforced error is +1 for one player and −1 for the opponent, and points that end in unforced errors are replayed; winners are +2.
- Rallies that extend beyond 10 shots are worth +2.

Conclusion

Navy Seals toss into a swimming pool a fighter pilot dressed in full combat gear and strapped in his cockpit seat. The idea is to provide an experience that will help the pilot respond with confidence in a critical situation. If he must ditch his plane in the ocean, he has been conditioned to act from experience and memory. The Navy wants its people to experience each crisis in a controlled environment. This process of education is, in many instances, merely a process of repetition.

Similarly, drills should allow a student to repeat a stroke so often that she becomes comfortable with it. Under the pressure of a match situation, the player realizes she has hit the same shot a thousand times before. A person can acquire this sort of confidence only from experience. Now the player just needs to learn how to win because the structure and experience of producing shots is in place.

Chapter 11

Physical Conditioning

Sports training has developed a lot in the past 40 years. Moreover, physical capacity is now a mandatory part of any sports program.

So many everyday athletes, including those who just play tennis recreationally, pay little attention to the physical part of training and how important it is for reaching the level of excellence they're aiming for. Players must be able to cover every inch of their side of the 7,200-square-foot tennis court at various speeds and in all combinations of body positions with balance. Players of all levels and abilities take lessons on their strokes and strategy, not realizing their physical conditioning from head to toe will have a major influence on who wins. When you are physically fit, your shot selections are much more realistic, and you think on the court in a different way. Before you take another lesson, spend a little time with a physical conditioning specialist. Just a few tips can change how you play the game.

Athletic and personal development is at the epicenter of IMG Academy, with highly qualified performance experts delivering science-based training and curriculum in disciplines like sports nutrition, physical conditioning, mental toughness, leadership, vision training and more.

To ensure each person is destined to succeed by enabling and inspiring them to rise up to their full potential is the chief purpose of IMG Academy. This purpose permeates all aspects of athletic and personal development on our campus. As it relates specifically to physical conditioning, we use a "no stone unturned" approach, addressing every critical aspect that affects performance. World-leading experts in areas like strength, speed and movement, and body management work in conjunction with experts in areas like mental toughness and vision training to provide an interdisciplinary approach that ensures every athlete can move closer to realizing his or her full potential.

This approach also reduces the likelihood of incurring an injury that will sidetrack, if not derail, an athlete's progress toward his goal. Evaluation, pregeneration, and sound training programs that are age and developmentally appropriate and a systematic regeneration and recovery program all contribute to maintaining health and a high level of functioning, for both short- and long-term athletic development.

Pregeneration Training

Pregeneration prepares the body to better accept the stresses of the impending training session. This indispensable facet of the training program takes on a preventative role, like flossing your teeth prevents dental problems. Done daily, pregeneration allows each player to better adapt to the training stimulus about to be undertaken.

Whole-Body Vibration Training

Regular application of whole-body vibration using a vibration platform can better prepare the body for training. The proper frequency is selected and a 30-second bout of vibration is applied while the athlete assumes various positions on the platform (e.g., half squat, bent hang, lunge, figure four) to target specific muscle groups. The vibration stimulates receptors, and the muscles relax and become more compliant. Additional benefits include an increase of blood flow to the muscles through dilation of the blood vessel walls. With the correct frequency, amplitude, and duration of vibratory stimulus, an athlete can achieve a heightened endocrine response, increased skeletal density, and increased power output.

Myofascial Compression Techniques

Tennis players are at risk for many musculoskeletal injuries including muscle and ligament strains resulting from the ballistic nature and repetitive movements of the sport, which lead to muscle tightness, reduced joint mobility, and stress on the noncontractile components and the musculoskeletal system. Commonly affected areas include the lower limbs, back, shoulders, elbows, and wrists. Many of these injuries can be prevented through a daily myofascial compression protocol—which also allows athletes to compete at their highest level.

Myofascial Compression Techniques (MCT) is a form of self-myofascial release that systematically restores tissue elasticity, fluidity, and function. This technique results in pain reduction, injury prevention, and performance enhancement. MCT targets the fascia (connective tissue) that surrounds and embeds the muscle fibers, known as myofascia. This continuous web from toe to fingertip within the musculoskeletal system requires total support (muscle plus fascia) for efficient movement. The foot is the foundation of this system, and any dysfunctions along this integrated chain will cause imbalances, pain, and muscle inefficiency above or below the dysfunction.

The methodologies associated with MCT require building compression into a targeted muscle along a cylindrical surface and taking the associated limb through several ranges of motion (rolling, pulling, pivots, and cross-frictions). The compression results in the production of an inhibitory response in the muscle spindle (the sensory nerve receptor within the muscle), while also addressing associated myofascial dysfunctions (such as trigger points, adhesions, and other muscular challenges).

This process coupled with deep nasal breathing can open up the circulatory and neurological pathway, allowing for improved sensory relay of proprioception, efficient movement, delivery of oxygen to the muscles, and increased muscle viscosity.

MCT for tennis players should wake up the body and release the following muscles. This protocol will ensure proper function for the demands of the sport;

- *Soleus*: This calf muscle is a major contributor in the biomechanical chain that is frequently overworked.
- *Quadriceps*: Shortened quadriceps cause the pelvis to tilt forward and the buttocks to shift back, placing strain on the lower back.
- *Psoas*: When the psoas is overactive and shortened, the upper body is pulled in front of the pelvis, which exacerbates the anterior pelvic tilt and places compression on the spine (at the L4–L5 area), decreasing the ability of the gluteal muscles to function. In an attempt to maintain force production, the body will begin to use the hamstrings for hip extension.
- *Piriformis*: This small muscle can become overstrained because of pelvic tilt and weak glutes. When the piriformis goes into spasm or tightens, it can impinge the sciatic nerve, impeding neural drive to the lower limb
- *Latissimus dorsi*: The latissimus dorsi becomes overloaded from repetitive overhead movements or when the hips and lumbar region are not adequately stabilized.

- *Thoracic spine*: Proper functioning of thoracic spine muscles contributes to movement, range of motion, and breathing. Rotation is the primary motion allowed throughout the thoracic spine. When these muscles are dysfunctional, this rotational ability, as well as control of the shoulders and upper extremities, becomes compromised. Improper technique (specifically the backhand) created by lack of thoracic spine mobility can be a predisposition for tennis elbow.
- *Pectorals*: The body's tendency to rotate the shoulders forward during daily activities can shorten the pectoral muscles.

Myofascial Compression Techniques should be adopted both before (pregeneration) and after (regeneration) training or competition. An important component of the dynamic warm-up process, pregeneration prepares the tissues for the upcoming demands by increasing tissue tolerance, optimizing the length–tension relationship, creating more efficient movement, and increasing muscular force output. Regeneration is an important cool-down method that consists of a total body flushing that helps promote circulation of metabolic wastes, create tissue pliability, and initiate the recovery process.

Using MCT with tennis players provides the athletes with self-care tools to help them prevent injuries and perform at their optimal athletic ability by improving biomechanical efficiencies, reducing pain, and enhancing movement and recovery.

Rotex

Dr. Joe LaCaze brought the Rotex to the world of athletics, and it was quickly embraced by coaches, therapists, and athletes in numerous sports. This device consists of a turntable positioned on a stainless steel platform. The tension to rotate the turntable may be varied according to the level of the athlete's needs. In the basic form the athlete positions the Rotex near a wall in such a way that her back can rest again the wall. She places one foot on the foot pedal and the other on the turntable. While maintaining a drawn-in position and a neutral pelvis, the athlete internally rotates at the hip joint in order to turn the turntable. She holds an isometric contraction for up to 30 seconds. Multiple repetitions can be performed. This exercise strengthens the often weak hip internal rotators. Strengthening the weak muscles increases balance between internal and external rotators and loosens the hips. Additionally, the internal obliques are strengthened without engaging the external obliques.

Long-Hold Static Stretching

You may be used to seeing the terms *warm-up* and *stretching* used together, but at IMG Academy we have long chosen not to use long-hold static stretching in our pregeneration protocol and our active dynamic warm-up. In the mid-1980s, renowned speed and movement expert Loren Seagrave (now director of track and field at IMG Academy) proposed that the nature of placing a muscle or a muscle group in a stretched position and holding that position for an extended period of time had a negative impact on power production. The mechanism by which long-hold static stretching causes the muscle to relax is now well understood. The stretch stimulus is applied to the stretch receptor embedded in the intrafusal muscle fiber. The intrafusal muscle fiber, unlike the extrafusal fiber, which is responsible for muscle contraction and force production, controls the tension on the stretch receptor. When tension is applied to the stretch receptor over a longer duration, the gamma efferent nervous system causes the tension on the intrafusal muscle fiber to lessen. This in essence reduces the tension on the springlike stretch receptor, rendering it less effective. This desensitization of the stretch receptor reduces the stretch–shortening phenomenon and thus reduces force. For example, if you test your vertical jump and then perform a long-hold static stretching program, on poststretch retest regardless of how hard you try, you will not be able to match your prestretching mark. Why switch the nervous system off just before it must function maximally? If one of our athletic trainers or physical therapists suggests a preexercise static stretching program to address a specific challenge an athlete is working through, we incorporate these exercises on an athlete by athlete basis.

Active Dynamic Warm-Up

As opposed to the traditional static passive warm-up, which is often characterized as "jog a couple laps and stretch," the active dynamic warm-up not only prepares the player's body for today's training session or match but also increases work capacity by improving all the biomotor abilities that profoundly affect performance during the most important matches later in the season. A well-constructed active dynamic warm-up addresses all the benefits of the pending performance. The active dynamic warm-up increases core muscle temperature, reduces muscle viscosity, increases muscle compliancy, and activates the neuromuscular system.

Core Muscle Activation Exercises

The active dynamic warm-up frequently begins with a series of core muscle activation exercises designed to wake up these critical stabilizers by dynamically challenging the neuromotor system in all planes of motion. This ensures less energy is leaked by a sloppy, unprepared core. A thermogenic activity increases blood flow through the muscles. Jump rope is popular, but many other activities can be employed to ensure a variety of stimuli.

Closed-Chain Muscle Activation Exercises

Next is a series of closed-chain muscle activation exercises to engage the muscles acting on the hips and knees. Closed-chain exercises are usually done in a standing position so that the athlete must balance and stabilize the joints. A multiplanar approach is used: Body-weight squats, lunges, side lunges, crossover lunges, and transverse lunges contract the muscles through a full range of motion under a light to moderate load. By the principles of autogenic inhibition and reciprocal inhibition, the muscles will relax on reflex without desensitizing the stretch receptor. In fact, this approach wakes up the nervous system. Typically, the athlete performs 5 to 10 repetitions of each exercise.

Transit exercises now move the athlete from point A to point B. Initially the intensity is a subjective half effort. As the session progresses, intensity increases. The distance covered can be as short as 10 yards or meters or as long as 100 yards or meters; the distance is determined by the athlete's sport as much as physical conditioning level, maturity, and space available in the facility. Fundamental movements such as running, sliding, galloping, and skipping, including backward skipping, can be used. Select movement patterns that utilize all planes of movement and then progress to patterns combining various planes of movement to challenge the nervous system and address all muscle groups. Often the return activity has a slightly different nature than the simple transit exercises. These exercises employ a secondary benefit and thus become transit-mobility and transit-stability routines. The intensity is less. Exercises such as the straight-leg march, walking knee hugs, and stork stands constitute the mobility portion; when the range of motion is deeper—walking lunges, low walk, low side slides, backward low walk—the focus is stability.

Open-Chain Muscle Activation Exercises

Open-chain exercises, unlike their closed-chain counterparts, are usually done while lying down or kneeling. Examples include leg raises and hip circles while reclining supine, side-lying, prone, or kneeling. Typically 5 to 10 repetitions of each exercise are performed. Students should engage the core and maintain postural integrity. This needs to remain a partial focus for all exercises until the feed-forward mechanism for core stabilization is automatized.

Transit Exercises With Mobility and Stability

In these transit exercises, the second section is often made more sport specific. Intensity is again ramped up. Here are some examples:

- *Tennis*: Knee-to-shoulder lateral walk (frogger) or hamstring hand-walk (inchworm)
- *Basketball*: A-skip or backpedal
- *Football*: Spider-man crawl or straight-leg bound

Dynamic Mobility Exercises

This group of exercises may resemble some of the muscle activation exercises. The key difference is that these movements have higher angular velocities because the system is now better prepared to execute through greater ranges of motion. Swinging exercises and movements that encourage circumduction about the hip and shoulder joint appear in this unit.

The duration of the active dynamic warm-up is at the discretion of the coach. When the players are learning the exercises and their names, the duration is protracted. Once experienced, a player can execute a thorough warm-up in 20 minutes; if the warm-up that day is focused more on work capacity and biomotor development, it can be extended to a full hour by adding medicine balls, agility ladders, and hurdle mobility exercises.

When a review is done of the effects of the active dynamic warm-up, it is easy to see that the exercises will promote strength and power, neuromuscular coordination, flexibility, and general endurance. After all, the active dynamic warm-up is not only active and dynamic but also continuous so that the heart rate is maintained above critical threshold for 20 minutes or more. When critical threshold—the heart rate that provides an aerobic stimulus—is maintained for at least 20 minutes, improvements are seen in energy system development.

Warm-Up Objectives

Like any other machine, the body should be prepared before engaging in intense or strenuous exercise. The warm up should achieve a change in a number of physiological responses in order for the body to work safely and effectively. Below is a list of the main targets of the warm up:

1. Increase the body temperature, specifically core (deep) muscle temperature.
2. Increase heart rate and blood flow.
3. Increase breathing rate.
4. Increase elasticity of muscular tissues.
5. Activate mental alertness.

Warm Up 1

- Bridge series: plank (right side, left side, rear) 30 seconds each
- Leg raise series: (front abduction adduction) 10 times each
- Hip raise series: fire hydrants (circle clockwise, circle counter-clockwise), scorpions, ham string reach, and row the boat 10 times each
- Forward skip with arm circles and backward skip with arm circles 30 seconds each

- Glute bridge and single-leg glute bridge 5 times each
- Hip flexors and SL hip flexors 10 times and 5 times
- Forward skip with arm chops and backward skip with arm chops 30 seconds each
- Parachutes 10 times
- Forward skip with arm hugs and backward skip with arm hugs 30 seconds each
- Leg swing series: same leg same arm, same leg opposite arm, alternate leg opposite arm, and prone scorpions 10 times each
- Knee hugs, power kicks, cradles, and stork stretch 5times each leg
- Right-high shuffle with arm swing and left-high shuffle with arm swing 30 seconds each
- Right-shuffle lunge and left-shuffle lunge 30 seconds each
- Right-low shuffle with arm swing and left-low shuffle with arm swing 30 seconds each
- Body weight squats 10 times and transverse squats 5 times each leg
- Forward and backward lunges 5 times each leg and transverse lunges 5 times each leg
- Acceleration run and backward run 2 times

Warm Up 2

Perform the following exercises for 30 seconds each:

- Walking knee hugs
- High-knee skip
- High-knee run
- Heel ups
- Straight-leg skips
- Straight-leg deadlift walk
- Backward run
- Backpedal
- Backward and forward lunge walks
- Inchworm
- Cradle
- Heel-up with internal rotation
- Walking heel up
- Walking heel up with straight leg deadlift
- Overhead lunge walk
- Backward lunge walk twist
- Straight-leg crossover

Achieving Work Capacity

Many training theoreticians have recognized that in order to achieve high performance, work capacity must be at a high level. All the biomotor training prescribed increases work capacity. Work capacity is not just being able to survive the training session that day, nor is it just having superior levels of general endurance. It is the ability to maintain quality of movement and intensity of movement under ever-increasing volumetric loads.

The concept of intensity is well known and easy to understand. Intensity is a percentage measurement of maximum, the 100 percent value. Quality, on the other hand, is less understood. It is a percentage measurement of perfect. If work capacity is inadequate, then the quality of movement execution suffers and the player ends up rehearsing less than optimal technique. This slows player development because the correct motor patterns can't be established through quality high-intensity sessions. In a match when quality of execution breaks down and intensity falls off, the player performs less than optimally, specifically in tennis, which is an acyclic, short-term intermittent workload. A well-developed work capacity is fundamental for any tennis player.

Biomotor Training

Work capacity is improved by systematically developing all the major biomotor abilities and the various subclassifications of the biomotor abilities. This section addresses the biomotor abilities required for tennis.

Strength and Power

Although sometimes used interchangeably, strength and power are very different capacities. Strength is the ability to apply force or overcome a resistance. For movement to occur, the nervous system must send an electrical signal via neurons to groups of cells. Each neuron and all its associated muscle cells are called a motor unit. To increase the force, more motor units must be recruited. In this way the player can train the neuromuscular system to recruit more motor units to produce more force. In addition to this, depending on the type of training prescribed by the coach, the player may increase the contractile protein inside each muscle cell, thereby increasing the amount of muscle force that can be generated. When the cross-sectional area of the muscle enlarges, this is known as hypertrophy. Muscle hypertrophy is more easily realized in male players than female players. Both avenues to increase force must be developed; however, tennis is a sport that is classified in terms of power to body weight. A tennis player must move the mass of the body quickly. When the mass increases, the force must increase proportionately to accelerate at the same rate. As a general rule in power-to-body-weight sports, if a player adds 1 kilogram (2.2 pounds) of body weight, the additional weight, if muscle mass, must produce 2 additional kilograms (4.4 pounds) of force against the ground. This axiom should raise an immediate alert for unnecessary upper body hypertrophy in the sport of tennis, although it is very well known that a firm wrist and a strong shoulder are necessary for good strokes.

Power, on the other hand, is expressed as rate of force development. If a player is able to lift 100 kilograms (220 pounds) in the squat and the bar is displaced 1 meter, the amount of work performed is 100 kilogram-meters (kg-m). If the amount of time required to lift the bar is 1 second, then the rate of force development is 100 kilogram-meters per second. If another player can lift the same 100 kilograms over a 1 meter displacement but requires only one half second to do so, the result is 100 kilogram-meters / 0.5 second, or 200 kilogram-meters/second. The second player is twice as powerful as the first. Power training improves the rate at which force can be applied, increases muscular strength at both slow and fast contraction velocities, and improves coordination and movement efficiency. For maximum adaptation, a significant strength base is necessary before performing the exercises involved in power development.

Other subsets of strength and power that are important to develop include balance and stability, absolute (maximal) strength, relative strength, and reactive strength.

Balance and Stability

Balance is directly related to the central nervous system, the system that guides and controls every movement. It provides an insight into the notion of body awareness (proprioception); better body awareness equals a better feeling for technical skills.

Players of all ages can benefit from body-weight exercises. Many can be incorporated into the active dynamic warm-up. Young players in particular should use body weight for the majority of strength and power training. Stability in joint systems refers to a well-supported joint and core strength (thirty-five muscles attach to the lumbo-pelvic-hip complex, ribs, and scapulae). Stability in joint systems can be lost in players of any age primarily because of unrehabilitated injury. For this reason, balance and stability training using body weight is appropriate for all ages.

Absolute (Maximal) Strength

Absolute muscular strength refers to the maximal strength a person can develop regardless of body weight. High levels of maximal strength are desirable but not to the detriment of relative strength—a large engine in a small chassis should be the goal of many speed–power athletes. Training for maximum strength also puts large structural loads on a player's body and must be introduced at an appropriate age only after technique has been mastered.

Relative Strength

Strength to body weight is the definition of relative strength. It is calculated by dividing a person's absolute muscular strength by his body weight. As body weight increases, particularly in tennis, since moving the body is of paramount importance, strength levels must match the task demands. Males generally have a greater absolute muscular strength than females because of their increased muscular mass. When relative muscular strength is considered, however, there is little difference between males and females.

Reactive Strength

Also referred to as reactive ability, reactive strength is the coupling of eccentric strength with concentric strength. The exercises that promote reactive strength are known as plyometrics. In terms of moving the body, plyometrics are jumping exercises. To develop reactive strength, the body's mass must be accelerated by gravity so it attains a negative vertical velocity before landing. Because the body mass remains relatively constant within a training session, the variable that is manipulated is velocity upon landing. A mass traveling at a specified velocity has momentum. The greater distance a mass falls, the more time gravity has to accelerate that mass, and consequently the greater the momentum that must be overcome to rebound from the ground.

This type of activity trains the player to be more explosive. Technique of execution is critical. Athletes should land on dorsiflexed ankles and absorb the force with the glutes and hamstrings. They should not shift the knees forward or internally rotate at the hips, causing the knees to collapse inward. Selection of drop height is also critical. This is clearly a case of more is not better. Measure the vertical jump height as the athlete rebounds from the surface. When the athlete's jump height drops off markedly, consider reducing the drop height by 6 inches (15 cm). A better system is to measure the ground time required to turn the center of mass around after landing. An excessively long time indicates a height that may be excessive.

Neuromuscular Coordination

Neuromuscular training creates better body awareness, balance, and coordination in order to increase reaction time and effectiveness. There are seven distinct types of neuromuscular coordination players can improve to increase movement efficiency. Through deliberate practice and rehearsal, players can improve the sequence (type of fiber) and order (size of fiber) in which they recruit and relax muscles and muscle groups. The timing of when the signal arrives to the motor units is critical for maximizing force production and eliminating breaking forces and wasted movement. The intermuscular coordination between the agonist (prime mover) and its antagonist (helper) must be such that one muscle group isn't working against its counterpart. Intramuscular coordination integrates the messages sent from the receptors in the muscles with the volitional messages of the motor pattern to maximize motor unit recruitment and the use of stored elastic energy. Synchronization involves having all the motor units fire at the same time, which generates greater force in smaller amounts of time. Finally relaxability is the ability of the muscle to contract, relax, and contract again. This quality can be increased with training and reprogramming of the nervous system.

Speed and Agility

Speed and quickness are two of the most revered qualities in any sport, and tennis is no different. There are seven distinct aspects of speed in a multidirectional sport. Tennis is characterized by rapid acceleration, deceleration, change of direction, reacceleration, conversion, force application, and reaction, all happening in less than 10 yards or meters. In many sports, maximum velocity is another indispensable aspect of speed, but it has limited use in tennis. That said, young tennis players need to learn the neuromotor pattern for efficient running at maximum velocity as well as how to use stored elastic energy in the muscle while running at high speeds.

For more than 20 years, the slogans for speed dynamics haven't changed: "Speed is a skill." "Speed can be taught just like any other skill by coaches who know how to teach it." "Any coach can make you tired." "A player doesn't get faster just by working harder." The key is to recognize the difference between training and coaching. Training is a physical stimulus that has a positive impact on biomotor abilities. Coaching is teaching. Maya Angelou's favorite quote for teaching coaches is "Train animals, educate people." Coaches should not assume their players will accidently figure out how to move more efficiently and consequently be faster and quicker.

Reaction

In tennis, as in any sport where an opponent is directing an object toward you at a high velocity and that object must be intercepted, anticipatory reaction is important. A tennis player gets cues by watching everything that occurs on the opponent's side of the court. The opponent's body position, the path of the racket, the angle of the face of the racket, and innumerable other perceptible variables tip off where the ball is heading. Further, anticipated tactics and strategies reduce choice reaction time and increase decision accuracy.

Force Application

A tennis player must apply a large force in a short time in the proper direction and through the optimal range of motion. Anticipatory reaction time may allow the player to shift the base of support relative to the center of mass to even better apply the force in the proper direction, a technique used by soccer goalkeepers. Simultaneous double-foot force application is superior to stepping in the direction of the intended movement, resulting in a single-foot force application.

First Two Steps

The first two steps, whether they are forward, lateral, or backward, are often sufficient to reach the ball and strike it. The key point with acceleration is that the first two steps must land behind the center of mass to effectively apply force for both forward and backward movements. For lateral movement, the touchdown must be lateral to the center of mass in the direction opposite of the movement. The player who has perfected applying force through the inside edge and outside edge of the foot saves time as there is no need to pivot or pick the foot up to reposition it.

Deceleration

Deceleration is complex in tennis because often the ball must be struck during deceleration. Deceleration strategies must be rehearsed on a stable surface and then on the playing surface of the impending match. It should go without saying that the dynamics of hard courts, clay courts, and grass courts vary widely, and there is minimal transference of deceleration skill. The key component of strength here is stabilization.

Deceleration training is important to help tennis athletes move more efficiently on the court as well as to reduce the likelihood of injury.

Change of Direction

Change of direction is set up by the efficient placement of the base of support (the foot position) and the center of mass. The player must be in a stable position to strike the ball and then displace the center of mass into a position where reacceleration can take place. The key component of strength here is reactive strength.

Reacceleration

Reacceleration is often two or three steps off the change of direction. Strategy and tactics along with anticipating the next shot influence the decision of where the player will accelerate next. Power and superior technique play hugely into the success of this aspect of speed.

Conversion

Conversion is an athlete's ability to apply all momentum generated by force, application, and acceleration in a linear movement transforming the chemical energy into mechanical motion.

Nick's Tip

Agility is the ability to change the direction of the center of mass, often within a confined space, by systematically repositioning the feet relative to the center of mass. This skill can be introduced in patterns that then become more a choice by the player in response to game play.

Flexibility

Many coaches would agree that unrestricted range of motion is a goal of a performance training program. When muscles are in a relaxed and compliant state, they are able to withstand eccentric loading without contracting prematurely or tightening up, which is often called splinting. In splinting, the muscle becomes shortened to prevent excessive eccentric load. Dr. Willem Kelley shared with me 30 years ago his opinion that a tight muscle is almost always a weak muscle. The goal of a training program, especially an active dynamic warm-up, is to cause muscles to contract under load to relax and consequently become stronger. When the length of a muscle is determined by the state of relaxation of the contractile mechanism in the muscle cell, the coach can use the nervous system to lengthen the muscle so it relaxes. When the length of the muscle is determined by the length of the connective tissue, the coach can prescribe eccentric stretching programs that target specific muscles for a maximum of six minutes per muscle. After the six minutes the connective tissue becomes unresponsive to the stimulus for approximately six hours. Keith Barr compares this phenomenon to a flush toilet. Once flushed it can't be flushed again until the tank refills.

Energy System Development Training

Most players think of fitness and conditioning as the development of the energy systems that provide the energy for muscle contraction. Tennis requires high-intensity exercise bouts of short to medium duration with relatively short rest periods between points and longer pauses between games. All the energy systems are contributing energy all the time. The percentage of each system depends on the intensity and duration of the rally.

The central molecule that must be present to supply energy to the working muscles is adenosine triphosphate (ATP). Once an action potential (electrical signal from the nervous system) stimulates the muscle's motor end plate, enzymes inside the cell break apart the ATP molecule by cleaving one of the phosphate groups, leaving adenosine diphosphate (ADP) and a lone phosphate. This releases the energy that is necessary for muscle contraction, and the muscle cell contracts. Energy from other substrates cannot be used directly to cause muscle contraction. Metabolism of the other substrates combines the ADP and the phosphate to yield ATP.

ATP–CP System

ATP and another high-energy phosphate molecule, creatine phosphate (CP), are collectively known as the phosphagen system. Creatine phosphate can be cleaved enzymatically to yield its energy to recombine ADP and phosphate. Creatine doesn't have any metabolic by-products that interfere with muscular function. It burns cleanly, so to speak. Creatine stores can be increased with properly designed training programs. During high-intensity agility activity, the body relies primarily on the ATP–CP system.

Depending on the creatine phosphate stores, the energy provided by CP to replenish ATP can last from 8 to 15 seconds. The key to having the body store more CP is to deplete the stores repeatedly within the training session and to do this multiple times during the week. Very high intensity bursts of 5 to 6 seconds followed by relatively short rest (e.g., 20 seconds) adequately deplete the CP. This method simulates a short rally and mimics the time between points, and is often preferred for the tennis player over extended high-intensity bouts from between 10 and 15 seconds. This latter method can be effective but has the drawback of relying more on the glycolytic system, which accumulates a negative by-product.

Glycolytic System

The glycolytic system, also known as the anaerobic lactic system, doesn't require oxygen in order to metabolize glucose or its stored form, glycogen. A specialized enzyme breaks down glycogen, yielding a small amount of energy and pyruvic acid. Pyruvic acid is then metabolized further in the mitochondria, the powerhouse of the cell, given that certain conditions exist. If pyruvate is not metabolized, it is converted to lactic acid. As glycolysis continues and the exercise intensity remains high, the acid level of the cell increases. Acid is poison to cellular function, interfering with metabolism in several areas and with the contraction mechanism itself. Training of this system is accomplished by exercises with moderate to high intensity which last more than 10 seconds and less than 12 seconds.

Aerobic System

Aerobic simply means with oxygen. The pyruvic acid by-product of the glycolytic system is transported into the mitochondria of the cell, where it undergoes a complex multistep chemical process called the Krebs cycle in order to rebuild ATP. The best way to increase a player's aerobic capacity is through shorter bouts of exercise with a limited amount of recovery. Tennis-specific movements can be incorporated with non-tennis-specific movements in a 5 to 20 second circuit of relatively intense activity followed by equally short rest intervals. Changing the activities enhances the effectiveness of the training. The SpeedTracs Speed Station is ideal for on-court metabolic training of groups of athletes, all under control of the coach. This multi-station system can be used to develop resistance, strength, plyometrics, and explosiveness using a variety of bands and other components attached to a central pillar.

Nick's Tip

Long, slow distance training can also increase aerobic function, but because tennis is an explosive dynamic sport, it should be minimized in training, especially for younger players.

Movement-Specific Training Drills

The movement-specific training drills focus on all the training concepts outlined in this chapter.

Cross Drill

Objectives

- Improve general movement.
- Improve agility and footwork.

Procedure

- Set up four cones. Cones A and B are 15 feet (4.5 m) apart on the service line, having the T as their center (middle of cones). Cone C is 15 feet from the T on the center service line, and cone D is 15 feet from the T closer to the baseline.
- Player starts at the T facing the net.
- Player performs side steps between cones A and B four times and then sprints to C. At C he performs a volley and then sprints backwards to D, where he performs an overhead and sprints back to the T.
- Duration of drill: 15 seconds.

Square Drill

Objectives

- Improve change of direction.
- Improve agility and footwork.

Procedure

- Place four cones in the court 15 feet (4.5 m) apart to form a square.
- From cone 1, facing the net, player sprints to cone 2. She performs small adjustment steps before hitting a stroke and side-shuffling to cone 3. She moves around cone 3 and backpedals to cone 4, where she split-steps and sprints to cone 1.
- Duration of drill: 15 seconds.

Baseline Linear Drill

Objectives

- Improve forward and backward movement.
- Improve transitions.
- Improve agility and footwork.

Procedure

- Place one cone about 5 feet (1.5 m) in front of the baseline and a second cone 5 feet behind the court.
- Player starts at the baseline.
- Moving forward and backward to the cones, he performs the strokes (live balls can be added).
- Depending on the dominant arm, the player starts on one side of the cone (e.g., a right-handed player starts on the left side of the cones and performs a forehand at both cones).
- Duration of the drill: 30 seconds.

Horizontal Displacement Drill

Objectives

- Improve the movement.
- Improve agility and footwork.
- Improve stamina.

Procedure

- Player starts at the doubles sideline facing the net.
- She side-steps to the center service line and then sprints back to the starting position.
- Player turns and sprints across the court to the opposite doubles sideline and then side-steps to the center line.
- She sprints back to the same doubles sideline and then back to the starting position.
- Perform the drill three times.

Nutrition for Tennis

As tennis becomes increasingly more competitive at every level, good nutrition and hydration are more important than ever. The type of fuel used before, during, and after matches has the potential to affect endurance, power, concentration, and fatigue.

Before the Match

Carbohydrates are the body's primary fuel during a tennis match. Consuming adequate carbohydrate foods will help you maintain energy levels. Eat a complete meal two to four hours before match time. Meals should be rich in carbohydrate, moderate in protein, and low in fat and fiber to prevent upset stomach. Grab a quick carbohydrate snack 30 to 60 minutes before a match to help meet immediate fueling needs. Aim for two to three cups of water in the hour before start time. Make sure urine is light like lemonade, not dark like apple juice.

During the Match

Although fluid needs are individual, a general rule is to aim for 5 to 8 ounces (150 to 240 ml) of fluid every 15 minutes during a match. For training lasting less than 60 minutes, water or low-calorie sport drinks will meet hydration needs. For training and matches lasting longer than 60 minutes, choose sport drinks containing 6 to 8 percent carbohydrate and electrolytes.

After the Match

Immediately after a match, it is important to eat carbohydrate and lean protein to allow the body and muscles to recover. Carbohydrates refuel energy stores depleted during the match, while proteins help rebuild and repair muscles after a match. Great postmatch nutrition choices include low-fat or skim chocolate milk, sports drink, low-fat Greek yogurt, fruit, and water.

Rehydration should begin as soon as a match has ended. For every pound of body weight lost, 16 to 24 ounces (500 to 700 ml) of fluid with electrolytes should be consumed. Educating players to hydrate before, during, and after training and matches is crucial to guarantee success in their recovery strategies.

Conclusion

Keep in mind one factor that will never change - to hit the ball you must move to the ball quickly balanced, and repeat this over and over. Techniques, even if great, without movement and balance, makes it difficult to be a winner.

Chapter 12

Mental Conditioning

"When I step onto the tennis court, whether positive or negative thoughts are on my mind, I try to keep focused on the game."
—Björn Borg

Though a cliché, deep inside we all know it to be true - ninety percent of performance, of winning, is mental. At IMG Academy, no athletic development program is complete without a complementary mental toughness program. In this chapter we first take a look at the mental demands of the sport and then move on to the core tenets of developing your own mental conditioning program. Taking the time to become more self-aware will allow you to put a mental routine into place that will help you from letting your head unravel your physical effort, and instead turn your mind into your most powerful weapon.

Mental Demands of Tennis

Hitting the tennis ball is only a fragment of what tennis is all about. Knowing how to handle pressure, adversity, gamesmanship, and the fear of failure are critical elements of a successful tennis player's repertoire.

Handling Cheating

During the more than 60 years that I have been teaching tennis, I'm sure I have seen matches, and even tournaments, won or lost on the basis of cheating or gamesmanship. I have also on many occasions witnessed points and even games won through manipulative, unethical tactics.

Tennis has many opportunities for cheating, gamesmanship, and unethical behavior. For example, actions such as calling a ball out that is in, questioning every line call, taking too long between points, and quick serving are all tactics that display disrespect for tennis and a lack of personal etiquette.

Buried deep within the old saying "Winning tells something of your character, but losing tells all of it," lurks the psychological cause of cheating. Make no mistake, cheating is not a modern phenomenon. Plato, the ancient Greek philosopher, recognized this human weakness by observing that "you can discover more about a person in an hour of play than in a year of conversation." Over the course of human evolution, why have many of us come to believe that cheating is a reasonable way to avoid defeat? Why have youngsters become convinced that they must win at all costs? Why have they been led to believe they are OK only if they win? Are they afraid that a loss will disappoint those who love and support them? And how do we begin the process of rebuilding the self-esteem and character of our youth so they may better serve themselves and humanity in their adulthood?

Clearly, this problem has been around so long that it will not be resolved quickly. Parents, educators, and role models have a huge responsibility. We must address the root causes of cheating because these issues are steeped in poor self-esteem and a lack of self-respect that will not serve our children well in adulthood. We must stress the value of having integrity, the quality that places more importance on effort than result. We must assure our kids that heroes and winners who cheat are frauds. As General Colin Powell put it, "The healthiest competition occurs when average people win by putting in above-average effort."

At IMG, the staff and I have had lengthy discussions with our staff about this. Our findings are not what we think, but what we know to be true. The majority of tennis players will deal with cheating at some point, and there are a host of reasons why. For some, parents never stop asking why they "didn't win" because they are paying substantial money for their lessons, equipment, travel, and fees. Players are also under a great deal of peer pressure, and their friends want to be with winners. The pressure to win at any cost can be powerful. Acknowledging these factors and the reality of life and how to deal with cheating is important. It is easy to assume that the world is a fair place, but the reality is that it is not. How we teach students to deal and manage will shape their experience not just in tennis, but also in life itself.

Those who would teach kids when and how to cheat don't deserve the power that has been given them. They have been entrusted with the responsibility to mold the values that our children will use as adults. They have been given the authority to provide for the emotional direction of children's lives. They have been offered an opportunity to provide nutrition for the minds of young people and then have fed them poison. As surely as small doses of poison will steal the lives of children, learning to win by cheating will steal their futures. Parents, if you or your tennis pro tolerate or encourage cheating, you are both guilty of preventing your child from enjoying the true benefits of this wonderful sport Let your children know that they must work hard for victories and compete with integrity. Children must be made to realize that, in the final analysis, cheaters lose.

Neutralizing Gamesmanship

Certain tactics used to disrupt an opponent's momentum or game, however, are acceptable but borderline ethical behavior. For example, a player may attempt to change the tempo of play and upset an opponent's rhythm.

Although at times it may be difficult to distinguish between gamesmanship and acceptable tactics, some actions are obviously unscrupulous, if not obnoxious. I still encourage my players not to jump to conclusions and to give any opponent the benefit of the doubt. But when a situation arises in which dishonesty is clear, the defense should be to ask your opponent if she is sure of the call. At no time should you scream at your opponent or an official or accuse your opponent of foul play.

To neutralize an opponent who employs gamesmanship, I encourage my players to pay attention to their own game and not become caught up in their opponent's behavior. If your concentration begins to fade, focus on the ball and think only of the point being played. As Andre Agassi used to say, "The previous point is over. It's history. The most important point is now only the next point."

Overcoming Frustration

"I'm not getting any better. . . .It's boring to lose match after match. . . .I can't hit with any power. . . .I'll never be able to hit a slice serve. . . .I'm frustrated." All these negative statements born out of frustration will bring a player's performance and improvement down. You have to believe you can do it! With a few simple pointers, all of you can improve and enjoy the game within your own style of play.

Frustration can happen to anyone at any time, no matter what you are doing. The key is understanding that you will have ups and downs in life, as well as in tennis. As Charles Swindoll was quoted, "Life is 10% what happens to you, and 90% how you react to it." Your attitude is determined by your perspective. Think of the difference between someone frustrated by windy conditions compared with a child fighting cancer. The simple truth is that we are lucky to have the opportunity to do any variety of activities, let alone tennis. Embracing your ability to choose your attitude will set you up for success. There are sources of frustration around every corner, so embrace your attitude and what you can do about it.

Staying Focused

Developing the ability to focus, to center or concentrate, can be difficult because you must filter out your normal awareness of the surrounding environment. In this regard I have had experiences with several top players.

- *Maria Sharapova*—Her focus is all tennis. Whether it's her between-point routine where she's looking at her strings or she has her eyes glued to the ball during play, she's on a mission.
- *Novak Djokovic*—Sometimes called "the joker," he's not afraid in a critical moment to turn to the fans and put on a show or look for support. Sometimes, taking yourself out of the moment and absorbing the energy and taking a break can help refocus things.
- *John McEnroe*—He argued consistently throughout his matches. Statistics showed he was able to focus on the ball right after these outbursts and win 80 percent of the points. Many opponents thought he did this to break their concentration.
- *Boris Becker*—To stay focused, Boris relieved frustration with controlled gestures of anger. For example, if he missed a shot, he slapped his leg and yelled some German phrase. Or he glared at the umpire, walked up to him, and let everyone in the stadium know that he was putting him on notice.
- *Jimmy Connors*—He put on a complete television show with every point, every set, every match.
- *Billie Jean King*—She frequently mentions that during a match she was so focused and so into the next point that she would forget whom she was playing. Her attention centered on the ball and the point she was currently playing.

I could go on forever, but it all boils down to one factor: being ready. Are you ready for the next ball, the next stroke, the next point, or whatever you are doing? Are your mind and body focused on being ready to get into gear without losing the edge?

I have learned many things from my students:

- What's happened is history. You have no control over the past.
- We are all human and subject to breakdowns.

- The most drastic penalty you can get is one point against you.
- There are many ups and downs in tennis matches. The players who can keep positive and compete through the downs without giving up mentally have a great advantage.
- Remember, it isn't over until it's over.

Another tough area is learning to stay focused when winning, even though it seems pretty simple—just finish the match. But victory is often elusive, and it can escape the faint of heart. Giving away a match after leading 5-2 in the third is possible through a combination of events. First, your opponent is at the threshold of defeat and is going to bear down harder than ever. Your rival's renewed focus may eat at you, causing you to play more cautiously. You may completely abandon the game plan that got you to match point. Some call it a shift in momentum, and when momentum starts rolling against you, anything can happen, and it usually does.

A cliché applies here: "Never change a winning game, except perhaps to intensify it." Don't change from a baseline style to serving and volleying. Stay with the game that enabled you to succeed. Obviously, winning one point at a time and not thinking about the score are the habits of winners. Choking, or giving away a match or game, is something every athlete must cope with. No one is immune. Some mask the feeling better than others do. Losing when victory seems imminent occurs in all sports. There isn't a formula, but there is one thing you can do to avoid giving away a match. Train yourself through quality practice sessions, and learn to put a match away when ahead. Remember, quality practices generate quality matches.

Facing Fear

Throughout my experience, one factor has repeatedly come into play—many people do not like to compete because they fear losing. For some, telling their parents they lost is unbearable. The shame and embarrassment can generate tremendous fear. Indeed, the visibility of results online and how quickly news can be shared through Twitter and Facebook can exaggerate this sensation of how we're perceived by others.

Expectations can deter players from giving their best. Competition often changes people, especially when they must play in front of a crowd or with their parents looking on. Competition can completely alter a person's style of play and prevent the person from doing what feels comfortable or what she has practiced.

The key rests with two very simple questions.

- How do you define success?
- How do you define failure?

The reason these two questions are so powerful is that they typically generate the source of our fears. When you ask most players, they will tell you the following:

Success = winning

Failure = losing

The mistake people make here is that they define *winning* as the result of the match. If this is your approach, you are setting yourself up for failure. Every tennis player, indeed, every person, will lose at some point or another, but this is not the same as failing. When you ask the best pros in the world, they will tell you something more like this:

Success = a winning mind-set and competing every point. Failure = a quitting mind-set, not giving my best effort

The differences are subtle but incredibly powerful. Imagine the power of walking on the court knowing that you can't fail! You play to win, no matter what the score. When you watch the best competitors on the tennis court, like Nadal or Sharapova, you have no doubt that they play to win. Every match, every point, every ball. This does not mean they are losers when they lose a match. Winning is a mind-set and attitude, not the score of the game. Indeed, many of the best players in the world have a tremendous work ethic and embrace this competitiveness regardless of who they are competing against, whatever the round, whatever the tournament. With this shift in your thinking, you can remove a great deal of fear from your life. You cannot control the outcome of the match, but you compete to win regardless of the result.

Making Changes

If you are getting your butt kicked in all directions, I have a very simple answer that consists of two choices.

1. Keep getting it kicked! You cannot play on my team or work for me.
2. Change it. Do not change your entire game plan, but boil it down to just a few answers.

One of the most difficult tasks any tennis player faces when competing is how to change a losing game. Most good players are stubborn and tenacious. Unfortunately, this stubbornness often makes them stick with a losing game plan.

As an overall strategy for success, any winning plan should include a tactic that changes the rhythm of play, for at least a few games. Michael Chang, whose strength was from the baseline, was as adept at making this change as any of the world's leading players. When his baseline strategy failed, he invariably did his best to mix staying back and approaching the net, giving his opponent something to think about, something to distract his rhythm, something to derail a groove, something, anything, to disrupt momentum.

If this exercise was good enough for Michael Chang and other top-flight pros, it's probably worthwhile for your strategy. Develop a game plan. Of course, you'll want to design it around your physical assets and mental capabilities, but don't underestimate the importance of changing a losing game.

There is nothing easier than losing a tennis match. As anyone who has coached aspiring pros will confirm, tennis players can find any excuse to lose. I've heard them all—loose strings, cheating, crowds, not feeling well, any number of crazy excuses. Seldom, if ever, did a player lose and confide in me that she had simply played dumb or been outthought by the opponent.

While you are playing a game, it is never easy to understand why you're losing. But you can pick up some clues, and they are not necessarily the score. Look to see how and why you're losing points. If you are netting the ball, then the change is simple—concentrate more on the ball than your opponent does, take the ball early, and hit the ball higher to take the net out of the equation. If you're hitting short and allowing your opponent easy put-away shots, hit the ball higher and deeper. If your opponent is hitting winning shots from everywhere on court, even though you're hitting deep and to the corners, you can't do much other than wait until your opponent cools off.

Much of this is simple, little more than common sense. The real art in changing a losing game comes when you're playing well, perhaps even at your best, and you're still losing. Assume for a moment that you have a character similar to Michael Chang's, that you are a focused player with strong resolve and a disciplined mind. You are a fit baseline player whose strategy consists of retrieving every ball until you wear your opponent down. Assume also that you're playing well. Unfortunately, so is your opponent, who happens to be fitter. If your opponent is fitter and you're both baseliners playing well, the odds are not in your favor. This would be an excellent time to change your tactics, perhaps throw in a few serve-and-volley points or storm the net when your opponent least expects it. If you're losing, you have nothing left to lose. The upside is that by disrupting your opponent's rhythm, you might upset her concentration. This circumstance may allow you to crawl back into the game.

If your opponent becomes flustered and the score turns in your favor, you have a difficult choice. You can return to what you're most comfortable with, or you can stay with the change. My recommendation is that you revert to your strengths and win or lose by doing what you do best.

The same is true if your preference is to serve and volley. Don't be so stubborn or stupid that you will not change a losing game. Try something different. Stay back a game or two, push if necessary (particularly if it's a temporary strategy), and all the while think of yourself as a winner.

The art of changing a losing game is to get inside your opponent's head and disrupt her concentration. If your opponent is distracted by your tactical change, then you've taken the first step to winning. Having tipped the balance in your favor, it's up to you to hold the momentum through the final point of the match. Do this and you've beaten your opponent physically and mentally. What could be more satisfying?

Be stubborn, practice hard, be disciplined, but don't let a losing game force you into the back draw, at least not without trying some degree of change. Change a losing game and intensify a winning one. Following this advice will carry you well into the twilight of your game. Try it, and you'll be surprised at how easy it is to turn a potential loss into a satisfying win. The bottom line is that to be a champion, you have to be a warrior. Sometimes this means doing something different. Be ready to grind it out and fight to the end.

Dealing With Pressure

Today we all face pressure just to survive. Many years ago, life just seemed to go on each day, and many of the social problems that exist today were absent.

Good communication is required to identify the different types of pressure for various students. Until this happens, little progress can occur. Pressure can come from yourself, outsider (verbally or by facial expressions), innuendoes, or simply from a specific activity (e.g., competition). Everyone can improve in this area. You must accept reality, and you must understand that to survive daily activities you have to stay involved. This is a starting point for finding ways to play the game and cope with pressure.

Setting Goals

If you are going out to practice, have a plan of what you want to work on. Don't go out and just hit. Convince your playing partner that you'll get more out of the session by working on particular drills or rallying exercises. When you go out to play, have a few small goals in mind. Most important, don't judge everything by the result. Look deeper and analyze different aspects of your game to see what has improved and what needs more work.

Although most people will set goals, we're often not very good at keeping them visible and evaluating our progress. Use this goal identification form (see figure 12.1) to record your goals and share them and your progress with your coach.

In addition, here are a few key points in relation to goals:

When setting goals, be specific.
Specific goals convey information to both you and your coach. The more specific you can make a personal goal, the greater the chance you will be motivated by it. Select no fewer than three goals and no more than seven at any one time. Use the following list samples for your goal statements.

Figure 12.1   Goal Identification Form

Name:_____   Date: _____

Tennis Skills Goals	Date Completed
1.	
2.	
3.	

Physical Fitness and Conditioning Goals	Date Completed
1.	
2.	
3.	

Daily Living Skills Goals	Date Completed
1.	
2.	
3.	

Personal Goals	Date Completed
1.	
2.	
3.	

Bollettieri, Nick. *Nick Bollettieri's Tennis Handbook, second edition.* Human Kinetics: Champaign, IL.

Physical Game

To improve the accuracy of my first serve

To increase the percentage of my service return

To get more depth on my ground-stroke rallies

To win more first points in a game

To improve my fitness so I can perform fully in long matches

To add variety to my second serve

Mental Game

To relax better on important points

To become more disciplined in preparing for my matches

To remain focused between sets

Learn how to measure goals so you can better follow through.
Review your practice and match-play performances. Compare your ratings with those of your coach, and determine similarities and differences.

Break down personal goals.
Break goals into simpler components if they become too complicated to accomplish. To attain goals, you must know what actions to take. Know and determine why your goals are relevant. Determine goals in terms of short-term and long-term attainability.

SMART goals have five characteristics found in the letters of the word *smart.*

- *Specific*—You and your coach known exactly what the goal is.
- *Measurable*—You and others can measure your progress toward the goal.
- *Attainable*—You are able to make progress and attain the goal.
- *Relevant*—By attaining the goal, you will have become a better tennis player; the goal is relevant to your development as a tennis player.
- *Timely*—You have a clear understanding of when you expect to attain the goal.

Discuss your goals with other people.
Use others to give you feedback and monitor your short-term and long-term goals. Discussing your goals with other people is an effective way to get them involved positively in your game. Seek help, guidance, and ongoing support and monitoring from others. Learn to monitor your progress continually.

Establish a benchmark.
Establish a benchmark to know where you began to measure your progress. Determine your progress toward each of your goals. Knowing where you are and where you came from will allow you to measure your progress effectively. Know where you are heading. Be flexible and able to adjust your goals based on your progress. Learn to define and monitor the quantity and the quality of your practice and progress. Quantity refers to the number of times you practice. Quality refers to the effort you expend to achieve your goals. Making changes in goals is characteristic of the mentally efficient tennis player. Be open to accepting the feedback of critics. They can be your best friend.

Achieve Self-Motivation

When you are self-motivated, you have the interest and desire to attain important goals. The more aware you are of yourself, the more self-motivated you will be. Self-motivation means you have taken personal initiative to set goals for yourself and do what is necessary to attain them. You do not want other people to be your primary source of motivation. Others can help you set conditions for improvement, but they can't make you take advantage of them. Your motive for action comes primarily from within, not from an external source. However, you must be honest with your self-evaluation.

Develop an increased focus on what is important both on and off the tennis court. When you are self-motivated, you have positive energy that helps you control all aspects of your training. Being self-motivated allows you to block out negative distractions. Being self-motivated will give you more physical and mental energy. Identify personal goals that have meaning to you. You will be able to remain self-motivated when your goals are ones you can control. The driving force to attain a goal comes not from outside but from within. Create a master list of goals, and select the ones especially important for you. Select enough goals so that you can stay focused and motivated.

It's really important for you to begin with asking why you play the game. What's something that gets you really excited about the game? Perhaps the feeling of hitting that perfect ball? Or maybe the dream of walking onto Wimbledon Center Court, playing for your school, or defeating an older sibling? Regardless of what the dream is, it should be something compelling and exciting for you. This can act as your pilot light, which always burns and allows you to ignite your passion and motivation. When you look at Maria Sharapova, Rafael Nadal, or Novak Djokovic, you can see that they always have that burning passion that will motivate them through thick and thin.

There are three elements that help people maintain long-lasting motivation. First, highly motivated people feel as if they are among the best at their sport. The adage "competence before confidence" rings true. Here, they have some control and a feeling of competence that they can perform well. Second, they feel connected to others in their sport. This may be a positive connection to their coaching team, perhaps others in their training group, or even their competition. But there's a feeling of community or camaraderie that increases that connection. Finally, the third element is the idea that there is some control over their career, and that they have some autonomy over what they do and are involved in decisions and the future of what they are doing. A sense of ownership and investment means you are more likely to see things through. This can be important for coaches and parents to also keep in consideration, because if these elements can be allowed to flourish, it sets the foundations for the internal drive that is so important for long-term success.

Developing a Mental Conditioning Program

By looking at the big picture, you can recognize that tennis influences all aspects of your life, just as events in your life influence your tennis development. Consider yourself not only as a tennis player but also as a unique person who exists beyond the game. Tennis can be a worthwhile part of growing up, a routine aspect of your life, and a favorite pastime. By taking a personal perspective, tennis will provide you with a range of personal development benefits.

Over the last four decades of working with juniors and pros at IMG Academy, we have witnessed success come in the form of many different faces. We continue to innovate and evolve our mental toughness programming to include the latest science-based research. Our mental experts' mission is to help individuals reach their full potential by training a high-performance mindset. What we've learned is that regardless of the sport people play, there are two common characteristics of athletes:

They want to grow.

- They are hungry to improve.
- They have a positive attitude.

They are coachable and motivated to get better, always looking for opportunities to develop and compete. Look at Roger Federer, who has continued to add to his game and to seek advice from coaches despite holding more Grand Slam titles than any other man.

Get in Shape for a Better Mental Game

It makes no difference whether you play sport or not. Whether you are a child or an adult, if you are physically fit, your approach to everything you do will improve and you will have higher productivity. It's not a secret that a tired body results in frustration and poor decision making. So, don't postpone getting into shape (or back into shape), and take one step at a time. Exercise really is one of the best medicines, reducing the likelihood of injury and many diseases.

You may not want to admit it, but the single most important aspect of your life is staying in shape. This holds on court and off. You owe it to your health (and your tennis) to set aside a few minutes each day. Once you find the time, it is not that tough to get in shape. If you can attend aerobics classes or gym sessions, or work out at home, fantastic. But if you do not have the time or cannot afford such things, don't panic. You can do plenty of simple activities that require little time or money. Take a few minutes each day to jog, swim, ride a bicycle (even a stationary bicycle), jump rope, take a walk, or use the stairs instead of the elevator. You can do simple stretching exercises, push-ups, sit-ups, and other exercises at home to shape up.

Using the physical fitness and condition rating scale (see figure 12.2), rate your physical fitness attributes—stamina, speed, strength, mobility, weight, and diet.

Figure 12.2 Physical Fitness and Condition Rating Scale

For each item, rate yourself in the space to the left. Rate what you believe is your current level of development. Use this scale:

1 = excellent   2 = good   3 = average   4 = fair   5 = poor

Stamina

___ Running

___ Breathing

___ Pulse rate

Speed

___ First-step quickness

___ Speed endurance

___ Coping with tiring situations

___ Quick recovery

Strength

___ Muscle tone

___ Endurance

___ Power

Mobility

___ Stretching

___ Lunging

___ Range of arm motion

___ Joint flexibility

Weight and Diet

___ Current weight

___ Body-fat composition

___ Prematch diet

___ Nutrition during the match

___ Postmatch diet

They want to perform.

- They love to compete.
- They thrive on the task of their sport.
- They focus and manage their thoughts and energy when the pressure is on.
- They are confident in their ability and enjoy the battle.

Take one of my longtime students, Tommy Haas, who is still competing at the very highest level at the age of 37, having overcome many injuries and setbacks. His love of competing is fierce, and he's continued to develop his mind and body to compete and win, 18 years into a career on the pro tour.

Many people consider these characteristics something you either have or do not. However, at IMG Academy, we have learned they are skills that can be nurtured and developed. While every individual has a unique makeup, everyone can maximize their mental skills if they are open to change and can be disciplined enough to put in the effort and create habits of consistency.

Change is possible when you consider that increasing people's motivation allows them to better connect with something they feel passionate about. People can become more consistent when they use routines to help them focus. Repetition builds strength, and this applies when we repeat negative thoughts and behaviors as well as positive. If we develop good habits early, we can increase the chances of success for that athlete.

At IMG, we think of the high-performance mind-set as a series of skills and principles that help players achieve high performance. The subsets of growing and performing are addressed in this section, but understand that these are largely outcomes. Maria Sharapova achieves great consistency in her matches, Kei Nishikori has strong coachability, Max Mirnyi has great readiness, and Tommy Haas has world-class concentration. However, they all have their own strategies to achieve these outcomes. Interestingly, the absence of these assets can create problems, too. What happens to the player who is not motivated? Or the player who has no control? Or poor consistency? It's pretty rare for players to do all of these well, all the time. How often are players actually training to improve these parts of their game, though? When you truly consider how important each of these aspects are, you begin to start respecting them more and more. The fact is, the best players typically play the mental game better than most of their competition. How much attention are you giving your mental game?

Becoming Aware of Yourself

Awareness is the first and perhaps most important step in training the high-performance mind-set. If you are not aware or not willing to look at yourself honestly in the mirror, then it's going to be impossible to push hard and get close to reaching your potential. Personal awareness refers to your ability to know yourself as a tennis player and as a person. You can develop your strong points even further. Developing a sound and thorough personal awareness will help you identify your strong points, limitations, and areas for improvement.

Be honest with yourself. You will be a better player if you have a vision. Challenge yourself to be a better player, and focus on what is important and what you need to work on. You can obtain information about yourself by asking focused questions. The tennis skills inventory (see figure 12.3) is divided into tennis skills. I recommend that you complete this inventory by yourself and then discuss it with your coach and others.

Once you've evaluated your tennis skills, rate your daily living activities and personal routines using the personal profile form (see figure 12.4). Learn what has prevented you from doing as well as you would like in tennis or in other areas of your life. Identify your strong points, determine areas that you need to develop, and become aware of your current personal limitations. Get an outside check on the accuracy of your opinions. A personal mission statement outlines what you want to do as both a tennis player and a person over the next two years.

Your mission statement should be broad based and clear. It should not refer to external, self-centered achievements. A mission statement is for your personal use and benefit, not for discussion by others. Visualize yourself realizing your mission. Update your personal awareness profile two or three times a year.

Encouraging the Conditions to Grow and Perform

Once you are aware, the next step is to train and exercise those skills. Repetition builds strength, and one of the secrets of a strong mental game is training your mind as well as your strokes, along with your body on the court. Let's take a look at how to train the guiding principles of both mind-sets of growing and performing (see figure 12.5 for the guiding principles).

Committing to Continuous Improvement

We often talk about having a growth mind-set. This is the idea of being personally committed to using information about your progress and performance in tennis and other areas of your life. If your personal growth is in motion, it will remain in motion until some external force stops it. If it is at rest, it will remain at rest until you take action. A person who does not seek improvement in a planned way is likely to become stagnant mentally, emotionally, and physically.

Figure 12.3 Tennis Skills Inventory

In the space to the left of each item below, rate your current level of skill development. Use this scale for each item:

1 = excellent   2 = good   3 = average   4 = fair   5 = poor

Ground-Stroke Play
___Forehand crosscourt
___Forehand down the line
___Backhand crosscourt
___Backhand down the line
___Backhand lob
___Forehand lob
___Forehand inside out

Transition Play
___Forehand approach shot crosscourt
___Forehand approach shot down the line
___Backhand approach shot crosscourt
___Backhand approach shot down the line

Net Play
___Forehand volley crosscourt
___Forehand volley down the line
___Backhand volley crosscourt
___Backhand volley down the line
___Overhead

Return of Serve
___Forehand in the deuce court
___Backhand in the deuce court
___Forehand in the ad court
___Backhand in the ad court

Specialty Shots
___Forehand angle crosscourt
___Backhand angle crosscourt
___Forehand drop shot
___Backhand drop shot
___Forehand touch volley
___Backhand touch volley

Serve
___First-serve flat
___First-serve slice
___First-serve topspin
___Second-serve slice
___Second-serve topspin

Style of Play
___Serve and volleyer
___Aggressive baseliner
___Baseliner
___All-court game

Movement
___To the wide forehand
___To the wide backhand
___To the short forehand
___To the short backhand
___On volleys
___For overheads

Bollettieri, Nick. *Nick Bollettieri's Tennis Handbook, second edition.* Human Kinetics: Champaign, IL.

Figure 12.4 Personal Profile Form

Name:_____ **Date:**_____

My current strong points are the following (specify physical and mental tennis skills, physical fitness and conditioning, daily living skills):

1.

2.

3.

4.

5.

My current needs for development are the following (specific physical and mental tennis skills, physical fitness and conditioning, daily living skills):

1.

2.

3.

4.

5.

Limitations that I need to address and rectify are the following (particular knowledge, skills, attitudes):

1.

2.

3.

4.

5.

I plan to discuss my profile with_____.

Bollettieri, Nick. *Nick Bollettieri's Tennis Handbook, second edition.* Human Kinetics: Champaign, IL.

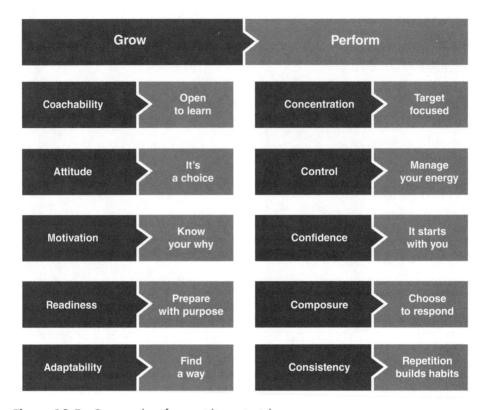

Figure 12.5 Grow and perform guiding principles.

To improve yourself continuously as a tennis player and as a person, you must approach the task in a planned, systematic way. By constantly improving your mental, emotional, and physical skills, you will be sharp, productive, and able to maintain a competitive edge. Committing to continuous improvement will steer you away from a complacent attitude and psychological helplessness.

Progress feedback is information that indicates your growth or improvement from one point in time to another. Performance feedback is the data that indicates the results of your play. Ask your coach to provide an opinion about how you are progressing in the area of self-confidence in match play. Watching videotape can help you compare your current performance to a previous performance. Identify the things you are doing well. Make notes about areas in which you want the opinion of your coach or others. Consider the things you need to improve. List specific items that you want to discuss with your coach. To conclude your meeting, summarize your thoughts and impressions.

You can use all this information to take initiative for continuous improvement. In addition, you may want to discuss your answers with your coach. Acquire new physical or mental skills that will help your game, become more respectful and patient with other people, and believe in yourself more consistently.

Maintaining Quality Interpersonal Relationships

Tennis is an individual sport, so people don't often think of the team involvement in tennis. At IMG Academy, we have always recognized the importance of the individual, but we also fundamentally believe in a group and team approach to individual development. In a quality interpersonal relationship, you gain benefit from another human being while providing that person with something valuable in return. You build a quality interpersonal relationship by respecting, trusting, and having a sincere interest in helping another person. If you want to accomplish something worthwhile in tennis and reach your personal best, you need the help of others. You should seek to develop quality relationships with all kinds of people yet know when not to associate with particular people. Having caring relationships with others fulfills a critical but often neglected personal need. When you are mentally efficient, you can address this need.

It is important to gain the cooperation of others. Helping others and being helped by others is a mutually profitable experience. When you respect others and yourself at the same time, you are more likely to enjoy playing tennis and practicing. By eliminating or reducing a self-centered approach to your existence, you can maintain quality relationships with many people.

Your personal network consists of all the people who are important to you and with whom you want to maintain contact. Identify the people with whom you want to develop or maintain quality interpersonal relationships. Place the people in your network in categories, and record that information so it is readily accessible.

Specify your own needs and interests to these people. Determine which needs your network of people can fulfill. Now specify the needs and interests of the people with whom you want to maintain quality interpersonal relationships. By focusing your attention on the other person, you will avoid having a self-centered relationship. One way you can specify the needs of others is simply to ask each person what he or she expects from the relationship. Anyone will appreciate getting respect, a listening ear, help when needed, and compliments.

Assess the status of your relationships. Identify specific actions you need to take to improve each relationship. Feedback will come to you in many different forms, from different sources, and in a variety of circumstances. You will receive oral feedback and written feedback. You will expect some of the feedback you receive; other comments may come as a surprise. The way you accept personal feedback from others will influence future performance and the quality of your relationships. We suggest that you accept all criticism about yourself in a positive way. You can take or leave opinion for what it's worth, depending on the reliability of the source.

Feedback can be positive and expected.

Feedback can be positive and unexpected.

Feedback can be negative and expected.

Feedback can be negative and unexpected.

Make sure you understand the feedback, no matter what type it is. Be a good listener. To maintain quality interpersonal relationships, you must give feedback to others. Do unto others as you would have them do unto you. Be specific and clear when providing feedback. Look for nonverbal signs. Provide additional information to the person.

When conflict occurs in an interpersonal relationship, try to manage it effectively. Conflicts between individuals often develop because the people involved are not aware of whether they are disagreeing over means or ends. A conflict can be a positive experience and a growth situation for the people involved. Interpersonal disagreement can happen in any setting. Discuss first the areas you agree on and then talk about those you disagree on. Discuss how you can reach an agreement. Restate the compromise as a personal action and follow through on it.

Building and Maintaining Self-Confidence

When you are self-confident, you believe in your ability to follow through and accomplish the goals set for yourself. With self-confidence, you are able to maintain poise and perseverance—two important indicators of a self-confident state. *Poise* is the ability to avoid becoming upset with yourself or with what is going on around you. *Perseverance* means follow through with your plans no matter what the obstacles. When you believe you can compete on the court with players of your ability level or better, your self-confidence promotes and sustains performance.

Trust yourself. Have faith in your training and ability. Balancing the mental and physical aspects of tennis allows you to reach your potential. Believing in yourself helps eliminate negative self-perceptions and feelings of failure, fear, and intimidation. Practice building and maintaining your self-confidence regularly. Make a personal commitment to yourself. Do not doubt yourself or your ability. Strive to improve and play your best.

You must be realistic, of course—you cannot be perfect. But you should challenge yourself to reach your best. Separate your performance in sport from your self-worth in life. Determine your own level of self-confidence (see figure 12.6). Believe that you have the skills necessary to perform well or, if you don't, be able to develop them within your training program. Sport is dynamic. You will have to continually change, learn, and refine during development. Determine when you are confident and when you are not.

Figure 12.6 Tennis Self-Confidence Survey

Name:_____ **Date:**_____

When am I in a confident state (e.g., during practice, prematch warm-up, match play, other)?

In what aspects of my game am I usually confident (e.g., baseline play, midcourt play, net play, mental approach, serve, other)?

What is it that makes me confident?

When am I not confident?

In what aspects of my game am I not confident?

Bollettieri, Nick. *Nick Bollettieri's Tennis Handbook, second edition.* Human Kinetics: Champaign, IL.

Determine the Factors That Benefit You

Determine which factors help you be more confident and which factors hinder your confidence. Know your current skills. You must maintain skills by using consistent, high-quality practice habits. Conduct a routine inventory of your skills. Get opinions from others who are interested in your development.

Examine Your Skill Levels

Appraise your situations and results realistically. You alone determine how you react and view a particular situation. You alone interpret the situations and events in your life positively or negatively. No one is perfect. Those who believe they are perfect approach life unrealistically and set themselves up to fail.

Acknowledge Your Mistakes

The first step to building self-confidence is acknowledging your mistakes. Try to reduce the frequency of making mistakes. Don't be adversely affected by things beyond your control. Focus on what you can control. Making every situation in tennis and life a learning experience is a healthy, positive way to approach sport and life. Put a particular situation into a fuller context to gain perspective. You alone control your ability to be (or not be) self-confident.

Recognize What Your Senses Tell You

Learn to recognize and monitor three important senses—visual, auditory, and kinesthetic. Learn what factors inhibit or enhance your self-confidence. Learn to identify the situations in which you have the least amount of self-confidence. Once you have identified your low-confidence situations, recognize the feelings associated with them. Learn what negative statements you may be associating with a particular situation. Muscle sensations can also be identified and associated with particular low-confidence states.

Learn to monitor your senses during and before competitive play. Learn to use breathing to your advantage in practice and match play. Learning to regulate your breathing will increase your self-confidence. Use breathing to relax and eliminate negative, unproductive performance states. You need to control what you think and be able to detect differences in your muscle tension. Practicing progressive relaxation will help you learn how to control and relax muscles. Become aware of how your muscles feel when you are tense and how they feel when you are relaxed. Practice the progressive relaxation procedure often.

Control Your Thoughts

Learn to control thoughts to improve your self-confidence. Negative thoughts can adversely affect your game mentally and physically. Learn to say no to negative thoughts. Focus your mind on a positive thought. Use the technique of letting go of negative thoughts. Remind yourself that you can control thoughts and make them positive.

Visualization is a personal process involving the forming of mental images, or pictures, about your tennis performance. The more often you use visualization, the better your chances of being motivated to hit and execute a specific shot. Through visualization, you can put yourself in positive states of thought and emotion. Make the mental images relate to your goals. Make a list of your personal goals and the associated mental images. Describe the images on the positive image form (see figure 12.7).

In addition, visualization should be scheduled, not random. Collect visual images of yourself that you can refer to for reference and reinforcement. Look at your still pictures and videos regularly. Add to your positive images throughout the tennis season. Positive affirmations will aid in maintaining motivation, help you concentrate on what you are trying to accomplish on court, and allow you to reestablish your focus if you lose it. Identify specific positive states that you want to attain as a tennis player. Write a positive affirmation for each specific positive state (see figure 12.8).

Developing Positive Self-Esteem

Self-esteem is what you think about yourself. You can think about yourself either positively or negatively. Judging yourself by things over which you have no control is setting yourself up for a negative situation. You need to know and believe that you are unique. You must be able to separate the quality of your performance from your overall worth as a person. You should be able to counter and eliminate negative ways of viewing activities in your life.

You can avoid developing a poor opinion of yourself and devaluing yourself as an individual by practicing and following through on activities that develop and maintain your self-esteem. Your true value does not come from playing tennis. Make a vow to look at yourself in an accurate, positive way. It is important to have an accurate view of what you can and cannot do. Be realistic in what you attempt to do.

Usually, the way we make judgments about who we are comes from what people tell us about ourselves. It is important for you to engage in a variety of activities beyond tennis. You should use yourself, not others, as a basis for comparison. Be satisfied with small but steady gains in all that you do. You risk lowering your self-esteem if you maintain or create irrational beliefs about yourself. You have to be able to let go of self-defeating beliefs. You can be confident about being able to perform well while recognizing that you will never be perfect.

It is important to recognize your anxiety, accept it, and take steps to reduce it. Identify irrational beliefs and dislodge them. Personal aware-

Figure 12.7   Positive Image Form

Name:_____ **Date:**_____

Style of play:_____

Positive image:_____

Situation when I will use this image:

Positive image:_____

Situation when I will use this image:

Positive image:_____

Situation when I will use this image:

Bollettieri, Nick. *Nick Bollettieri's Tennis Handbook, second edition.* Human Kinetics: Champaign, IL.

Figure 12.8 Positive Affirmations Form

Name:_____ **Date:**_____

Style of play:_____

Positive state:_____

Positive affirmations:

Situations when I will use these affirmations:

Positive state:_____

Positive affirmations:

Situations when I will use these affirmations:

Positive state:_____

Positive affirmations:

Situations when I will use these affirmations:

Bollettieri, Nick. *Nick Bollettieri's Tennis Handbook, second edition.* Human Kinetics: Champaign, IL.

ness of your beliefs can help you dispel them. Substitute an appropriate belief for each irrational belief. Negative self-talk usually leads to lowered self-esteem. Positive self-talk means you make statements that put you in a favorable light. If you routinely employ positive self-talk, you are likely to be positive about yourself and enhance your self-esteem. Identify the various situations in which you examine how you talk to yourself (see figure 12.9). For each situation you list on the form, describe the statement you made to yourself. When you are practicing or playing in matches, you can foster positive self-talk by substituting the positive for the negative. Self-esteem has to do with unconditional acceptance of yourself despite mistakes you think you have made. Change the perspective that you have about the mistake. View a mistake as a signal to yourself. Everyone makes mistakes—that's part of life. Learn from each mistake and move forward.

Practice Mentality

Venus Williams, Serena Williams, Novak Djokovic, Maria Sharapova, and Rafa Nadal have the mentality of Bjorn Borg, Martina Navratilova, Martina Hingis, Chris Evert, Monica Seles, Boris Becker, Tracy Austin, and many other great past champions. They approach practice with great intensity, set goals, and have an all-business mind-set.

Be patient with yourself, establish your goals, and work daily on achieving them. You should strive for perfection but understand that you will make mistakes along the way. If you don't make mistakes, you will never get better. The player who can best manage mistakes and failures is the one who will most often achieve greatness. Avoid doubting your abilities and being negative about yourself.

There is no substitute for hard work. Practice intelligently by working on specific developmental goals. Accept constructive criticism from your coach and those who understand the game better than you do. Practice the way you want to play your match, and play your match the way you practice. The coach should demand you do this. If you don't apply your shots in practice, you will not be able to do them under pressure.

Possessing Self-Discipline

Serious athletes are disciplined in their sport and in other areas of their lives. When you plan what you need to do to attain your goals and then follow through, making adjustments as required along the way, you are actively developing self-discipline. Self-discipline involves following through on activities not directly related to your primary goal yet important to accomplishing it.

Personal planning offers several meaningful benefits. Being self-disciplined promotes positive, constructive thoughts and behaviors, provides

Figure 12.9 Self-Talk Assessment Form

Name:_____ **Date:** _____

Situation	Self-statement	Rating (+/-)	Personal action

Bollettieri, Nick. *Nick Bollettieri's Tennis Handbook, second edition.* Human Kinetics: Champaign, IL.

positive reinforcement, allows you to use your time effectively, gives you a sense of self-control, and involves you taking action and moving forward.

Make a commitment to developing a personal plan. A personal plan is a statement of the actions you will take to accomplish something. Implementing a long-range plan for your tennis development will require patience and perseverance as you make progress toward your goals. A game plan includes one or more specific goals to develop and implement during match play. Game plans involve the use of strategy and tactics.

A continuing education plan targets your development beyond and outside tennis. You can plan all the goals and actions for your tennis and your life. Decide which kind of goals will be part of your personal plan. On the personal planning form (see figure 12.10), list the goals your plan will focus on. Specify personal actions you will take. Establish a timeline for starting and completing the action. Make sure you have a way of knowing you have completed the listed personal actions. Describe any personal obstacles under the comments section of the form. List the people with whom you expect to discuss the plan. It is valuable to have others review and support your plan. Show another person your plan and discuss it in detail. Seek this individual's constructive criticism and comments about your plan.

Take a systematic approach to monitoring yourself. If you are not satisfied with how you have followed through, you can troubleshoot possible reasons. Use the information from your troubleshooting activity to make changes in your plan. Don't be afraid to make changes. Flexibility is an indicator of a self-disciplined approach. Find the most effective and efficient means to achieve your actions and goals. You may have to readjust the timeline for attaining a goal.

Nick's Tip

Self-reinforcement means doing something positive for yourself. Compliment and reward yourself for a job well done and enjoy reinforcement from others. Reward yourself occasionally with something tangible or material.

Establishing a Routine

A routine is a standard way of doing something that contributes to your overall effectiveness. Routines help you maintain self-discipline, a sense of balance, and order. A productive routine helps you follow through on your personal actions to attain your goals.

Figure 12.10 Personal Planning Form

Name:_____ **Date:** _____

Customized plan of action: _____

People to discuss this plan with _____

Goal	Personal action	Timeline	Comments

Bollettieri, Nick. *Nick Bollettieri's Tennis Handbook, second edition.* Human Kinetics: Champaign, IL.

You can develop routines around life areas that are important to your daily effectiveness in tennis and school. You have the option of perceiving a situation as a challenge or as a source of stress. Assess your current routines in relation to the areas you have identified (see figure 12.11). Make changes in your routines as necessary. Evaluate the productiveness of your routines on a scheduled basis.

Consistency Is King

There are many different types of routines. The key is developing your awareness, recognizing the things that work well for you, and starting to build deliberate habits that are under your control, regardless of where you play, your opponent, or the situation. These habits should help you be in the optimal mental and physical shape, prepared to be at your best when your best is needed. An easy way to categorize them is before, during, and after play.

Before Play

Being prepared covers a wide range of elements. Over time, create a checklist so you can consistently do the things you need to in order to be successful. I'm not talking about eating at the same restaurant every time or wearing your lucky socks. These habits can be dangerous because you build a reliance on something you don't truly have control over. Strong routines can be consistently under your control yet still flexible and adaptable to your situation and environment. The strength of the routine is it allows you to be comfortable in a potentially uncomfortable situation—to be an anchor that brings you back to your optimal state and allows you to be at your best in the current situation. The staff at IMG share these nine broad suggestions as a checklist for our students to start from, but the truth is you need to also examine your preparation and identify what helped you during your best tournaments and what hindered you during your worst (see figure 12.12).

During Play

Between-point routines are perhaps one of the interventions that can make the biggest immediate difference in your mental game. It is easy to get swept away by the emotions of tennis and the roller coaster of ups and downs a match can take. In watching professionals play, it is easy to see that the players who manage themselves better between points typically win the match. When you look back to the legends of Pete Sampras, Boris Becker, Monica Seles, and Steffi Graf, they were all masters of the game between points, as well as the points themselves. This is part of the reason

Figure 12.11 Routine Evaluation Form

Name:_____ **Date:** _____

For each item below, give yourself a rating in the space provided to the left. Use this scale:

    1 = excellent   2 = good   3 = average   4 = fair   5 = poor

_____ Overall, I am able to manage my entire life.

_____ I devote adequate time to study, which allows me to be successful in school.

_____ I do not put off what I am supposed to do in school.

_____ I make sure I am ready to train in a quality manner.

_____ I can prepare for matches efficiently.

_____ I am able to add appointments to my schedule without difficulty.

_____ I am able to say no to people when time does not permit.

_____ I do not take on more things than I can handle.

_____ I am able to plan a weekly schedule for my life.

_____ I spend quality time with family and friends.

Bollettieri, Nick. *Nick Bollettieri's Tennis Handbook, second edition.* Human Kinetics: Champaign, IL.

Figure 12.12 **Match Preparation Checklist**

____ Do I have a game plan?
- Goals for the match are clear
- Goals are understood
- Goals are planned out with coach

____ Have I been making smart eating and drinking decisions?
- Intake at the appropriate time, at least an hour before match
- Eating the correct amount
- Hydrating several days before match

____ Have I been getting plenty of rest?
- Quality sleep
- Feel rested and full of energy

____ Have I packed all the equipment I need?
- Essentials for the match (e.g., racket, uniform, shoes)
- Extra necessities (e.g., sunscreen, blister kit, socks, iPod, towel)

____ Have I warmed up my body?
- Stretch muscles
- Increase heart rate
- Break a sweat

____ Have I taken my warm-up strokes?
- Comfortable with strokes
- Play out some points

____ Have I prepared my mind?
- Clear mind of distractions
- Visualize game plan
- Be positive

____ Am I confident in my ability to win?
- Focus on playing the game
- Control the controllable

____ Am I achieving the correct intensity level?
- Monitor intensity
- Find your best zone

Bollettieri, Nick. *Nick Bollettieri's Tennis Handbook, second edition.* Human Kinetics: Champaign, IL.

Concentration Is the Name of the Game

The cliché "one point at a time" could not be more true for the sport of tennis. In fact, that phrase may be the one most commonly used by coaches and players alike, but don't mistake this simple act as an easy thing to do! Consider the task of focusing for a whole match. How confident would you be of focusing for two hours straight? Once in a while, players have this kind of experience where they feel locked in and in the zone, focusing for hours on end. Much more frequently, players drift in and out of their focus, and frequently their performance follows this same ebb and flow. However, there is an important statistic when it comes to focus. The length of each point is on average 5 to 7 seconds. On the ATP and WTA tour, the length of time between points has been shortened to 20 seconds, but the fact remains that you have far more time between points than the average point itself. Tennis gives players a gift. The task is actually not to focus for a long period of time—it is to become really good at *refocusing*. Ask yourself how confident you are in focusing for 7 seconds? That sounds a lot better than the task of several hours!

they were so successful when playing high-pressure points. Strong routines helped them keep their focus and energy so that the pressure didn't get to them; they simply focused on what they needed to do and would play some of their best tennis. The good news is that the opportunity to have a strong routine is there for everybody. Again, this is a simple concept, but it is not easy to be disciplined and stick to a routine point, after point, after point. Follow these three steps to help develop your own individual routine (see figure 12.13).

Step 1: Release

It's that first reaction immediately after a point when you will see the biggest emotional high or low that can really fluctuate and affect your ability to think and recover before the next point. Jim Loehr spoke a lot about this concept in his "16-second cure" to get ready for the next point, beginning with a positive physical response and followed by a relaxation response. Notice that figure 12.13 shows traffic light colors, where the red for release represents the idea of "stop!" You want to clear the mind and be ready before you move on. Taking a deep breath, focusing on positive body language, and walking back to the fence and away from the court is the best way to end your last point and begin the next. Maria Sharapova teaches a master class in her between-point routine and mentality for those willing to watch and learn. Watch how consistent her reaction is, whether winning or losing the point, she turns, takes deep breaths and walks to the back of the court with strong positive body language every time. This is

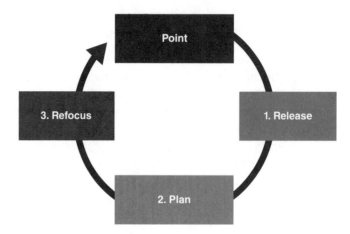

Figure 12.13   Establishing a between-point routine.

your opportunity to clear your head, recover physically, and be in a better position to shift your focus to step 2, the plan.

Step 2: Plan

The plan is where you see Rafael Nadal at his towel, or Maria Sharapova looking at her strings deep in thought. Here the key is to not overthink, but to keep things simple and get yourself ready. Referring back to the traffic light colors, yellow means you're now getting ready and switching the mind on in preparation for the green light.

I often ask players to consider two questions. The first is what did you learn from the last point? Is there anything you can adjust or do better? Whether you are winning or losing, a simple positive cue or self-instruction can help you play better. The second question is focused on what you want to do on the next point. Although you can't predict everything that will happen, have a game plan or purpose for what you want to do with the ball. It's amazing how often you will execute that plan if you simply have a clear picture of how you want to begin the point and take control.

Step 3: Refocus

A football team breaks from the huddle knowing the plan and what play they want to run. When they step up to the line of scrimmage, it's like the tennis player stepping up to the baseline. Whether serving or returning, this is where you begin your physical and mental cues to be absolutely ready for this next 5- to 7-second burst. That's it! You now have a green light to play the next point.

Remember how short that average point really is. Some points will be longer, some shorter, but challenge yourself to be absolutely locked in and focused on the present moment the whole time. Many pros use a physical act, or trigger, to reinforce this focus. For example, Maria Sharapova brushes the hair from her face, left to right, before bouncing the ball high two times. Rafael Nadal adjusts his underwear right before he bounces the ball. These are not superstitions or nervous tics; these are deliberate cues that remind them to be ready, relaxed, focused, and confident. Ready, set, go! As you walk to the baseline and take a deep breath, develop a physical and mental cue that gets your mind and body ready for the point at hand. By being consistent with your routine every time, you will develop a conditioned response that is positive, relaxed, and focused for every point. Remember, repetition builds strength.

These three steps could apply to either the serve or return game. There is a lot more emphasis on the serve game because the server has control and dictates the start of play. However, the great returners of the game, such as Andy Murray, Novak Djokovic, Jelena Janković, and Viktoria Azarenka, all take an aggressive mentality and exert a consistent, focused approach to each and every point. Although they know they won't break every time or win every point, they are patient and ready for any opening or weakness. Begin integrating these three steps into your routines, whether serving or returning, and you will soon find your mental game much more consistent.

The Power of Breath

We have long known the importance of breathing and meditation; however, the application in tennis is hugely important and sometimes undervalued. Let's look at breathing from two perspectives.

Between Points

As simple as it sounds, taking deep breaths is typically better than taking fast, shallow breaths. Indeed, a player who's stressed out on the court often rushes from one point to the next, red in the face, breathing quickly, thinking too much, and getting uptight. Now picture Maria Sharapova turning her back to the court; looking at her strings; taking deep breaths as she dances on her toes; staying calm, loose, and clearing her mind before the next point. The same goes for changeovers. Deep breaths from the pit of your stomach, under calm control, allow your lungs to physically fill up to their capacity, but they also exert control and focus over your conscious mind. By bringing the mind and body together with the act of breathing, you typically calm both by getting more oxygen into the system and also giving the mind something to focus attention on. This focus keeps you from thinking about that last unforced error, or becoming too excited about potentially winning the match. Instead, you create a calm and clear mind that's ready to go.

During Points

It is interesting to compare and contrast the feeling of playing your best tennis with some of your worst. If you think about the two extreme situations, the following scenarios often come up. The best tennis feels smooth, with a full stroke and follow-through, breathing out as you hit. The worst tennis feels tight, awkward, and rushed, and you might even have your jaw clenched and be holding your breath!

Science tells us that exhaling as we exert force gives our output of power a great mechanical advantage. The funny thing is we get not only a physical advantage but a mental one too. By focusing your eyes and energy on the ball and breathing out as you hit, you are keeping your mind and body synchronized. Indeed, this pattern appears across different sports. The weightlifter breathing out as she exerts force. The karate kid breathing out as he breaks bricks with his bare hands. The boxer exhaling as she punches the bag. In coming back to the example of best versus worst tennis, people often describe the best tennis as having virtually nothing on their minds except the ball and perhaps the target they are hitting to. There's a feeling of a physical and mental rhythm and just the ball. Quite the opposite is true during a bad game; the mind is often racing a mile a minute, with far too many thoughts, including doubt. Focusing your energy on the rhythm of the ball and breathing out as you hit can be a powerful ally for controlling your breathing and controlling your energy.

After Play

You get ready before a practice or match, and of course you put a lot of preparation into the match itself, but what about afterward? It's incredibly easy to pack your racket in your bag and walk away. Again, this is where champions separate themselves from their rivals. Your mind and body need to recover to be ready for the next match or tournament. To win a Grand Slam you need to win seven matches in a row. Qualifying might add three or more matches. To be at your best, time after time, takes a lot of energy and consistent preparation. That preparation begins immediately after your last performance.

You obviously need to recover physically, and there are many ways to do that, from cooling down to stretching to using ice baths, but your nutrition and hydration are also important elements that will help your muscles regenerate. Mentally, you need to recover and rebuild for your next opportunity. It's easy to overanalyze, in the same way it's sometimes easy to underanalyze and never learn from your mistakes, or to understand why you are successful. A simple strategy we like to use at IMG Academy is to ask our players three questions:

- *What did you do well?* No matter how bad a performance was, there's always a positive, even if it was having the courage to get on the court and compete. Get in the habit of seeing and understanding your strengths and what you are doing well. Be balanced in your approach and your evaluation of yourself and the practice or match.

- *What will you do better next time?* It can be painful to look at your mistakes, but the best performers aren't afraid to look in the mirror and see where they can improve. Did you simply get outplayed? Whether you won or lost, this is the opportunity for change and growth. What can you do better?

- *What did you learn?* This is the opportunity to turn both positive and negative lessons into actionable steps for practice or the next round. What did this experience mean to your development as a player and person? Do you have a clear sense of what this experience has taught you and how to translate that into action?

When it is all said and done, more is usually said than done! Routines allow you to be more systematic in your approach and leave less to chance. Most athletes work far too hard to leave things to chance. The better prepared you can be, and the more consistent your thoughts and actions, the better your chances of success.

Making Excuses

I could write volumes about excuses. For the most part, excuses result from predicting outcomes. Legitimate excuses are certainly valid, but most are not true. They occur before, during, or after competition. Many excuses come from covering up losses. In this case, a coach needs information to complete a case history of the student. An excuse can be either a cop-out or a valid explanation. The coach must determine what is real and what is imagined. Look for similar patterns at school and outside sport. Excuses are typically about avoiding responsibility and ultimately about a fear of failure.

Match-Play Mentality

Don't fear making mistakes or hitting the ball out because this will make you tentative. Use your forehand as often as reasonably possible as the basis of your ground-stroke attack. Your backhand can also be a weapon, but there is something about ending a point with a huge forehand that intimidates even the best players. Andre Agassi provides the perfect example. His backhand was a weapon, but when he wanted to dominate play, he hit as many forehands as possible. Show versatility in your ground strokes by mixing up the pace with spins and other kinds of shots to keep your opponent off guard. Set up combinations of shots that highlight your forehand strength. Build points around your strengths and stay positive, even when you are down. Being confident is essential to accomplishing your goals.

When developing habits, take one new thing at a time and be patient. Remember, when you either add or take away something from your stroke, your success and confidence may drop for a while. Don't worry! You should expect this decline, but it should be temporary if you are willing to work hard. Once you overcome it, you will be playing at a higher level. This is the only way you can become better.

Mental Toughness

A good foundation for mental toughness begins at home. Parents arguably play the most important role in shaping a child's attitude and openness to learn and improve.

It's been shown that human beings learn just as well, if not better, from positive support as they do from negative reinforcement. Here are a few tips when it comes to your child, the tennis player:

- Tell your child what he or she did well and suggest what to try in the future vs. belaboring what was done incorrectly

- Do not compare your child to a peer. Be sure to evaluate progress against only his or herself.

- Examine your own behavior in stressful situations during practices and matches. Remember to set the standard you want to see emulated.

- If you have hired a professional coach, let them do their job. Work with the coach to reinforce the lessons you are teaching your child.

Conclusion

Your commitment to creating a sound mental conditioning program can start right now. Begin with self-analysis and create a routine that works for you. Share it with your coaches, parents, and others who are interested in your improvement and dedicated to helping you reach your goals.

Chapter 13

Game Plans and Match Strategy

The most successful players define their game plans around their strengths but also consider protecting their weaknesses.

Strategy is more than a few sentences about how you want to play. I suggest starting out with a simple plan and being open to making adjustments as the flow of the match develops.

Match Strategy

The basic foundation of strategy begins with learning how your shot selection affects court position, recovery position at the baseline and net, reasons for using shot combinations, and patterns of play. The objective is not to persuade you to abandon your style of play. Instead, use what you have and become more effective by changing your shot selection, altering your recovery position, and adding more strategy to your game. Without changing your style, you can become more consistent at winning by learning to control the center of the court and improving your shot selection in match play.

Basic Court Positioning

This section discusses the factors influencing the server and returner's positions, and your position at the baseline.

Server's Position

In singles the server will usually take a position near the hash mark on the baseline to begin points. By staying back to play the point, the server can quickly recover to a position that is halfway between the opponent's best possible returns (figure 13.1). Note that the server may at times take various positions along the baseline. The kick serve by a right-hander to the ad service box will likely have the server extend his serving position several feet to his left. For example, Andre Agassi liked to stand out wide when hitting a high kicking topspin serve. Lefties will cheat several feet to their left particularly when serving to the ad side. John McEnroe and Rafa Nadal, on the other hand, although left-handers, don't move too far from the center line and are still able to get their serves out very wide in the ad box.

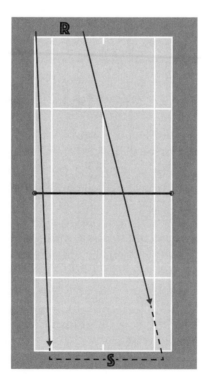

Figure 13.1   The server should stand halfway between the returner's best shots.

Returner's Position

The returner's position is influenced by whether the server is right- or left-handed, the server's ability to produce spin, and the power and range of the server's placement. In general, the returner will position in the middle of the range of possible serves. By adjusting her position, however, the returner can influence where the server will serve. Taking a different position can pressure the server and protect the returner's weakness by forcing a serve to the returner's strength. Whether you stand in front of, on top of, or behind the baseline will depend on your strengths and weaknesses and those of your opponent (figure 13.2). Today, players stand several feet behind the baseline (Rafa Nadal), stand on top of the baseline (Serena Williams), vary their position depending upon the server (Novak Djokovic), or stand around one wing to use a strength or protect a weakness (Roger Federer to protect his backhand).

You should take a position on the return that allows you to reach various serves yet gives you a chance to establish some control of the point.

Contact and Recovery

The objective of recovery is to position halfway between the opponent's best possible shots. When your opponent is in a corner and hits down the

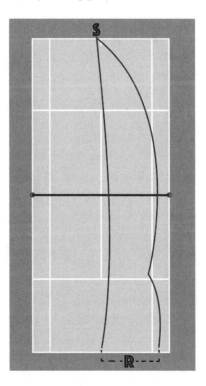

Figure 13.2 The returner should position to cover the server's best serves.

line, he cannot force you any wider than the singles sideline. Anything wider is out of play. The opponent who hits a crosscourt angle from that position, however, could force you much wider than the opposite sideline. So if your opponent is in the deuce-court corner, you need to cover against the crosscourt angle by positioning several steps to your right of the hash mark. This position puts you at an equal distance from your opponent's down-the-line and crosscourt shots.

In addition, controlling the center of the court is the foundation on which all strategies are built. This process involves understanding the concept of recovery. Your recovery position is based on the shot you hit and the location you hit it from. The objective of correct positioning is to eliminate open-court opportunities for your opponent as you build the point. You must learn to defend your court against an opponent's attack, just as you would in other sports. In basketball, a good defense makes it difficult for the opposing team to get the ball up court, take an open shot, or break to the basket. If you leave parts of the court open, your opponent has an opportunity to take control and score.

Once you get into the habit of finding the correct recovery position, you will find it easier to control the center of the court. The look of the court will be your guide to finding the correct recovery position. At no time should you look down at your feet to find your recovery position. Instead, you must watch the ball and your opponent as you move to position on recovery and find your way by the look (or perspective) of the court. Initially, you will feel out of position when you are in the perfect recovery spot. You must train yourself to respond to the look and feel of the correct recovery position.

When you hit balls down the center of the court, you should recover to the baseline and a little to the left or right of the center hash mark opposite to your strength. This is a modern-day tennis position allowing you to hit your weapon as much as possible. Again, this position will generally put you halfway between your opponent's two best shots. The depth of your position will vary based on the strength of your shot, your style of play, and the surface. For example, players tend to position themselves farther behind the baseline on clay courts than on hard courts (figure 13.3).

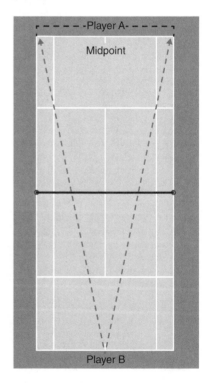

Figure 13.3 Player A should position himself halfway between player B's two best shots.

Although the recovery position behind the hash mark is appropriate for a ball hit toward the center of the court, when you hit to a corner the recovery position changes based on the direction of your shot (figures 13.4 to 13.7).

A common misunderstanding is that you should always recover back to the middle behind the hash mark in a rally, no matter where the ball is hit. Players who do this often find themselves out of position with no control of points. Even quick-footed players can look slow on the court when they don't know where to position themselves. Don't forget, however, that top players will use this general principle but will also shade to the left or right slightly in the direction opposite their strength in order to be able to hit their offensive weapon as frequently as possible.

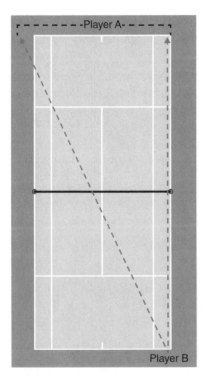

Figure 13.4 After forcing player B into his forehand corner, player A incorrectly recovers behind the hash mark in the center of the court. Player A has left an open court for player B to hit to.

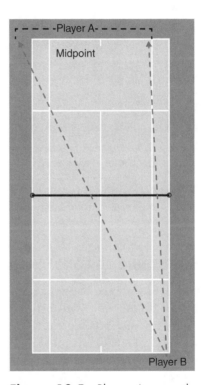

Figure 13.5 Player A correctly recovers to the midpoint of player B's best shots from the forehand corner.

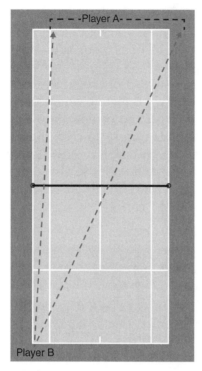

Figure 13.6 Having forced player B into his backhand corner, player A recovers behind the hash mark in the center of the court. Player A has put himself out of position and left open court for player B.

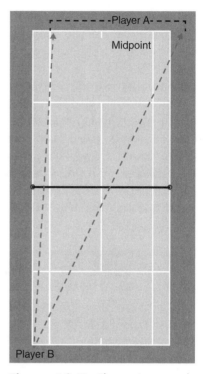

Figure 13.7 Player A correctly recovers to the midpoint of player B's best shots from the backhand corner.

Court Position and Shot Selection

After your shot leaves your racket you have only until the ball reaches your opponent to recover your court position. On average, it takes your shot less than 1.5 seconds to reach your opponent. How far can you expect to move on recovery given that small amount of time? Most players can travel only two or three steps in 1.5 seconds. For this reason, it is important to understand and execute shots that are good for your position when building points. Some players start their recovery steps while they are still hitting their shot. Kei Nishikori for instance can start his recovery in the middle of his shot. Only a few players can do this. The execution of a recovery step immediately after the shot is essential because of the limited time you have to reach your opponent's shot.

A shot that is good for your position is one that you hit in a direction or in a way that allows you to recover before your opponent's next shot. For example, when in a corner of the court, hitting in a crosscourt direction would yield the shortest distance to the correct recovery position (figure 13.8).

When in the middle of the court, you can hit a shot in any direction and still have time to recover. No matter which direction you choose to hit, you will be only a few steps from the correct recovery position. Depending on where you are positioned, you can hit to any of the three shot selections and recover in time (figure 13.9).

Another option, when in the corner of the court, is to hit a high loop down the line. This shot takes more time to travel to your opponent because of the spin, slower pace, and trajectory, thus allowing you more time to reach the correct recovery position. The objective of hitting the ball in this situation is to force a change of direction in a rally, not end the point. In this example, you use the way you hit the ball, not the direction that you hit it, to buy time to recover (figure 13.10).

In summary, you now know the following:

- When you are near the center of the court on the baseline, you are close enough to all recovery positions that you can hit in any direction and have time to recover.

- If you are forced into a corner, hitting crosscourt provides the shortest distance to your correct recovery position. You use the longest part of the court by hitting from corner to corner, which gives you a time advantage, and you have the benefit of hitting over the lowest part of the net.

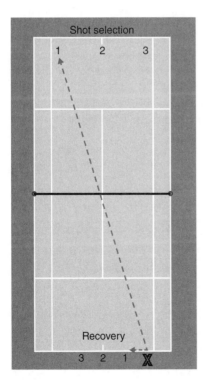

Figure 13.8 Hitting a shot in a direction that is good for your court position.

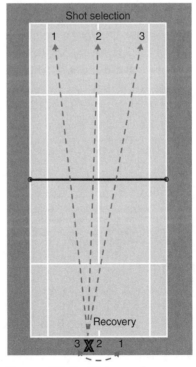

Figure 13.9 Hitting a shot to any of the three shot selections and being a few steps from the correct recovery position.

• If you hit down the line from a corner, your shot should be a high, deep ball that allows you time to recover and continue the point.

Shot Patterns

Crosscourt patterns result when players protect their positions as they build a point. Neither player wants to leave an opening or waste energy running the extra distance to maintain good court position. Thinking of what you've learned so far, you can understand why professional players often maintain crosscourt patterns in a rally. They are extremely cautious about driving balls down the line unless there is a defensive return from their crosscourt rally. When you are hitting from inside the baseline, however, you can hit down the line with less risk, and you will be able to recover to the correct position quickly. Early in every match, a player must make a basic decision about whether a forehand-to-forehand pattern or a backhand-to-backhand pattern will be more advantageous in highlighting the player's strengths or attacking the opponent's weaknesses.

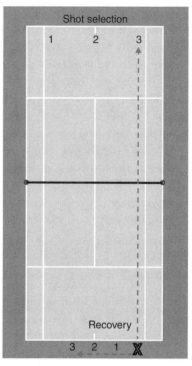

Figure 13.10 Hitting the ball down the line produces the greatest distance to the correct recovery position.

Crosscourt patterns for both the forehand and backhand offer the following margins for safety:

• The ball has the longest distance to travel.
• The ball crosses the net at its lowest point.
• The largest area of the court is available to hit into.

This pattern is very common, especially if the players are hitting high-trajectory shots with penetrating spin, forcing the opponent to hit the returns from above the shoulders and several feet behind the baseline. The player who hits a defensive short ball from this pattern leaves 90 percent of her court wide open for the opponent.

The following shot-pattern drills make the players get into an actual play simulation and force them to follow the drill. Keep in mind that these drills are positive for the most part, but when the match starts, pressures of competition will play a huge role in the performance. These drills try to get you as close as possible to actual match situations in the hope that you will perform in the same way when under match pressures.

Down the Line vs. Crosscourt

Start off each rally by hitting the first ball down the center of the court. Your opponent will then start into a pattern. One player is designated to hit everything down the line. Play 10 points and then reverse the shot patterns so that both players experience the two patterns.

The down-the-line player must work harder to stay in the point because she must continually hit shots that result in unfavorable court position. This exercise allows both players to experience how shot selection affects court position and recovery.

Forehand Crosscourt and Recovery

Both players begin in a crosscourt forehand rally (for right-handed players). Alternating the start between players, one player begins the drill by hitting the first ball toward the opponent's forehand corner. The focus is on achieving full recovery after every shot and being consistent rather than powerful.

To create a game out of this drill, simply add scoring. Each player begins with 15 points. For every unforced error you commit, you lose a point. The first player to reach 0 loses the drill. This method of scoring helps you develop consistency.

Backhand Crosscourt and Recovery

This drill is similar to the forehand crosscourt and recovery drill except that players use a backhand pattern. Score the same way, and compare the results of the two drills to determine your most consistent side.

Forehand Crosscourt and Attack

To the second and third drills, we now add the element of attack. Again, players work in a forehand pattern, and the player who attacks and wins the point at the net is rewarded.

The scoring this time starts at 0 and plays to 20. Each player gets 1 point for winning a point and 2 points for winning the point on a volley, overhead, or opponent's forced error. Alternate the start of each point between players.

Backhand Crosscourt and Attack

This drill is run in the same manner as the previous drill except that players use the backhand pattern. Compare the results of the two drills to determine which pattern works better for setting up your strengths for attacking the net.

Building Points

The concept of building points begins with an understanding of how the parts of your game contribute to a game plan (more on the game plan later in the chapter). The idea is to start a point, set it up, create an opportunity, and finish the point.

Nick's Tip

Tennis is one of the few sports where your opponent's errors advance *your* score!

Why must you build points? Every time you go for an outright winner and make an error, your opponent's score improves. In basketball, if a player takes a shot and misses, the offensive team has a chance to rebound the miss and take another shot. At worst, the other team gets the rebound and advances toward their basket. Missing shots in basketball doesn't put points on the board for the opponent. In tennis, however, it is much easier to beat yourself because each time you make an error, your opponent scores. This scoring system means you must be selective about when and how you try to end a point. Think of how a basketball team builds a play. An inbound pass begins the action. A player dribbles down the court, and the team sets up in formation. As the players pass the ball around, they are constantly trying to create a good opportunity to score. When they find an opening in the defense, they seek to capitalize. In the same way, while rallying, tennis players are constantly probing their opponent and trying to create opportunities to seize the offensive. Both players are exchanging deep crosscourt balls, but one of the players hits a short reply in the vicinity of the service line. The receiving player must seize the opportunity and score on his next shot.

Phases of Building Points

Understanding the four phases of building points will help you organize your strokes and shots.

Phase 1: Start
The point starts with the serve and return. It is important to understand the objective and mentality for phase 1—using the serve and return effectively to get the point started. You want to establish control of the point from the first ball. Players are inconsistent in phase 1 because they use the serve and return to try to end the point. Aces and return winners may result from well-placed shots, but they should not be the focus for most points.

Establishing a mind-set of getting the point started properly in phase 1 will improve consistency. Being more creative with your options will make you more effective in starting points.

Phase 2: Setup

If the point does not end on the serve or return and neither player advances to the net, then the point progresses into phase 2—the baseline rally. Just as a basketball team passes the ball around to search for opportunities, in the rally both players use pace, spin, and trajectory options, while working with shot patterns and directions, to try to create opportunities.

Again, players who make many errors in the rally are often trying to end the point from low-percentage situations. The objective is to work on the setup until you create a high-percentage opportunity. Your objective in the rally is to establish offensive control of the point and be mentally prepared to hit as many shots as necessary to set up an opportunity. You must stay alert and be able to identify opportunities so that you can quickly capitalize on them when they happen. It is important to use shots and patterns that permit you to maintain correct position while rallying. You want to avoid giving the opponent open-court opportunities during the setup phase.

Phase 3: Opportunity Ball

An opportunity ball can present itself immediately off a serve or return, but it may appear on another point only after a 12-shot rally. You should recognize several opportunity-ball situations—the short ball, the open court, and the angle or drop shot.

- *Short ball*—The short ball, the most recognizable opportunity, often results from a penetrating ground stroke or from a defensive shot by your opponent. The short ball offers you the option to go for a controlled but very aggressive shot or to advance to the net on an approach shot.

- *Open court*—An open-court opportunity usually occurs when you use a combination of shots that pulls your opponent out of position in the court. Open-court opportunities will also occur if the opponent chooses to hit shots that are not good for her court position.

- *Angle and drop shots*—Angle and drop shots force the action out of the rally, setting up the opportunity to end the point. Much of the time, your sharp angles or drop shots will pull your opponent off court or catch her at net.

Phase 4: Finish

The choices you make with the opportunity ball set the stage for what occurs in phase 4—finishing the point. An aggressive shot-maker is more likely to try to end the point with an outright winner, whereas players who use other styles of play will prefer to advance to the net.

By advancing to the net, you are relying on the quality of your approach shot to create a difficult situation for the opponent to either lob or pass, make a forced error, or set up a ball that you can volley or overhead away. The most successful players, such as Roger Federer and Novak Djokovic, will not be showoffs but will hit big and not go for the lines.

The way of thinking for phase 4 is to capitalize and finish strong. You are no longer building the point; you are closing. Be realistic. You can't outslug Serena Williams. You can't outserve Milos Raonic. Pride can make even the top pros stubborn about this. Boris Becker, for example, tried to beat Andre Agassi from the baseline, where Agassi is superior. Becker lost eight times in a row. Today it would be like Milos Raonic trying to beat Novak Djokovic from the baseline.

Realize that not every point will reach all four phases. Winners and errors anywhere in the building process will end the point. Some tactics, such as serve and volley, are designed to eliminate phases of building a point by applying immediate pressure.

Strategic Options When Building Points

While building points, you have strategic options available within each phase. Using these options to create variety in your game plan will help you control points and keep your opponent guessing.

Serve Options
Many players think of a first serve as hard and flat and a second serve as spin. This way of thinking produces predictable serves, allowing the returner to anticipate what's coming. In baseball, if a pitcher were to throw nothing but fastballs, the batters would soon know what to expect and would start hitting the ball out of the park. By using a variety of pitches and changing speed, spin, and placement, the pitcher keeps the batter guessing.

In tennis, the server has the same options. On the first serve, using flat, spin, and kick serves; changing speeds; and varying placements will reduce the returner's effectiveness. Mixing spins and pace will make it difficult for the returner to establish timing. Andre Agassi, one of the best returners in history, loved to hit returns from the biggest servers, but even Andre would be caught off guard by a change-of-pace serve. In addition, changing placements on the first serve will open up opportunities to attack weaknesses and allow you to anticipate the direction of the return. The wide slice serve in the deuce court or down the T in the ad court is a very effective serve.

By maintaining a high first-serve percentage, you can keep pressure off yourself and avoid having to hit too many second serves. Missing too many first serves gives the returner an advantage. At times you may have to go for more against an aggressive returner (like Maria Sharapova or Serena Williams).

To reduce double faults, use spin serves and aim for the center of the box. Spin allows you to swing aggressively while maintaining consistency. Options include using slice and kick serves as well as mixing placement for variety, but using too much variation can upset the regular rhythm of your swing, causing faults if not double faults. These possibilities are all the more reason to get the first serve in on big points (i.e., game point or break point).

Return-of-Serve Options

Getting the point started on return of serve is challenging against a consistently strong server because you have only fractions of a second to react and execute. Your court position is the key. Where you are positioned varies based on the server's strengths, your ability to return, your style of play, and your strategy. In general, you should position yourself halfway between the extreme possible placements of the serve. There are different opinions on the return of serve: (1) No matter what, hit your return crosscourt and get the ball in play. (2) Go for a big return even off a big serve (like Andre Agassi). It's up to you. Each player must know what he can do and feel confident in his decision as to which style to use.

Your return position in relation to the baseline will vary according to your tactics, your strategy, and the server's ability. Most players simplify when returning a first serve by using the pace already on the ball and hitting to a predetermined target.

Returning a second serve allows you to stroke more aggressively. On the big points, good returners often use their position to add pressure to the server's second serve, influencing both where and how the opponent hits that serve.

Your shot selection as a returner for both first and second serves will depend on your strategy. Hitting crosscourt on the return works well for getting into the rally, whereas going down the line on a second serve allows you to get into the net and immediately close out the point. Many players today challenge the server by standing close to the baseline and trying to take time away from the server on the return. You and your coach must determine where you should stand on first and second serves. There is no golden rule. Everyone is different.

Baseline Rally Options

Based on the shots and patterns that are good for your court position, here are some options to consider in the rally.

Early in a match you must decide whether to use the forehand crosscourt pattern or the backhand crosscourt pattern to build points. To make the decision, analyze your strengths and weaknesses as well as what opportunity you seek to set up. There is no set pattern for all situations. Many times you must do what you're most comfortable with.

To anticipate what will happen, know that if you hit a ball crosscourt your opponent is likely to hit back crosscourt or toward the center of the court. If your opponent hits the ball toward the center of the court, you can hit to either corner to set up a pattern. If your opponent hits deep down the line in the rally, you should automatically think about hitting crosscourt to take advantage of the open court or at least take control of the point. Once again you must at times feel your way into each point, but try to get into situations that favor your style of play.

If the opponent hits regularly down the center of the court, you have an opportunity to hit corner to corner and put your rival on the run as you control the center of the court. As you learned earlier, if you choose to hit down the line to force a change of direction in the rally, you need to hit the ball in such a way that you will have enough time to recover and continue the point. Remember, if your opponent hits down the center of the court, you must hit your weapon most of the time.

As you work in crosscourt patterns to create an opportunity ball, you have options to adjust the spin, pace, and trajectory of your shots. Working with this variety will make it difficult for an opponent to establish rhythm. Use angle shots to force your opponent wide to set up further open-court opportunities.

Opportunity-Ball Options
An opportunity ball can be any offensive situation that presents itself and allows you to progress to ending the point. How you choose to work with that opportunity may vary from point to point. Your match mentality and style often determine your choice. Here are options to consider for the various types of opportunity balls.

The short ball offers several options, one of which is to attack the net with an approach shot. As you learned earlier, the shot direction you choose on the approach affects your position at the net. Hitting the approach down the line or down the middle when you are positioned near the center of the court will provide the shortest distance to good position at the net. Using the short ball to approach puts pressure on the opponent as you finish the point at the net. Some players prefer to use the short ball to try for an outright winner toward any court opening, but they run a greater risk of making an unforced error. Follow the path of the ball that you hit from a short ball, and get into position for the volley.

The open-court opportunity ball usually occurs because you used a combination of shots to open the court. You can then finish the point with an offensive shot. Another open-court opportunity could occur because your opponent chooses to hit a shot that is not good for her position, thus being out of position to recover. When you have an open-court opportunity, you should not aim for the lines with your point-ending shot. You risk making an unforced error. Be offensive with your shot, but leave some margin for error.

Using angle and drop shots can force your opponent out of the rally by bringing her into the net or off court, putting the player in a defensive situation. Your angles and drop shots need not be outright winners; you can use them to set up for finishing the point.

A textbook finish to a point has the player in control, taking the first opportunity ball and advancing to the net. This sequence puts the opponent into a forced situation. If the opponent on the baseline is unable to produce a winning passing shot or lob, she will either commit a forced error or hit a shot that you can put away with a volley or overhead. Many players will do this from a tentative second serve.

The player attacking the net uses the opportunity ball to force the opponent to execute winners, relying on the fact that if the approach shots are forced, the baseliner will make more errors than winners or will produce shots that can be put away.

Be careful, however; some players are extremely effective at hitting passing shots and lobs. They look forward to the challenge. These players will often bring you to the net so they can pass you. The net position is then a difficult place to be. You are caught in a defensive situation and not in control of the point.

When at the net, it's important to establish a position that keeps you in reach of the down-the-line or angle pass yet able to guard against the lob. When facing a net player, you must interchange the down-the-line pass with angles and lobs to create opportunities. Keep an eye on the position of the net player. If your opponent plays close to the net, lob until she moves back. Your passing shots will then become more effective. In the long run, moving in closer to the net will gain you more points than protecting against the lob.

Game Plan

Being a military man, I was taught to have plans and backup plans. Having a plan and a backup plan is extremely helpful in preparing for a match. It allows the player to understand how to apply his strengths against his opponent's weaknesses and defend his weaknesses against his opponent's strengths. Some players, however, get confused when asked to implement a plan. They are more effective just hitting and reacting.

Player Qualities and Style of Play

Building an effective game plan begins with being truthful in your self-assessment and trusting in your coach's assessment of your strengths and weaknesses. Strengths and weaknesses go beyond merely the skill set to include the following:

- Having great emotional control under pressure and having more patience than most opponents.
- Being willing to adjust your game according to the flow of a match; knowing when to play aggressively and when to play defensively.
- Not becoming easily discouraged when you fall behind or the momentum swings the other way.
- Being more consistently focused for every point and having great discipline in your decisions by managing risk and margin of error.

Nick's Tip

Coaches must understand all of the strengths, weaknesses, and habits of their players. All players are different, and to be an effective coach you need to know not only what to say but also how to say it. All my players were different. Some had significant idiosyncrasies that I had to accommodate in order to be "heard."

To become the best competitor you can be involves some deep soul searching to understand yourself so you can take everything into consideration when building your game plan. Many of the qualities just described have an influence on how your style of play is defined. Accomplished players always have a game plan or strategy they take into battle that reflects how their style of play and tactical strengths should best match up versus the opponent.

To understand the concept of style of play, think of cars on a highway. First of all, although you typically don't know who else is on the road with you, you can learn a lot about those strangers through simple observations. Personality, attitude, and driving style are often expressed by the driver's choice of vehicle. Those drivers with aggressive personalities, who live life in the fast lane, often choose to buy cars that match their personalities and suit their lifestyle, such as sports cars. In a way, what they drive tells a lot about who they are, how they will react, and their predictable patterns of driving.

A tennis player's style of play is much the same. The tactics players employ, the level of aggression in their game, the decisions they make, and their predictable patterns of behavior are often consistent with their personalities, as much as it reflects the strengths of their skill set. For example, look at two contrasting rivals that both trained at the academy, Pete Sampras and Andre Agassi. With a big serve and weapons around the net, the serve and volley style of play Sampras favored not only featured his skill strengths but also represented much of his personality. As an aggressive, counterpunching baseliner, Agassi's style of play also perfectly suited his competitive personality. If Sampras had tried to execute Agassi's style of play and game plan, he would have never been successful and vice versa.

A basketball scenario will further reinforce the point about personalities, styles of play, and decision making. With 5 seconds left in the game, if you had a choice of being the team that's up by 2 points and defending or the team that's down by 2 points with possession of the ball at their end and a chance to shoot to win or tie the score, which would you choose? I think if it were Sampras, he would choose to be the team up by 2 and defending. If it were Agassi, I'm pretty certain he would not only want his team to have the ball with a chance to shoot to win, he would want to be the player on his team who takes the final shot. Some of you may side with Andre and want your team to have the ball, but you wouldn't be comfortable with the pressure of being the player who takes the shot. Translating that back to tennis, those are often the players who think of themselves as shot-makers and want to play this style but don't have the skills and confidence to succeed as a shot-maker.

Here are the most common styles of play, how players win within each style of play, and how players overcome the various styles of play:

Defensive-based styles

- Pusher
- Baseline defender
- Counterpuncher

Offensive-based styles

- Shot-maker
- Attacking player

Balanced styles

- Aggressive baseliner
- All-court player

Pusher

Pushers play overly safe tennis to avoid errors. They rarely take risks, are happy to play longer points, and use consistency as their weapon. It's a very successful strategy at the beginner and lower to intermediate levels, where the player with the fewest unforced errors usually wins. The pushing tendency stems from a lack of confidence to play more aggressively. Plus, the pushers are often victorious in the early stages of competition. They provide little to no pace and will test your patience. Both feared and hated by opponents, pushers don't *beat* anyone, they just frustrate you into beating yourself!

Coaches must understand that winning matches at an early age just by pushing is not the path to future tennis success. Coaches should give players the courage to vary their game, and in the long run giving them a better chance of winning in later stages of their game, whether it be in college or the pros. This isn't easy for most parents to accept.

When playing against a pusher, you have to be very patient and not get too aggressive where you give away too many points. It typically doesn't work well to push back unless you are a skilled pusher yourself. They are used to opponents resorting to pushing and often prove to be the better of the two pushers. Force the opponent to have to generate offense by attacking and coming to the net, if you have the net skills to support that. The other option is to force her off the baseline and into the net where she is less comfortable using the drop shot, short slice, and angles.

Baseline Defender

The baseline defender is more evolved, seasoned, and experienced than the typical pusher. This player is very confident he can win strictly by being a tenacious defender from the backcourt. Capable of forcing conditions on the opponent, the baseline defender can strike with offense when forced to. He is happy to play long points, run every ball down, and beat you through consistency.

He is not rattled by your occasional winners, because that's exactly what he is challenging you to *have* to do. Baseline defenders must be very physically fit, be consistent on both sides, and play high-percentage patterns to avoid leaving open court for the opponent. This strategy is effective against shot-makers, who tend to make far more errors than winners. No two players fit this category better than David Ferrer and Lleyton Hewitt, but let's not forget other greats of the past such as Michael Chang. In today's game, this type of player will have great difficulty wining a Grand Slam.

Against the baseline defender, use patience and don't overhit the ball. Because your opponent is probably a retriever and won't hurt you, wait for a short ball to put pressure on the opponent to end the point. Take your time, use drop shots and angles to open up the court, and then go on the offensive. Control the center of the court with good footwork and consistent shots high over the net with good depth. If possible, look for a looping return, and hit forceful, swinging volleys to create your offense. Also remember you must take advantage of the first defensive opportunity given you by the baseline defender.

Counterpuncher

The counterpuncher understands most opponents prefer to be offensive. On the attack, the aggressor often becomes vulnerable, creating opportunity for the counterpuncher to strike. Counterpunchers often mix it up with a variety of balls during a rally and work to keep the ball out of the opponent's strike zone. They feed off your pace and will try to bait you into attacking them.

Content to assume the defensive position, counterpunchers will go deep into rallies and wait for the opponent to pull the trigger first. This leads opponents into many unforced errors. The counterpuncher understands that in the end, the opponent's winners will likely be far offset by much higher numbers of errors.

Keep in mind the counterpuncher can hit all variations of shots that drive opponents crazy. When forced, counterpunchers will aggressively come forward and hit volleys and swinging volleys. Andy Murray is a good example of a counterpuncher.

Shot-Maker

The shot-maker is often a high-risk, low-reward style of play. Many players like this style because it can be the most gratifying when they occasionally make the shot. Plus, it's perceived by many as the coolest way to play. The shot-maker can be dangerous because she'll go for spectacular shots at any time from anywhere. It's all about offense and striking big. "Go big or go home" is the attitude. If not, you're just a pusher! This thinking gives the shot-maker little option to play defense, even when it's the smartest play.

The shot-maker can create exciting shots and winning combinations but typically has a difficult time maintaining this level of brilliance throughout the entire match. She ends up attempting too many high-risk shots and in the end makes too many unforced errors to win the match. There are some exceptional shot-makers, however, who are able to combine their shot-making brilliance with solid play through the entire match. When this occurs the player can be exceptional. Examples include Roger Federer, Serena Williams, and Kei Nishikori. They can do it all.

Against a shot-maker, opponents just have to be patient, play consistently, and be prepared to weather occasional hot streaks during a match. Typically, the stats clearly show in the end that the shot-maker is really a shot-misser. It's the quickest way to crash and burn and lose to even a pusher.

Attacking Player

Attacking players often have strengths to start and close points but are often weaker in baseline rallies. They look to avoid long rallies and prefer to get to the net on every opportunity to close out points. They use a variety of combinations, usually off the start of points, including serve and volley, chip and charge off return, and approach and volley combinations, to set up their net game and force the opponent to pass or lob.

This style of play keeps constant pressure on the opponent to produce high-quality shots to win points or break down trying. The attacking player needs strong serve and return skills along with strengths at the net. The serve must also have other variations that throw off the returners.

The old label of the attacking player was "I'm coming to the net." Players such as Stefan Edberg, Yannick Noah, and Paul Annacone came in because they could not pay the bills from the baseline. This has changed. Pete Sampras, Novak Djokovic, and Serena Williams can all do whatever needs to be done. Let's focus on Roger Federer. This man can do it all, and now his coach, Stefan Edberg, has him using his attacking skills more and more.

Against the attacking player, do not panic. There are many things you can do: Keep your ground strokes deep with penetrating spin, and move the ball from side to side. Change position when returning serve. Add angles and slices to your rallies. When he attacks, do not panic but just play the ball. Do not try to anticipate where the attacker is going. Hit heavy, dipping balls to force the attacker to hit up when volleying. Vary your rallies with different spins. Come in before he does. You must improve your serve and at least get into a tie breaker. Do not show frustration no matter what.

Aggressive Baseliner

Aggressive baseliners have strong defensive skills but also look to dictate offense whenever possible. Movement strengths and athleticism are their biggest weapons. At times, they'll get you into long rallies to test your patience and wear you down. They'll hit corner to corner and carve angles to force you off the court. On any short-ball opportunity, they'll step inside the court and strike to the open court. The aggressive baseliner often uses a variety of two- and three-ball combinations to open the court and close. It's not uncommon for the aggressive baseliner to sneak-attack on high floaters and strike with swinging volleys. This style player also likes to counterpunch and loves a target at the net to pass. The aggressive baseliner is a movement specialist, typically with at least one ground-stroke weapon, and is usually very consistent on the other wing.

Against the aggressive baseliner, be assertive, take the initiative, and go up the line early in the point. Look to create offense quickly. Seldom hit the ball to the same area twice, except to wrong-foot the opponent occasionally. If your opponent attacks first, try to outrun her. If your opponent is overpowering you, move back and lob a few balls to make your opponent generate her own power. Use angles and dictate points by running around the backhand and hitting inside-out forehands. Also use some surprise attacks and come in.

All-Court Player

The all-court player is a Roger Federer type of player who has a balance of offense and defense and can execute the best of any style of play. Depending on the opponent's strengths, weaknesses, and style of play as well as the score situation, the all-court player will vary tactics to keep the opponent guessing. He is comfortable playing from any position on the court and capable of applying constant pressure. This player can be an aggressive baseliner, a baseline defender, an attacker, even a shot-maker when forced to. All-court players have a wide variety of skills, few if any weaknesses, can be very unpredictable, and rarely beat themselves.

Against the all-court player, try the following: Be prepared to anticipate when your opponent will stay back and when he will come to the net. Determine where your opponent plays best, and keep him out of that area. If your opponent prefers the net, lob the ball and vice versa. Make plenty of first serves even if you must sacrifice pace. Conversely, make offensive returns of serve and control the point from the start. Respond especially aggressively against second serves. When you have to hit a second serve, go for depth to neutralize the return. Take chances to win the point early.

Combating a Power Player

As the ancient Chinese war general Sun Tzu stated "When facing superior fire power, you don't prepare to attack, you prepare to defend. You must wait and work for conditions of vulnerability in the opponent before you attack."

A match between two power players (e.g., Maria Sharapova versus Serena Williams) is interesting to watch and analyze to see what little things determine the winner. One thing you can do against power players is to throw in a change of pace including deep, high, rolling shots and following them to the net to finish the point with a volley of a short return into the open court. For the most part the power game is usually built around one or two shots, the serve and the forehand. Power players will do all they can to hit their weapon. The opposition must find a way to make power players very uncomfortable by forcing them into long rallies without trying to outhit them.

A power player can be the most intimidating to play. If you are outgunned, it is likely you won't have much of a chance to dictate play. The most effective strategy would be to rely on counterpunching tactics and win by way of great defending. To understand how to play the power player, you must first understand his strengths and tendencies—his tactics more so than his technical aspects.

Power players love to discourage their opponents by hitting a high number of winners and playing quick points. Doing this achieves two things. First, opponents become discouraged because they cannot put the ball in play. Second, opponents make more unforced errors because the power player is hitting a constant barrage of winners. Power players seek to play quick points because their opponents then have little time to gain confidence or develop a good rhythm. The power player's foe thus becomes more uncomfortable as the match progresses. How do you counter and adjust to the big hitter? How do you get back into the match? When you understand what the power player looks for and thrives on, you can more easily develop a game plan to retaliate.

From a technical standpoint, early preparation is a must. Because the ball is coming hard and fast, you must pick the ball up when it leaves your opponent's racket. You do not have time to wait until the ball crosses the net or bounces on your side of the court. Prepare and move to the ball immediately. You must have good hip and shoulder turn, and the racket must go back in the same motion to ensure good balance and positioning. You must also remember to shorten your backswing, which will help you keep the ball in front and allow you to use your opponent's power. Play smarter, not harder! Don't try to outhit your opponent in a slugging match because you will lose. You must try to win off your opponent's mistakes, not off your winners. Strive to put as many balls in play as possible.

Be extremely patient. Remember, the power player loves pace and likes to play quick points. Therefore, whenever possible use change of pace to neutralize the power of the incoming balls. The power player will find it much more difficult to create pace off shots landing at the baseline with no speed. Also, don't forget the high looping ball. This shot drives power players crazy!

Last, try to move farther behind the baseline to give yourself more time to prepare for your next shot. If your opponent begins to hit angles, however, you must move closer to the baseline to reduce the amount of court your opponent has to work with.

Now that you have a plan to use against the power player, you should be less concerned with the outcome. Remember, it is easier to develop and implement a game plan if you understand what your opponent is trying to do. If you implement these tips each day in practice, victories will come sooner and more often than you thought possible.

Game Plan Skill Sets

Once you've identified your strengths, think about how you can feature those strengths as much of the time as possible. If fitness and consistency are strengths, you may consider testing the fitness of the opponent by playing longer points, moving her often, and keeping time between points short to give her less time to recover before starting the next point. If quickness and movement are strengths, focus on maintaining faster-paced rallies and taking the ball early on the rise to reduce recovery time during points. If your serve is a strength, try to use the serve as the front end of a two-ball closing combination. From the deuce court, Federer so often uses his slice wide to force the opponent wide and then looks to hit his second shot to the opposite corner for a winner, or he forces an error from the opponent. Your goal is to find the tactical combinations and shot patterns that highlight the strengths in your skill set.

The next task at hand in executing your game plan is to identify and consider the opponent's strengths and weaknesses. Think of ways to match up your strengths versus her weaknesses. Featuring your strength can mean running around the ball to set up your forehand as often as possible for any ball down the center or even slightly to the backhand side of the court. However, even though your forehand may be your mightiest of weapons, at times you may face opponents whose forehand is much mightier than yours. That means you may need to steer away from the forehand cross-court rally pattern and look to build more often from the backhand side.

The higher the level of play, typically the fewer blatant weaknesses your opponents have that you can exploit. For many years you could get away with weaknesses on the pro circuit. Not so today. You cannot hide a weakness any more. Your opponent will get to it. That's when game plans must be creative and players must dig deeper to create opportunities. Focus on getting your opponents out of their comfort zone and away from their preferred style of play if you can. For example, if you are playing a baseline player who prefers not to come in, you could attack with short balls such as angles and drop shots to force her off the baseline and in to the net. If your opponent seems to feed off your faster-paced ground strokes and you seem to be raising her level of play, try slowing down and varying the pace and spin of the balls you send over and see if you can disrupt her timing. Sometimes you can play into a weakness to the point that it's not much of a weakness for the opponent anymore. You might find someone's backhand is a weakness not so much in the rally, but when it's time to hit a put-away and the pressure is on, that's when the backhand fails her most. If that's the case, you may choose to rally more to the forehand side and attack the backhand in situations where you are forcing the opponent under pressure to come up with a point-ending winner.

Not exposing any of your weaknesses is an equally important aspect of your game plan. Some players are big hitters but may not move that well. The harder you hit, the less time you allow yourself to recover. Slower-moving hard hitters all too often expose their own weakness by always amping up the rally speed. They may be better off building points with more spin, net clearance, and margin for error, at a rally speed they can manage, to avoid falling behind in the pace of play in longer rallies. If your weaknesses are around the net, you will need to rely on other options when short-ball opportunities arise. Rather than the traditional approach shot and advancing to the net, you may have to look toward combinations from the midcourt depth, such as angles followed by a closing shot to the opposite corner.

Closing combinations are the exit strategies for finishing points in high-percentage fashion. Following are the most common combos used by the professionals.

Serve and Volley

Once a predominant style of play, today this tactic is mostly used as a surprise. The serve acts as an approach shot, while the volley is to close. This tactic enables you to avoid the opponent's ground strokes while applying immediate pressure on your opponent to have to beat you at net.

Slice Serve Wide and Opposite Corner

This is an effective tactic for right-handers like Federer in the deuce court and is a common combination for Nadal on the ad side. The slice serve pulls the opponent wide off the court on the return, opening up the court for a put-away to the opposite corner. If your forehand is your strength, it is a good opportunity to feature your forehand inside-out and inside-in to close like Nadal.

Serve T and Corner Put-Away

This combination is set up by serving big down the T, which often results in a shorter return down the center of the court. This creates the opportunity to feature the forehand inside-out or inside-in for the put-away.

Drive Return and Attack

This tactic is used to apply pressure to the second serve, forcing the server to hit a passing shot on her second shot. The returner will take the ball on the rise from on or inside the baseline, most often playing the percentage shot down the line or straight ahead, and then follow the return in to the net.

Chip Return and Attack

This tactic is also used to apply pressure to the second serve, forcing the server to hit a passing shot on his second shot. However, by chipping or slicing the return, the returner has a little more time to get in to the net because the incoming ball for the server has less pace. The returner will take the ball on the rise from on or inside the baseline, most often playing the percentage shot down the line or straight ahead, and then follow the return in to the net. Chipping the return creates a lower bounce, which often results in a high-volley opportunity for you to close out the point.

Corner to Corner

If your opponent has a tendency to repeatedly hit the ball down the center of the court, you have a great opportunity to run her corner to corner. This tactic positions you to control the center of the court and force your opponent to hit on the run. This will wear down your opponent's legs and exhaust stamina. Using this combination helps to set up other options such as the corner and hit-behind combination.

Corner and Hit-Behind

A very effective rally tactic against movement specialists is to pull them wide and hit behind them. This will force vigorous direction changes and wear down their legs. Hit-behinds are important to force players to second-guess their anticipation. They will be more tentative to act early on what they anticipate. This tactic is particularly effective when combined with the corner-to-corner tactic. Hitting behind also exploits movement and tactical limitations. When players hit low-percentage shots, or if they don't recover to correct positions, or if they turn their shoulders away from facing the net on recovery, they are vulnerable to the hit-behind. This shot is especially effective on clay and grass, where the surface is less stable.

Drive Deep and Swinging Volley

Aggressive baseline players often use this tactic to combat high, looping balls from pushers. Also, when you have forced the opponent back with a deep, penetrating forcing shot, look to move in behind your shot for a swinging volley opportunity. The swinging volley allows you to sneak-attack, get to the net, and close with a second volley or overhead.

Deep Down the Line and Short Crosscourt

This classic combination can be effective during the rally when you are positioned inside the baseline. It is most effective on short-ball opportunities, hitting a down-the-line approach, followed by a short angle volley or drop volley.

Deep Approach and Drop Volley

When your approach shot or first volley is deep and penetrating, and the opponent has been pushed deep behind the baseline, the drop volley is a great option to close. Using drop volleys forces the opponent to position close to the baseline to defend the short court. Now, when you choose to penetrate deep, you have a better chance to force an error.

Drop Approach and Volley

When your opponent is deep in the backcourt and you get a short ball to attack, typically your opponent will expect a deep, penetrating approach shot from you. This makes him very vulnerable to the drop approach. Be sure to close in to service-line depth behind your drop approach. If the opponent manages to get to it, you'll often get a high volley or overhead to close out the point.

Short Crosscourt and Deep Down the Line

The front end of this combination is a sharp angle or drop shot. The second shot closes the point by landing deep in the opposite corner.

Angle and Angle Behind

The front end of this combination most often is a sharp angle but could also be an angled drop shot. If it's a half-court or three-quarter-depth angle and the opponent chooses the percentage crosscourt shot, she'll need to recover aggressively. That creates the option to close with another angle hit behind the opponent. When she chooses to go down the line off your sharp angle or drop shot, finish with a crosscourt shot to the open court.

Drop Shot and Lob or Pass

This tactic is most effective when you use deep slices occasionally to set up and disguise the eventual drop shot. The drop shot does not need to be an outright winner, so build in some margin of error. Your objective is to attack short and force your opponent in to the net. With all his momentum continuing toward the net after reaching your drop shot, the practical choice of shots is to lob your next shot into his backcourt. At times, a passing shot to the open court works well to close this combination.

Chip Short and Pass

This is a common tactic for the counterpuncher who loves a target at the net. She'll intentionally hit the ball low and short with a chip or slice, inviting the opponent to attack the net. If the opponent takes the bait, choosing to approach, the counterpuncher sets up for the passing shot or lob to close the point.

Nick's Tip

Mixing up the speed and varying the spins can force your opponent's strokes to break down in a rally.

Dip It and Pass

The dip and pass is used when the opponent is attacking the net. The front end of this counterpunch combination uses heavy topspin to dip the ball down near the feet of the net player, forcing your opponent to half-volley the ball up. This sets up an opportunity for you to move forward and hit a second passing shot off an easier ball to close the point.

High Heavy and Drop

Hitting high, heavy spins in the rally keeps the ball above the opponent's preferred strike zone, often forcing her to position deeper in the back court. This sets up the opportunity to use the drop shot to attack the open short court. This is a particularly effective tactic on clay and grass surfaces.

Deep Slices and Drive Angle

This tactic involves slowing down the pace of the rally by repeatedly slicing deep. Once the opponent settles into the rhythm of the slower-paced crosscourt rally, he becomes vulnerable to a drive angle.

Dictate Center and Defend Wide

This concept helps players understand that when you are controlling the center of the court and have unforced conditions to work with, it's your best opportunity to play offense and dictate play. And when you are forced wide in the court, you need to be willing to play neutral or defensive shots to avoid making forced errors.

Nick's Tip

You must find a way to create confusion and doubt in the mind of your opponent. Show your opponent you are a warrior.

Statistics and the Game Plan

Tennis players tend to be rather selective in their memory about a tennis match. Some players have the ability to overlook the errors they commit and choose to remember just the great points and shots where they were successful. Then there are players who are much more hypersensitive to the errors they commit during a match. They expect themselves to be perfect and barely acknowledge their own successes but really feel the pain of making errors. Players that dwell on the negative often struggle with confidence and play tentatively under pressure. Regardless of what you choose to remember, you are accountable for every point you play when it comes to scoring and statistics.

One significant aspect of the game of tennis that makes it so different from most other sports is the fact that every time the opponent makes errors, it adds points to your score column. That difference has a great impact on game plans and strategy. Tennis players don't need to end every point with a glorious winner to advance their score. Waiting for the opponent to make a mistake is a very effective strategy. It comes down to what the statistics reveal about the ratio of success to failure. In other words, if I attempted a shot with a high level of difficulty and a low margin for error 10 times in a row, how often would I succeed and how often would I fail? For the women at the U.S. Open, out of all matches played in the draw, on average, only 19 percent of the points end with a winner. That means 81 percent of the points end in either a forced or unforced error. Strategically, it is far more significant to pay attention to the 81 percent error production than it is to focus on a 19 percent success rate. Think about it: 26 percent of the points ended in unforced error, although a player would never start a point with the intent to make an unforced error to end the point. Errors are the by-product of trying and failing. With more than 50 percent of the points at the pro level ending in forced error, what most often determines the winner of a match is which player more effectively forces the opponent to make mistakes.

There's no question that the most rewarding and fulfilling way to end points is by hitting winners, but if your game plan is built solely around that outcome, you can easily beat yourself. In the context of earned versus unearned points, if the opponent hits a winner or forces you into an error, the opponent has earned the point. If you have a relatively easy ball and make an unforced error, the opponent gains a point that was unearned. It is helpful to have a pulse on the flow of your match with respect to whether you are earning most of your points or whether the opponent has been giving most of the points to you through his errors. If you've been living off of unearned points from your opponent, that could dry up at any time if he makes adjustments to his game. Conversely, did your opponent gain his lead in the score because you are giving away too many unearned points? If so, you need to make adjustments in your play to avoid giving away the match.

Ending Points

Even though there are many ways to win points in tennis, when developing a strategy that fits your personality and your game, you have to first identify your objectives in finishing points.

Point-Ending Objectives

To understand the purpose behind your strokes and shot selection, first focus on your point-ending objectives. Close your eyes and play the perfect point in your mind. . . . How does that point end? Were you serving? Was the end of the point something heroic on your part, with you executing the perfect shot? The action you created in your mind likely represents your most desirable way to end points. Influences are what you want to do, what you can do, and what you should do in a given situation. If all fails with this plan, try again with more determination and subtle adjustments.

In a rally, suppose the short-ball opportunity arises. What are you going to do with it? What you probably *want* to do is step up and crush the stuffing out of it for a winner. What you *can* do depends on the pressure of the situation and your ability to execute the desired shot. What you *should* do is make the shot that works best within a game plan that favors you statistically. Although you may come out of a losing effort thinking your strokes let you down, the fact may be that you lost because you made poor decisions with the opportunities you had. Although it is a glorious feeling to execute a perfect high-risk shot, you will be accountable for all the failed attempts as well. Why doesn't Roger Federer just go for an ace on every first serve? Why don't Nadal and Djokovic just smack those returns away for winners? Well, the greatest players of all time understand that managing risk and building in margin of error are the keys to consistent success. They have a game plan that features a variety of shot combination options for staging the end of points.

The game plan is your overall strategy for taking down your opponent. It highlights your strengths and protects your weaknesses. For example, for a player with not so powerful strokes but great movement who is more physically fit than her opponent, her game plan should be built on a willingness to play longer points and to be more consistent than the opponent. The objective would be to outlast the other player and test her level of patience and consistency. Game plans adjust to court surfaces, playing conditions, and opponents. To execute a game plan, you must trust its effectiveness enough to stick with it and not let your raw emotions dictate your decisions under pressure. And when the primary plan is clearly headed for failure, call on your backup plan, which should be part of your overall game plan. When the plan goes in every direction, clear your mind, relax, and just hit the ball.

Think of your skills, strokes, and shots as the tools you have to work with. For your game plan to flow smoothly, each tool must function in harmony with the others. The concept of point structure shows you the purpose behind each tool and how it best functions within your plan (see table 13.1). Champions are those players who can switch gears without losing a beat. Clear your mind and just play with the tennis ball, not against the tennis ball.

Understanding that the serve and return are intended to get points started puts you into a mind-set that will improve first-serve percentage, decrease double faults, and get more points started on return. When you attempt to go for aces and winners with your serve or return, your percentage of getting points started drops dramatically. To work successfully with a game plan, you must understand the decisions you have to make. You must know and be willing to go with what you *should* do. What you *want* to do should support that decision. And hopefully, you have the skills to

Nick's Tip

A game plan establishes an objective for every shot, organizing your skills into shot patterns and combinations so you can build points toward a desired outcome. There will be times in a match when you must consider a change. Sometimes there is no other option.

Table 13.1 **Point Structure and Strokes Used**

Point structure	Stroke inventory
Start	Serves Returns
Set up	Ground-stroke rallies
Attack	Approach shots Angles Drop shots
Finish	Volleys Overheads Passing shots Lobs

execute. You must adjust to the other player's game, his serve, his return. Keep in mind that a majority of players have similar patterns of play. You must know these patterns.

Players who don't tend to build points often make poor decisions, look to get out of points too quickly, and far too often rely on high-risk shot attempts to end points. If you are one of the hopeless many who still work with no real game plan and rely on defying the odds with winner after winner, you should not expect to win matches often. One of the big differences in how the game is played at the pro level versus how it is played by juniors is that great professionals will make decisions and play for the glory of winning in the end. Junior players unknowingly will play for the glory of playing an unbelievable point over and over again, at the expense of winning in the end. Once again, do not be stoic. Live with your game plan, but do not die with it.

Point-Ending Outcomes

If you were to chart match statistics, the end of every point would fall into one of three categories:

1. *Winners*—A winner occurs when you successfully execute a shot that goes untouched by the opponent to end the point.

2. *Forced errors*—A forced error occurs when your shot forces the opponent to execute without having time to set up mentally or physically, causing the opponent to make an error.

3. *Unforced errors*—An unforced error occurs when the opponent has time to set up mentally and physically for the shot and the opponent makes an error.

When you compile all the statistics at the end of a match, you will find some interesting results. On average in a professional match, only 20 to 30 percent of the points end in a winner. That means 70 to 80 percent of the points end in either forced or unforced error. The game of tennis at all levels is ultimately an exercise in error management. If you focus on creating winners with every opportunity, you will be at high risk of making so many errors you essentially give the match away in the end. Nothing feels better than hitting an outright winner, but nothing feels worse than turning a perfect opportunity into an unforced error. Even the easy sitters are easy to miss when the pressure is on. Winners are even more difficult to execute consistently when the opponent is forcing you to go for it. Are the unforced errors in one or two parts of your game? If so, is it because of physical, technical, or emotional deficiencies?

Against stiffer competition, just keeping the ball in play and waiting for the opponent to make an unforced error will not be enough to win the match. Good players may give you a few unforced errors, but rarely will they give you enough to determine the match. Because you have no control over when and how often the opponent makes unforced errors, you cannot really build an entire game plan focused solely on it.

Players who can force the opponent either to produce a winner or to commit a forced error put the odds in their favor. Forced errors constitute more than 50 percent of the point outcomes at the pro level. So, to be the player who can more effectively force errors on the opponent puts you well on the road to a winning game plan.

As you work through the stages of point structure in setting up the situation for your desired outcome, you build your points using shot patterns that allow you to recover behind each shot. The ball travels from baseline to baseline in less than two seconds on an average ground stroke. The time it takes for the ball to reach the opponent is all the time you have to recover before your opponent hits the next ball. How many steps can you take in less than two seconds? Not many. If you do not reach full recovery in time, you leave the court open for your opponent. If you use five shots to set up and end the point, you need to recover behind four of them.

Preparing for Tournament Play

Michael Johnson was one of the greatest sprinters in the history of track and field. At dinner one night I asked him what made him a champion. Here is what he said. "My coach and I worked to have me forget all of the training, my competition, and the results. He had me focus exclusively on the times I need to hit for each segment of the race and said the results would take care of themselves." Although Johnson wasn't thinking about his practice because he was well trained, his body performed naturally because of the muscle memories he built.

One of the greatest sources of confidence is feeling that you are fully prepared. You can develop this belief by training with a purpose, by meeting short-term goals leading up to the event, and by conditioning your body and mind for the test ahead. By developing reliable and consistent routines in preparation for a match, you can alleviate some of the prematch doubt that affects many players.

The physical part of the routine should include adequate sleep the night before the match, a proper diet, specific plans for transportation to the match site, stretching exercises, and a specific prematch warm-up. Most tennis players learn, over time, to bring the requisite physical items that will help them be ready—extra rackets, shoes, water, towel, snack, extra strings, extra shoelaces, extra socks, hat, sunscreen, bandages, glasses, extra shirts, extra shorts, a warm-up suit, grips, and so forth.

With the body ready and the physical necessities on hand, it's time to prepare the mind. Despite almost universal acknowledgment that a large part of tennis is mental, few players have developed a consistent, reliable mental preparation plan for their matches. Athletes should begin their mental preparation the night before the match.

Think about your game plan, and spend time visualizing the progression of the match in your mind. Consider the following:

- What will you do with the various opportunity balls?
- What shot combinations do you plan to work with most?
- How will you respond to questionable calls?
- How will you respond if adverse weather conditions cause a delay?

It is helpful to anticipate a long and difficult battle ahead of you so that mentally you go in prepared for the long haul if the match goes deep into three sets or more. Never let yourself go into battle underestimating the opponent, or you may set yourself up to fail. Avoid looking ahead in the draw or you may overlook the opponent you play next who could very well take you out.

On match day players should set aside a few minutes in their prematch preparation to get their minds focused on the upcoming task. Exactly how are you to accomplish what you've set out to do? Be specific about how you are going to use your strokes and physical presence to dominate the opponent. Regulate your prematch arousal level to be neither too anxious nor too relaxed. Relaxation and breathing techniques can help deal with overstimulation. Psych-up strategies are useful for days when you feel flat.

To build confidence, begin to gather more information during the warm-up. Become familiar with the court surroundings, and look for anything unique about the court's surface with regard to speed, reaction to spin, slippery areas, and so on. Assess environmental conditions, such as the sun, shade, wind, and placement of spectators. Take advantage of the warm-up to assess your opponent. Although you want to be courteous and enable your opponent to warm up adequately, this is a free look for five minutes at every part of the opponent's game, providing great insight for your game plan. This is a time to gather information, not a time to judge whether the opponent is better or worse than you. By making judgments, players may either lose confidence or become overconfident.

Despite good intentions and well-thought-out plans, circumstances will inevitably cause players to make changes on match day. We strongly encourage players to develop contingency plans to deal with unforeseen problems or distractions. Thinking about potential problems and writing down solutions can be helpful.

Here are some examples. What will you do if your opponent is rude to you before the match? How will you respond if your opponent is over-friendly and talkative? How will you deal with a conflict with your coach, playing partner, or parent that takes place just before the match begins? How will you react to drawing a player you've never beaten before? How will you cope with distractions, such as an opponent who cheats or a crowd that cheers more loudly for your opponent than it does for you? Adversity can strike in a myriad of ways before or during a match. Being prepared to handle all circumstances can help you perform optimally. Dealing effectively with uncontrollable situations can help you stay focused on the things you can control—attitude, concentration, and effort.

Fighting Back When Losing

Carl Sandburg said, "It's never over until it's over." Or maybe it was Yogi Berra. Either way, the message is clear—keep fighting, keep trying, and maybe you can turn around a hopeless game, set, or match. When it's easier to quit than come back, the real winner keeps fighting until the final whistle. Vince Lombardi, the legendary Green Bay Packers coach, said, "We never lose, we just run out of time." All competitors should have this winning attitude.

How do these clichés relate to tennis? Well, coming back from a likely defeat is an attitude. You see evidence of this attitude posted on locker-room walls: "When the going gets tough, the tough get going." Mental toughness separates great players from good players. Whether winning or losing, great players will fight and claw for each point. They will not give up, regardless of the score. When great players lose, they leave heart and soul on the court. These players can look at themselves in the mirror after the match and say, "I gave it my all—I have nothing left." If you have this attitude, any loss means you got beaten.

This type of mental toughness is evident in successful players like John McEnroe, Jimmy Connors, and Chris Evert—players who never thought they were beaten. This belief, even though each developed it in a different way, prevailed when defeat was near. Evert says she played not to lose. Connors played only to win, often forgetting to serve and battling until he left everything on court.

Tennis players can develop a successful mental game by forming good habits and continually focusing on mental preparation and concentration. Sports psychologists tell athletes to visualize winning shots and winning points one at a time. Maintain your rituals whether winning or losing, staying focused by taking deep breaths, and adjusting your racket strings.

To summarize, winning is a state of mind, a belief that somehow, something is going to happen that will enable you to prevail. The score is secondary. You should manage each point, each game, with the entire contest in mind. If you can accomplish this, you'll end up a winner regardless of the score. Refer to chapter 12 for more information on mental conditioning.

Conclusion

In boxing, if someone is punching you and you don't move, you deserve to be knocked out. You have to find a way to dodge and move. Similarly, tennis is a game of strategy. Offensively, you have to figure out how to apply your strengths to your opponent's weaknesses. Defensively, you have to figure out how to protect against your opponent's weapons. The correct strategies will help you win many matches.

Chapter 14

Rackets, Strings, and Grips

By understanding your individual equipment needs, you will stay healthier and win more matches.

There are so many changes with equipment that I must speak up loud and clear. It's not the size of the desk but who is sitting behind it that matters. The numerous changes that are occurring with tennis equipment are literally changing the game. Equipment can make a difference in your play, but if your opponent has the same equipment, it still boils down to you to make it happen.

This chapter covers the equipment needs of players at all levels. Keep in mind that these general statements focus on helping all players get the most from today's complex, high-tech racket products and services. Experimentation with this knowledge will help you fine-tune your specific equipment needs.

Remember, there isn't a bad racket, string, or other tennis product manufactured today, but players can make bad choices when they don't understand product specifications and design objectives. By understanding your individual equipment needs, you will stay healthier and win more matches.

Strings

Let's start with the facts. The energy created in a tennis ball that meets a racket breaks down into the following components:

- 60 percent of the energy comes from the string bed (the strings in the racket).
- 30 percent of the energy comes from the ball (a rubber object in motion with its own energy).
- 10 percent of the energy comes from you and your racket frame (frame only, not the strings).

This proves the importance of proper stringing, correct tension, string type, quality of strings, and age (freshness or resilience) of strings. With this in mind, let's start with the most important item in hitting a tennis ball, the strings.

The 10 Commandments of Strings

Whatever type or brand of string you use, the following 10 commandments of strings apply. Study each carefully. They will help explain the many differences in today's string selections and how they can affect your game.

1. Lower string tension generates more power (providing that excessive string movement doesn't occur).
2. Higher string tension generates more ball control (with less power, placement of the ball improves).
3. A longer string, or string-plane area, produces more power.
4. Lower string density (fewer strings in the string pattern) generates more power.
5. Thinner strings generate more power.
6. Strings with more elasticity generate more power and absorb more shock at impact.
7. Softer strings, or strings with a softer coating, tend to vibrate less.
8. Thinner strings produce more spin on the ball.
9. Lower string density (fewer strings) generates more spin on the ball.
10. The more elastic the string, the more tension is lost in the racket after a string job (prestretching will reduce this effect).

String Types and Construction

Not too long ago, players had just two choices in strings—natural-gut strings or nylon strings. Natural-gut strings have been used since tennis was invented. Most top professional players still use natural gut because of its amazing characteristics, which are found only in a natural fiber.

Today, many nylon strings are referred to as synthetic-gut strings. This name can be misleading. The most important point to remember is that all such strings are made from a nylon-based product. True, many synthetic-gut strings have special features that make them last longer than regular nylon strings, but in basic chemical analysis they are virtually the same product.

If the added features of a specific synthetic-gut string favor your game, feel confident in continuing to use that product. But remember, a freshly strung racket with the basic nylon string will greatly outperform an expensive synthetic-gut string that is old and has lost its resiliency.

The basic construction types in today's nylon or synthetic-gut strings can be classified into the following groups. Each construction technique is for a specific purpose.

- Solid core (polyester strings)
- Solid core (single wrap)
- Solid core (multiwrap)
- Multifilament
- Multicore (single wrap)
- Multicore (multiwrap)
- Composites
- Aramid fiber and hybrids (Kevlar and other materials)

Of these construction types, solid core with a single wrap is by far the most widely manufactured string, making up more than 70 percent of all strings manufactured today. The main reason for the wide acceptance of this string is its overall performance at a price much lower than the price of natural gut.

To help you find the best string type for your individual game, take a look at table 14.1. Refer to later sections on construction and gauge to fine-tune these recommendations.

To define each type of string better, let's look at a few of the more popular groups and their playing characteristics.

Table 14.1   Recommended String Type Based on Need

Need	Recommended string
More power	Natural gut, multifilament synthetic, thinner gauge
More control	Solid core, solid core (multiwrap), hybrid
More feel	Natural gut, multifilament, thinner gauge
Less shock and vibration	Natural gut, multifilament
Durability	Hybrid, thicker gauge
Firm feel	Solid core (single wrap), aramid blend

Solid-Core Synthetic Strings

Polyester strings fall into the solid-core category. Although they have been around for many years, polyester strings have recently found great popularity among players at all levels. Like all synthetic strings, they are available in different gauges (string thickness) and from a variety of manufacturers. The advantages and disadvantages are as follows:

Advantages	Disadvantages
Durability	Tension loss
Greater control	Less ball speed
Claims of exceptional feel	Increased shock and vibration
Resists notching	Difficult to install (for stringer)

Note that polyester string is less resilient than other synthetics, so a claim of more control also means the player cannot hit the ball as hard.

Solid-Core (Single Wrap) Synthetic Strings

Solid-core synthetic strings with a single wrap make up 70 percent of today's string market. These popular strings derive their durability from having a large solid core. An outer wrap of smaller filaments (or fibers) improves tension retention. The outer wrap assists in two ways by (1) helping to hold the tension on the string and (2) protecting the core from notching and other abrasions caused by impact with the ball.

Because of the string's popularity, a wide choice of gauges is available. Manufacturers price their strings competitively. If this is the best-playing string type for you, shop around. You can probably find the same string from several companies, differing only in packaging and pricing. The advantages and disadvantages are as follows:

Advantages	Disadvantages
Wide variety of gauges	Too many choices
Excellent value	Better strings overlooked
Very durable (thicker gauges)	Will go "dead" before breaking
Balance between power and control	Shock and vibration to arm

Multifilament Synthetic Strings

Multifilament synthetic strings are coreless and have multiple synthetic fibers twisted together in a manner similar to natural gut. Fibers vary in thickness and number. The biggest advantage of this type of construction is playability. These strings are technically difficult to produce and carry the highest price tag among synthetic strings. They are the best-playing synthetic-gut strings and most closely resemble natural gut in all characteristics. The advantages and disadvantages are as follows:

Advantages	Disadvantages
Exceptional feel	Tension loss
Increased power	Premature breakage
Less shock and vibration to arm	Susceptible to notching from topspin
Excellent for wide-body frames	

Natural Gut

Despite the countless number of synthetics on the market today, most players still judge natural gut the best, although many of the top professional players have moved to the polyester category or to a hybrid of polyester and natural gut. String manufacturers try vigorously to duplicate its exceptional feel and playability, but so far they have fallen short. Thus we often hear or read the statement "Plays most similar to natural gut."

Natural gut is made from high-grade beef intestine. Only the upper part of the intestine is used. The process is a delicate, hands-on procedure that requires up to three months from start to finish. Note that natural gut is a by-product of the beef industry. No cows are slaughtered just to make gut. The labor-intensive work needed to produce natural gut accounts for its high price compared with synthetic strings.

Natural gut is the best-playing string available; its power is unmatched. Natural gut will hold tension much better than any synthetic string, and it absorbs shock and vibration much better as well. The actual "dwell time" (time the ball is on the string bed) is longer with natural gut than it is with synthetics, so the player experiences a much greater feel. An old saying in the tennis world is this: "Once you have tried gut, you will never go back to a synthetic. You're hooked!"

Over the years, people have questioned the durability of natural gut. These doubts have arisen because some stringers don't know how to handle natural gut. Natural gut is extremely durable when handled correctly and remains playable longer than a normal synthetic string. Synthetic string will lose an average of 15 to 18 percent of initial tension in the first 24 hours after stringing. Natural gut will lose an average of only 5 to 8 percent. The synthetic string will become "dead" (lose its resiliency) after 15 to 20 hours of normal play, whereas natural gut will stay resilient for its entire life.

If you have had arm or shoulder problems, natural gut is the best remedy for you. It is made from hundreds of individual "ribbons" of the intestine, twisted together to form the string. Each ribbon acts independently as well as with others when a ball is struck. Each ribbon absorbs shock and vibration to deliver optimal power. Natural gut is considered a multifilament string and is available in many different gauges. All that you have learned about construction and gauge applies to natural gut. The following list further addresses its benefits and drawbacks. The advantages and disadvantages are as follows:

Advantages	Disadvantages
Power	Price
Control	
Tension maintenance	
Best for arm and shoulder	
Longevity of playability	

String Gauge

The gauge of a string is the thickness (or diameter) measured before traction (tension) is applied. Gauge is measured in millimeters and grouped into reference categories, which are what most people refer to when discussing gauge. By studying table 14.2, you'll see that opinion differs about where certain string gauges fall. It is important to understand these differences as you find out more about how the gauge of a string affects your game.

Of the gauges available, 16 gauge (1.26 to 1.34 millimeters) is the most popular. For most players this gauge delivers the best blend of power, control, and durability. Thinner strings play better (refer to the 10 commandments of strings) but are not as durable. Table 14.3 shows how string gauge affects playability. Remember what you have learned about how the construction of a string affects its reaction.

Remember that thinner strings are more elastic than thicker strings. This means thinner strings can store more energy at the same reference tension. The actual tension felt in the racket will be much different. If you string your racket at 60 pounds (27 kg) with a 15-gauge string (thick) and

**Table 14.2   Gauge Conversion
(USA and European String Gauge Specs)**

Gauge			
USA	Europe	Inches	Millimeters
13	12	.065-.071	1.65-1.80
14	11	.059-.065	1.50-1.65
15	9.5	.056-.059	1.41-1.49
15L	9	.052-.056	1.33-1.41
16	8.5	.050-.053	1.26-1.34
16L	8	.048-.051	1.22-1.30
17	7.5	.046-.049	1.16-1.24
18	7	.042-.046	1.06-1.16
19	4	.035-.042	0.90-1.06
20	3.5	.031-.035	0.80-.090
21	3	.028-.031	0.70-.080
22	2.5	.024-.028	0.60-0.70

Table 14.3   Playability Based on String Gauge

	Thicker string	Thinner string
Power	Less	More
Control	More	Less
Spin	Less	More
Durability	More	Less
Tension loss	Same	Same

like the way it plays but want to test a 17-gauge string (thin), you will need to adjust the tension accordingly. Players should experiment with gauges to find the best possible blend of power, control, and durability. A string of any given type of construction will play differently when used in a different gauge.

Tension

The most important thing to remember is that tension is only a number. What a particular stringing machine is set to when you are having a racket strung will be affected by the following:

- Prestretch
- Type of machine (e.g., drop weight, spring type, constant pull)

- Calibration of the machine
- Person using the machine
- String type being used (e.g., gauge, elongation, resiliency)
- Pattern of the racket
- Pattern used to string the racket
- Condition of the racket
- Exposure to the elements

Other variables such as elongation of the string over time and the amount of stress placed on the string bed during use (frequency and intensity of use) also affect tension. With all these factors, the number requested (tension) will be only a reference tension. The actual tension of the racket after stringing can vary from the reference tension by as much as 25 percent, almost always on the low side.

Let's look more closely at these factors so you can better understand their effect on the tension requested.

Prestretch

Some manufacturers recommend prestretching for highly elastic strings. Prestretching will make the string bed of your racket feel somewhat tighter at the same tension than it would feel without prestretching. This characteristic can be helpful to someone who wants a bit more control but can't afford to string tighter because of arm or shoulder problems. This process slows the initial string stretch (loss in tension) prevalent among this type of string. The process is accomplished by uncoiling the string set and wrapping the entire length of string around a smooth pole. The stringer then pulls both ends of the string in a slow, gradual motion, holding the string at full resistance for 20 or 30 seconds. The amount of force needed to accomplish a proper prestretch is 45 to 50 pounds (20 to 23 kg) of pulling force. A proper prestretch should result in the coil being taken out of the string so that it lies flat.

Many stringers prestretch natural gut so that it is easier to handle. Doing this will help reduce the initial tension loss in natural gut, but the prestretch will not have as great an effect on natural gut as it does on multifilament synthetic string.

Nick's Tip

If you are accustomed to having your strings prestretched, be sure to tell your stringer each time you need service. Don't assume your stringer will do it just because the string package recommends it!

Junior Rackets: Getting Your Child Started in Tennis

All too often the specialized equipment that kids need is either taken for granted or overlooked altogether. Most parents assume that because their child is just starting, any old racket will do. When their child gets better, they will treat the youngster to a better racket. This isn't good enough.

It isn't uncommon to see a child taking a first lesson using mom or dad's worn-out adult-size frame. The child is having a hard enough time just moving to the ball, let alone attempting to swing a racket that is too long and too heavy and has too big a grip. This struggle will leave a lasting impression on the child: Playing tennis is hard.

Racket manufacturers make frames called junior rackets that come in three lengths, referred to as the graduated-length method (GLM). These frames usually come with the following designations:

Length	Age
19-21 inches	4-6 years
21-23 inches	6-8 years
25 inches	8-10 years
26 inches	11 years and older

Unfortunately, the system doesn't work as well as it sounds. The biggest drawback is the low quality of the frame and strings. These frames are produced with one goal in mind—to make an inexpensive racket. The manufacturers are making a price-point frame that will introduce tennis to as many people as possible.

Parents must decide from the start whether tennis is something they want to introduce their child to properly or poorly. Your child can receive the best instruction money can buy, but if he can't hit a ball because the low-quality racket twists in his hands or lacks the stiffness to provide power, tennis will not be any fun.

If you want to start your child playing tennis, chances are you play tennis yourself. I encourage you to buy the least expensive adult racket you can find and *actually try to play with it*. The racket will probably cost $20 or $30; be made of aluminum; be prestrung from the factory; and have a slippery, low-quality grip. You will quickly learn why you shouldn't introduce your child to tennis with an inferior racket.

What are your options? From this chapter you learned that proper construction of a frame will lend more power with less effort and less twisting on off-center hits. And proper string selection and tension are crucial for playing success. And because of the recent push in "growing the game" initiatives, manufacturers are now making premium tennis rackets designed specifically for players who are 10 and under. Appropriate rackets, courts, and ball types make the sport fun for young players and set them up for success.

Machine Types

The first racket stringers were true artisans who used wooden dowels and makeshift awls to install strings. They achieved tension by wrapping string around the dowels and twisting until they heard the proper pitch from plucking the string. The stringer would then carefully install an awl into the frame hole, pinching the tensioned string to the frame. The entire frame was done this way. Because they achieved proper tension only by hearing a certain pitch, these early stringers varied from each other. Stringers gave unique attention to each racket, so players rarely changed from one stringer to another.

The first mechanical stringing machines used a drop-weight system. By applying a specific weight to a lever that held the string, tension could be applied more uniformly. By using the same drop-weight system, stringers could begin to duplicate each other's work more precisely.

These machines soon gave way to crank, spring-activated machines. The most popular of these was the Ektelon stringing machine (now manufactured by Prince and called the Neos). Many are still in use today and have been applauded for their years of reliable service and adequate consistency.

Electronic (or constant-pull) machines are today's state-of-the-art equipment. By pulling tension at a specific, precise amount, the machines have eliminated almost all human factors. These machines are the only ones that can account for the differences in elongation, friction, and resiliency of different string types. Electronic machines, by far the most accurate machines available today, are used at every major professional tournament.

Calibration

As mentioned before, tension is only a number. Reference tension and actual tension can differ by 5 to 25 percent. Accurate calibration will help reduce the difference between the two. Because of differences in construction, actual tension produced by the three types of machines will differ even when each is calibrated to be the same. Knowing the specific differences between these machines will help you request a reference tension when going from one machine to another.

For example, suppose you want your racket strung at a reference tension of 60 pounds (27 kg). You usually have your racket strung on an Ektelon machine (crank, spring activated). You should request the following for the other machine types (assuming that all machines are calibrated correctly).

Drop weight: 5 to 10 percent greater reference tension (63 to 66 pounds; 29 to 30 kg)

Electronic: 5 to 10 percent less reference tension (54 to 57 pounds; to 24 to 26 kg)

This does not mean an electronic machine strings more tightly than a crank, spring-activated machine. It only means that an electronic machine strings more accurately to the reference tension requested. Elongation, friction, and so on have less effect on this type of machine.

The closer you can get your racket to the tension you prefer, the better off you and your game will be. Knowing that machines string differently at the same requested tension will help you achieve this goal. Don't become caught up in a number. Be intelligent and play with a string tension that is best for your game.

The stringer should calibrate the stringing machine every day before starting work. By knowing that the machine will perform the same from one day to the next, the stringer will be more consistent. It is your responsibility to ask the stringer when the machine was last calibrated and if it's OK. Each company issues specific guidelines about proper calibration techniques. Shy away from a shop or stringer who doesn't know when or how to calibrate the machine. Chances are that stringers like these are not as serious about their work as you are about your game!

Stringers and Racket Technicians

The person using the machine must be skilled to achieve an actual tension that is close to the reference tension you request. Players sometimes refer to a stringer as someone who strings tight or loose. This usually refers more to the person's stringing habits, good and bad, than to the machine. Many stringers, for whatever reason, think they need to be fast to gain a favorable reputation from players. The opposite is usually true. Quality in doing anything takes time, and stringing a racket is no exception. If a stringer doesn't attend to details and, let's say, clamps off before the machine has finished pulling tension, the string job will feel loose to the player. The person using the machine and the calibration of the machine are the two factors that most affect tension, but there are others, as you'll learn in the following sections.

String Type

You learned in the section on string construction that different types of strings feel different. Even at the same reference tension (tension the machine is set to), different types of strings will vary in actual tension (tension of the frame's strings after stringing). Several variables can cause this difference:

- String gauge
- String construction or composition
- String elongation
- String resiliency (or elasticity)

The conclusion you can draw from this is that if you use a different string in your racket, your regular reference tension may give you a very different feel. You should do your homework or consult a professional about the differences first.

String Pattern of the Racket

Different rackets have different string patterns for a reason. Denser patterns (more main and cross strings) deliver greater string durability and more control because the strings move less on impact with the ball. Open string patterns tend to enhance power and spin on the ball when struck. Because it has more string, a dense-pattern racket will feel as if it is strung tighter than a comparable racket with a more open string pattern.

Let's take two identical rackets that differ only in string patterns. One racket has a dense pattern with 18 main strings and 20 cross strings. The other has an open pattern with 16 main strings and 18 cross strings. The requested reference tension is 60 pounds (27 kg). A player comparing the two would note certain characteristics (when comparing strings in the racket, not the frame) (see table 14.4).

Table 14.4   **Racket Characteristics Based on Pattern Type**

	Dense pattern	**Open pattern**
Power	Less	More
Control	More	Less
Topspin	Less	More
Durability	More	Less
Vibration	Same	Same
Shock*	More	Less

*Because a dense-pattern racket is less resilient and creates a tighter string bed, the player would feel more shock with it than with an open-pattern racket strung at the same tension.

Stringing Pattern

The two ways to install strings in today's rackets are typically referred to as one-piece stringing and two-piece stringing. When implemented properly, both are recommended by racket manufacturers. Some rackets call for one or the other. The stringer should know which is correct for a particular racket, but some overlook the distinction and don't understand why there is a difference. Some stringers will be lazy and simply install the strings into the racket as fast as they can.

As a serious tennis player, you should know the correct way to have your racket strung. Improper stringing is a major cause of premature racket fatigue and can create a different feel on the string bed.

Buying Multiple Frames of the Same Model

It seems that the more you play, the more rackets you'll have. If you are serious about your game, your rackets must be the same in every detail:

- Same model (head size, grip size, and string pattern)
- Same string type, gauge, and color
- Same tension (unless you feel the need for a little more or less tension in one)
- Same weight
- Same balance
- Same stiffness
- Same inertia (or swing weight)

No problem, right? You just go to your favorite sports store and pick up as many rackets as you need of the exact model with the correct grip size. Have your stringer string them with the same string at the same tension. How can you go wrong?

The chances of your receiving frames that feel and play the same are slim. The only thing you can be sure of is that the color will be the same. Every manufacturer has tolerances for production as well as multiple factories that make the same rackets. None of this means a specific racket is bad; it only means it may be different. You are trying to remove all variables to make your tennis game sounder. This is no exception.

If you are buying several new rackets of the same model, seek professional help to assure you that the frames in question are, in fact, the same or can be customized to be the same. Usually, the weight, balance, and inertia can be matched up. The only thing that can't be adjusted is frame stiffness. Be sure all rackets have similar stiffness.

This advice is especially important if you are buying a second (or third or more) frame sometime after your initial purchase. Take your old racket along to have it tested against the one or several that you are looking to buy.

If you have an old racket that you love and have finally decided to part with it, but you have no idea what to look for in a new racket, have your current frame analyzed by a professional racket technician who has the necessary test equipment. The technician will be able to test current new frames against your old racket and help you weed out some of the many rackets available today. Chances are you will find a racket similar to your old racket. Remember to demo any racket before you buy it.

The United States Racquet Stringers Association (USRSA) is the only worldwide organization that actively tests stringers around the world. Look for the worldwide symbol of a USRSA certified racket technician (CRT), the designation of the highest level of competence.

Racket (Frame) Condition

Another issue related to tension is the condition of the frame. An old and worn frame will most likely be fatigued and unable to hold the tension placed on it during the stringing process. The reference tension applied by the machine will be OK, but the actual tension will typically be much less than it was when the racket was new. The fibers of the frame can't withstand the forces placed on the frame and tend to give, causing the string bed to be softer than it should be.

On the other hand, a new frame that has never been strung will tend to string up looser on the initial stringing, mainly because the grommets haven't yet been "seated" or "conditioned" by having tension applied to them. Many professional players request that a new racket be strung 2 to 4 pounds (1 to 2 kg) tighter than normal.

Never attempt to string or play with a cracked or broken frame. You may cause serious harm to yourself or others. Discard the racket properly so that no one will attempt to use it.

Exposure to Elements

The elements play a big role in the tension of the strings in your racket. Heat is the most damaging. Exposure to excessive heat will reduce the ability of the strings to deliver the energy they had when fresh, before exposure.

We have all heard that you shouldn't leave your racket in the car on a hot day, especially in the trunk. What does this really mean? How long is too long? How hot is hot? The best way to explain this is by looking at test results about the effect of heat on a freshly strung racket.

Two rackets, identical in every aspect, were strung with the same string at 60 pounds (27 kg) of tension. Immediately after stringing, all possible measurements were taken on the string bed. The string beds of the two rackets were the same in all test parameters. One racket was then placed inside a car in the sun with the windows rolled up. The other was placed in an air-conditioned house. The weather was normal for a spring day in Florida, 75 degrees Fahrenheit (24 °C) and mostly sunny. The temperature inside the house was a climate-controlled 70 degrees Fahrenheit (21 °C).

A thermometer inside the car measured just how hot the car's interior became during the test. The temperature inside reached 140 degrees (60 °C)! The rackets were checked on the test equipment after 30 minutes, 60 minutes, and 120 minutes. Table 14.5 displays the results.

This was not an extreme test—people leave their rackets in the car all the time. We performed the test to show that heat becomes excessive in

Table 14.5   Effect of Heat on String Tension and Bed Deflection

Start	Fresh frame	Frame in car
String tension (machine set to)	60 pounds	60 pounds
Tensometer reading	60 pounds	60 pounds
RDC bed deflections	76 units	76 units
After 30 minutes	**Fresh frame**	**Frame in car**
Tensometer reading	59 pounds	55 pounds
RDC bed deflection	74 units	70 units
After 60 minutes	**Fresh frame**	**Frame in car**
Tensometer reading	58 pounds	50 pounds
RDC bed deflection	73 units	65 units
After 120 minutes	**Fresh frame**	**Frame in car**
Tensometer reading	57 pounds	47 pounds
RDC bed deflection	73 units	63 units

a closed-up car. What is it that causes the strings to lose so much tension and resiliency in such a short time?

Well, the molecules of the nylon under traction (tension in the racket) move farther apart and lose their ability to resist the force of the tension. Once this ability is lost, it will not return. Although the racket placed in the car had yet to strike a ball, for all practical purposes it was "dead" and should have been restrung. Two hours in the heat had stressed the strings as much as 20 to 30 hours of normal playing would.

You may be telling yourself, "If heat is this bad, then cold must be good!" All tests have shown that although extreme cold doesn't affect tension as heat does, it will make the strings (as well as the racket frame) brittle. If you live in a climate where you must leave your racket in the car during extremely cold (subzero) weather, you need to allow ample time for the racket and strings to warm up before playing. Remember, a racket is a nonliving thing that will lose heat faster than it will absorb it. Wait until the racket has a normal temperature to the touch. Thirty minutes should be enough. I hope you are playing inside! You will have plenty of time to stretch and prepare for your match.

When to String

Unfortunately, most people restring their rackets only when the strings break. The opposite occurs on the professional tour. Pro players restring before every match, and many do so during a match. What is best for you depends on the following:

- Are you above the novice level of play?
- Are you serious about your game? (Is top performance important to you?)
- Do you often break strings? (Will you be caught without a racket in a match?)
- Do you have arm or shoulder problems? (If so, fresh strings are a must.)
- Do you expose your racket to extreme conditions? (e.g., excessive heat, airline flights).
- Do you play primarily on clay courts? (Clay tends to wear out strings faster.)

If you answer yes to any of these questions, you probably need to be more aware of when to restring.

A good benchmark for normal recreational use is to restring your racket after every 30 hours of play. The more serious you are, the more often you should restring. Remember that 60 percent of the energy delivered to the ball comes from the strings. Even if you are just an occasional player who plays seasonally, you should restring before each season.

Stringing Process

Whether you are a stringer or someone who is having a racket strung, this section is important. It deals with the process of installing the strings into a racket and the basic things you should know.

Frame Inspection

The first item is a frame inspection. Before any racket, regardless of age, is restrung, a visual inspection of the following items should be conducted:

- Check for any visible cracks or stress marks in the frame. You should never restring or play with a cracked racket. If you are a customer just wanting to get your racket strung, knowing about any cracks will help answer questions that might come as a surprise later. If you are a stringer, checking the racket before doing any work can save you from trying to explain to a customer returning to pick up the racket that he has a broken frame. It is best to do this visual inspection while the customer is present.
- Check the condition of the grommets (plastic protective strips that protect the string and frame). You can often have these replaced for a nominal charge, and doing so will lengthen the life of both the racket frame and the strings.
- Check the condition of the grip. This is an excellent time to receive a complete tune-up of your racket. Also, be sure to check the butt cap for loose staples.

Stringing at Tournaments

Nearly all tennis players who travel will occasionally need to have a racket restrung by someone other than their regular stringer. Tournament players at all levels often have this need. For the professional player, it is the norm rather than the exception.

How you handle the situation will determine whether you gain the satisfaction you're looking for. What you really want is for your racket to feel like what you are accustomed to. Here is what you need to know:

What type of machine (electronic or spring activated) is your racket regularly strung on?

What pattern is used on your racket? (One piece? Two piece? Count the knots.)

What string do you use exactly? (Brand, gauge, and color are important!)

Does your regular stringer prestretch your string? (If you don't know, ask.)

If your regular stringer has made any comments, pass them along.

All too often people take proper stringing for granted and fail to pay attention to these simple issues. Have your stringer write you a "racket prescription" on a note card, and keep it in your racket bag. You will thank yourself when you need service from someone else.

Don't blame a stringer for spoiling your vacation or causing you to lose an important match because you couldn't play with your racket. Chances are that if you had known the answers to the preceding questions, you wouldn't have experienced a problem.

You should carry extra strings and grips of the exact type you use, especially if you use a string that is somewhat special or hard to find. Not every shop will carry the specific products you use.

All players who travel must be able to arrange for a restringing. Tournament players must do the following additional things.

- Immediately after arriving at a tournament, check in a racket for stringing. This is crucial! Don't wait until you *have* to get a racket strung. Chances are that the stringer will be busy, and you may not get your racket done as quickly as expected. More important, by having a racket done before you need one, you'll be able to judge the tension.

- Even if you need to get more than one racket strung when you arrive, have only one strung at first. When that frame is completed, test the tension. If you need to change your request, you will have wasted only one stringing.

If you prepare yourself successfully and professionally, be prepared to be professionally successful!

Cutting Out the Strings

The next step is to cut out the old strings correctly. To minimize the stress to the frame when relieving the tension, begin cutting in the middle of the string pattern. Cut mains and crosses together in a uniform system as you work to the outer edge of the racket. Cut at a diagonal direction going up, then down, then up.

Carefully remove the old string and again look closely at the grommet strips. Check the holes for any cracks, and check the bumper guard (on top of the racket) for excessive wear. Replace them as needed.

Tubing and Padding

If you can't find a replacement grommet kit for your racket, or have only a few holes that need attention, you can use tubing to protect the string from the frame. Any qualified stringer has plenty of experience using tubing and should have an adequate supply on hand.

Sometimes a stringer will install leather pads (referred to as power pads) in certain areas of a frame. These pads protect the string from breaking prematurely by creating a rounder turn for the string to follow, which helps alleviate sheer and grommet breakage. Pads are usually used with natural-gut strings in higher tension.

If you continue to break a string in the same area close to the frame and have tried replacing the grommets, try having power pads installed in that area. As with all special stringing variations or additions, consult a professional racket technician first.

Frame Mounting

Proper mounting of the racket in a stringing machine is essential for maintaining the integrity of the frame. Shy away from purchasing an inexpensive home machine because you want to save money on stringing. The stress load placed on a tennis racket during the stringing process is the most strain and stress it will ever experience. If stringing a racket causes its shape to change, chances are the machine is inferior or the racket was mounted incorrectly.

Knowing how to use a particular stringing machine is just as important as knowing how to install the strings. The manufacturer provides a complete set of instructions with the stringing machine. The stringer should understand and follow these instructions. If you have purchased a used machine that doesn't have instructions, call the manufacturer and request a copy before you use the equipment.

Racket Patterns

Now that you have checked and properly mounted the racket, you need to know what pattern to use. Every manufacturer has a diagram of the pattern for stringing every racket they sell. You may need to request one if you don't know the correct way.

There is only one way to string each racket. You need to know what holes the main and cross strings skip. The integrity of the racket frame will be seriously compromised if the racket is not strung as it was designed. In addition, a racket may be illegal for tournament play if the pattern isn't consistent. The USRSA provides a yearly digest to its members. Each edition is updated with all the newer models on the market. With this book, the stringer can quickly find the pattern for every racket.

String patterns fall into two broad categories—open patterns and tight patterns, which are distinguished by how many main strings (which run up and down) and cross strings (which run side to side) the racket has (see table 14.6). The difference in string pattern can dramatically affect several elements of play. We assume here that you are using the same racket, string, and string tension, varying only the string pattern.

Table 14.6   String Pattern and Impact on Play

	Tight pattern	**Open pattern**
Power	Less	More
Control	More	Less
Spin on the ball	Less	More
String durability	More	Less
String movement	Less	More
Shock to arm	More	Less

Don't be confused by some of the items listed. Because a dense string pattern will have smaller spaces between the strings, the string bed will play more firmly because the strings can't move as much as they can in an open pattern. Therefore, although the tension is the same, the feel will be that the denser pattern is strung more tightly.

A racket with a dense string pattern can be a real benefit to someone who has arm, elbow, or shoulder problems and can't control an open-pattern racket. If the player strings the racket at a lower tension, it feels better on the arm. By going to a frame with a denser pattern, the player can play with reduced string tension and still have the necessary control. This will help reduce the shock and strain that higher string tension places on the arm.

Be aware that if you change rackets, your trusty string tension may not stay the same. Even if you buy a racket with the same head size, be sure to check for string-pattern differences. The basic classifications for string patterns are as follows:

Open patterns	Tight patterns
14 mains and 16 crosses	18 mains and 20 crosses
16 mains and 18 crosses	20 mains and 22 crosses
16 mains and 19 crosses	16 mains and 20 crosses

Nick's Tip

Remember that the main strings deliver the power and the cross strings give control. More mains mean less power and more control.

If as a last resort you are attempting to string a racket for which you have no directions, look carefully at the existing string pattern. Do not cut it out until you are sure of the correct pattern. If the frame has no strings but has been strung before, look carefully at which way the grommets go. With luck you will be able to distinguish the mains from the crosses.

Custom Stringing Techniques

Undoubtedly, most stringers consider themselves the best. Many attempt to differentiate their work from the work of others by stringing in a special way. Usually the knots will be in a different place. Stringers may use creative knots or add pads on every frame. In any case, as long as these specialized techniques don't jeopardize the integrity of the frame or strings, you shouldn't worry.

In many cases these special techniques stem from knowledge about how certain strings react to particular frames, and the techniques can make an important difference. Be sure this is the case and that the stringer did not use a "special" technique only because she didn't know the proper way to string the racket.

Machine Maintenance and Calibration

Anyone who uses a stringing machine needs to clean and calibrate the machine at regular intervals. If you travel with a machine, you must have the calibration checked and adjusted before using it. Machines that stay put in a shop should be cleaned and calibrated daily.

Racket Grips

Here we discuss grip sizes, how to size a grip for your hand, grip feel, grip types, grip installation, and customization techniques.

Grip Sizes

The size of the pallet (the handle of the racket) when it has a grip installed is measured around the circumference of the grip. The smaller the measurement, the smaller the grip size. The most commonly produced sizes available today are the following (two numbers are listed for each grip size; the size in parentheses is how grips are usually described in European countries):

- 4 1/8 inches (L-1)
- 4 1/4 inches (L-2)
- 4 3/8 inches (L-3)
- 4 1/2 inches (L-4)
- 4 5/8 inches (L-5)

Proper Sizing of the Grip

The best way to determine your correct size is to hold the racket comfortably in your playing hand. Turn the racket over to expose your palm and fingertips. You should be able to place the pinkie finger from your free hand comfortably between the heel of your palm and the ring finger of the hand holding the racket. You should have enough room to just touch each.

If you overlap, the grip is too small. Having too small a grip is one of the primary causes of tennis elbow. If you are uncertain about which size to use, play with the larger one. By doing so, you will experience less twisting and torque and thus less shock to the arm. However, many of the better players are starting to use smaller handle sizes because it allows educated and elite-level players to move their wrists more freely. A larger handle size will firm up an over-wristy player.

Grip Feel

Two grips of a given size produced by different companies may feel different from one another. The circumference may be the same, but the sizing of the bevels (the eight sides of the pallet) will vary, which may cause an entirely different feel in your hand. You may experience discomfort when playing with a grip that is not the size you normally use.

When choosing a grip, find one of the proper size that feels correct. When changing from one racket to another (usually one from a different manufacturer), many people don't give the fit much thought. They will say, "I'm a 4 1/2-inch grip size. There's no need to check—that's what my old racket was." You always need to check the way a new or different racket fits your hand. Don't become caught up in a number.

Grip Types

The first rackets had no grip material at all on the handle. The grip was simply the wood as it continued down from the head of the racket. As the game and the technology of racket manufacturing progressed, players found it increasingly difficult to hold on to the racket because they were hitting the ball harder. Manufacturers started to produce rackets with a covering of natural leather over the pallet. Leather grips are still used today, but in recent years they have given way in popularity to synthetic grips. Each type has benefits and drawbacks.

Leather Grips

Because leather grips are made from a high-grade calfskin, they offer the best absorption of perspiration. Like any skin, the leather grip has many pores that breathe so it absorbs moisture well. The durability of a leather grip surpasses that of any synthetic grip. The biggest complaint about leather grips is that they have a much harder feel on the hand. The average recreational player may develop blisters and perceive more shock to the arm. On the professional tour, most players use a leather grip. Most rackets manufactured today come with a synthetic grip because the cost of a leather grip is much greater.

Synthetic Grips

Bright colors, various textures, tacky feel, and extra cushioning are some of the stated benefits of today's synthetic grips. Low durability, poor absorption, and a feel that quickly becomes slippery are more the reality. The synthetic grips feel good when new, but many recreational players fail to replace them regularly. Synthetic replacement grips are economical, and you can maintain the feel you loved when the grip was new by frequently installing a new one. If you tend to perspire a lot or play in a hot, humid climate, be aware that synthetic grips do not absorb moisture. They shed water at first and then become saturated and slippery. The benefit of the extra cushioning is a positive. If you want to reduce the vibration from your racket, a cushioned synthetic grip will help. Be aware that these synthetic grips do not have a life expectancy similar to that of the racket frame. A good guideline is to change the synthetic replacement grip every other time you have the racket restrung, if not more often.

Overgrips

With the overall appeal of modern synthetic grips, overgrips, or overwraps, have become popular. These thin grips are installed directly over the main grip of the racket. Inexpensive and usually sold in multiple-unit packages, they are intended for short-term use. Hundreds of overgrips are available, but they fall into two basic categories—sticky (or tacky) and dry (or non-tacky). Because each of us has a different pH balance, we produce different kinds of perspiration, so some grip styles will become more slippery than others. No type is better than another. By experimentation or by asking someone qualified, you will have no problem finding a perfect type for your specific needs.

Grip Installation

Any grip or overgrip must be installed correctly. If you are attempting this for the first time, you need to be aware of a few simple things.

- You must first remove the old grip.
- If you are replacing the main grip of your racket, you will probably have to remove a staple at the end.
- You will need scissors, a stapler, and grip tape (usually supplied with the new grip).
- Be attentive to how the original grip was installed. You should try to duplicate the wrap.
- All rackets come gripped right-handed from the factory.
- Always start from the bottom of the racket.

Almost all of today's replacement grips come with instructions. If you are installing a leather grip, you will also need some double-sided tape to secure the grip to the racket pallet. If you are putting on an overgrip, simply install it directly over the main grip of your racket. Try to follow the pattern of the main grip, starting at the bottom of the racket.

As mentioned earlier, all rackets from the manufacturers come wrapped right-handed. If you are left-handed, you should be aware that the grip on your racket is backward. If the handle doesn't feel comfortable on either side or if you tend to tear up grips quickly, chances are that you can solve the problem by having the grip installed for a left-handed player. If your grip is old or has been used, you will need to buy a new grip before making the change. When removing the current factory grip, notice the direction of the wrap. You will simply need to reverse the procedure and go the other way.

Grip Customization

If you can't get comfortable with the dimensional shape of your grip or you need to enlarge or reduce the size of the pallet, you can customize the grip. Few professional players use the grip size and shape their rackets come with. On this level, professional racket technicians remold the shape to one that is different and personal for each player. This technical service carries a premium price tag.

Although the recreational player wouldn't think of having this done, individual attention to grip shape is sometimes necessary. To increase grip size, several reliable options are available:

- *Add-ons*—Available at many tennis shops, the add-on is placed between the pallet and the main grip to add one full size.
- *Heat sleeves*—Installed on the racket pallet with a high-temperature heat gun, heat sleeves also add one full size.
- *Thicker replacement grips*—Some manufacturers sell a synthetic replacement grip somewhat thicker than normal, which increases the size.

Reducing the size of most modern rackets is more difficult. Many of the frames produced today don't have a foam pallet that can be shaved down. These solid, one-piece-construction rackets can't be reduced in size. You can try a thinner replacement grip or simply rewrap the existing grip more tightly to produce a slightly smaller dimension.

If you have a racket that can be shaved, you should seek a qualified person to do the work. Once the process has started, it can't be undone. If a mistake is made, you will have to replace the racket.

Other customizations for the grip of your racket include the following:

- Use a larger or smaller butt cap to create a larger or smaller feel at the end of the racket. Try a larger one if you have a hard time holding on to the racket when serving.
- If you have a two-hand backhand, you may want to wrap a new replacement grip far up the shaft. Most frames today apply grip material only high enough for one hand to have full touch.
- By wrapping the main grip tighter or looser, or by overlapping the material more or less, you can create a unique, personal feel.

Racket Selection

Racket selection is a very important part of the game. For players who are not comfortable with their rackets, it can mean the difference between winning and losing. Although racket selection is a highly personal decision, there are some basic truths that the player should use to make her personal decision. Here are some things to consider.

Frame Construction

The first tennis rackets were wood. Different types of wood created different feels or different kinds of playability. These first rackets varied little in head size, string pattern, or length. The biggest drawback to wood was its

The 12 Commandments of Racket Frames

Just as we offered the 10 commandments of strings, we offer the 12 commandments of racket frames, basic guidelines that apply to all rackets:

1. A heavier racket frame generates more power.
2. A heavier racket frame vibrates less.
3. A heavier racket frame has a larger sweet spot.
4. A stiffer racket frame generates more power.
5. A stiffer racket frame has a larger sweet spot.
6. A stiffer racket frame transmits more shock to the arm than a more flexible racket frame.
7. A stiffer racket frame provides a more uniform ball response across the entire string bed.
8. A larger racket frame (larger head size) generates more power.
9. A larger racket frame (larger head size) is more resistant to twisting.
10. A larger racket frame (larger head size) has a larger sweet spot.
11. A longer racket frame (total length) generates more velocity and therefore more power.
12. The string bed in a longer racket frame generates more spin because the long frame produces greater velocity.

weight and stiffness, which limited technical innovation. Equipment had little effect on the game for many years.

A big step for racket production came with the use of aluminum alloys, which allowed companies to make larger, stiffer, and lighter rackets. These new frames allowed the user to hit the ball harder and more accurately. Power quickly overtook finesse among tennis players at all levels. Soon after their introduction, aluminum frames had to share the spotlight with something even more powerful—composite frames made of graphite and fiberglass. The age of power tennis had arrived.

Keep in mind that racket frames vary in two ways—construction type and frame type:

Construction types	Frame types
Alloy (aluminum)	Constant beam
Fiberglass	Taper beam
Graphite	Wide body
Fused (alloy and composite)	Thin beam (player's frames)

Racket companies match the various frame types to the different frame constructions to attempt to bring out the best combination of attributes. Playing style has a crucial role in how a racket will perform. Keep in mind that there are no bad rackets, only bad choices in rackets.

By the laws of physics, all tennis rackets are governed by the following items:

- *Weight of the racket*—the total mass of the racket
- *Balance of the racket*—how the mass is proportioned
- *Stiffness of the racket*—flexibility
- *Inertia of the racket*—swing weight of the racket in motion

Beyond these principles are other items that can enhance how a racket will play, including head size, length, beam width, frame type, and material (construction type). Remember also what you have learned about string types and patterns and how they affect the playability of a racket.

Let's discuss each of the four items more closely.

Weight

Weight, or mass, is a measurement of the overall heaviness of the racket, measured without strings and recorded in grams. Some people still use ounces, but grams are more precise. To convert one to the other, use the following:

Grams to ounces: grams × .035 = ounces

Ounces to grams: ounces × 28.35 = grams

The tennis industry uses this general classification for the weight of rackets without strings (strings weigh 15 to 18 grams):

- Ultralight frames: less than 240 grams
- Lightweight frames: 240 to 279 grams
- Medium-weight frames: 280 to 320 grams
- Heavyweight frames: More than 320 grams

The current trend in the market is to make rackets lighter. Claims of "effortless power" and "easy to play with" are common. But the principles of physics apply to every racket—no matter how light or heavy. The 12 commandments of racket frames follow these principles, which we expand on here.

Remember that tennis balls always weigh about the same. A legally approved ball is 56.7 to 58.5 grams. So the lighter the racket, the closer the weight of the racket and ball. Thus, a light racket will deliver less energy to the ball than a heavy racket (when swung at the same speed). This simply means that for most people, a lighter racket will produce less power.

Another important thing happens as the two weights become more alike—shock to the wrist, arm, and shoulder increases dramatically. To understand this, think about pounding a nail into a piece of wood. You can use either a lightweight cobbler's hammer that weighs 5 or 6 ounces (140 to 170 g) or a construction sledgehammer that weighs 5 pounds (2 kg). If you were to swing each hammer at the same speed, which would drive the nail with less effort, with less shock? This is the principle behind racket weights. The point is that you should play with the heaviest racket that doesn't affect your normal swing speed. That racket will deliver the greatest impact on the tennis ball and have the least effect on your body.

Balance

The balance of a racket depends on its longitudinal (tip to butt) weight distribution. The balance is the racket's center of gravity. Balance is always read from the butt end of the frame and is usually measured in centimeters. Other common references are in inches and points (points are increments of one-eighth of an inch). Here is the conversion:

Centimeters to inches: centimeters $\times$ .394 = inches

Inches to centimeters: inches $\times$ 2.54 = centimeters

Racket balance is classified as one of the following:

- Head heavy (HH): More of the weight is in the head of the racket.
- Head light (HL): More of the weight is in the handle of the racket.
- Even balance (EB): The weight is evenly proportioned along the entire frame.

Two rackets of identical weight with different balance will feel completely different, discussed further in the sidebar Matching Frame Type to Playing Style. You first need to understand the characteristics of balance and its effect on your racket.

Keep the following example in mind when discussing racket balance. Let's take an ordinary 16-ounce (500 g) carpenter's hammer. No matter how you pick it up, it will weigh 16 ounces. If you hold it as it was intended to be held, by the handle, it feels head heavy and somewhat difficult to swing. Now hold it by its metal head. It feels lighter, and it is head light. It is very easy to swing.

In both cases you are holding the same mass, or weight, but by holding the weight differently you have a different perception of its mass. This is how to describe racket balance.

Stiffness

Stiffness, or flex, of a racket is a measurement of how much deflection will occur on the frame when a given force is applied. This is a technical way of describing how much the racket will give when you hit a tennis ball. We most often think of flex only in the longitudinal axis (from the head to the grip), but the ability of a racket frame to withstand force placed on it from side to side in the hoop area (where the strings are) also plays a crucial role in its stiffness and in the way it plays. This stiffness of a racket is known as *torsional stiffness*.

Without torsional stiffness, a racket couldn't withstand any twisting or torque when a ball is hit off center. Generally, the stiffer a racket frame is longitudinally, the stiffer it will be torsionally.

Racket companies attempt to make rackets that deliver the best of all worlds. They attempt to make frames that are solid on off-center hits (with high torsional strength) yet are comfortable and controllable (with lower longitudinal stiffness). These frames, typically called wide-body frames, have different beam widths in different areas.

The longitudinal stiffness of a racket provides power. The torsional stiffness gives control (less torque) and comfort on off-center shots. Both are important and work together to make up the feel of a racket on impact.

To understand the issue of racket stiffness, remember that the stiffer the frame, the less it will deflect on impact. Thus the string bed will have to do more work, and you will have to generate more power. This will cause greater shock to the arm and shoulder.

The less stiff the frame, the more feel you will have. Many players refer to this lack of power as control. A frame with less stiffness will cause less shock and vibration.

Rackets lose their stiffness over time. No matter how well you take care of it, you shouldn't expect a racket to last forever. Rackets lose their stiffness for several reasons:

- Improper stringing techniques (e.g., wrong pattern, inconsistent tensioning)
- Excessively high tension
- Excessive stringing of the frame
- Hitting the ball hard
- Exposure to excessive heat (especially in vehicles)
- Court abuse (e.g., throwing, hitting the net cord, bouncing on the tip)

If you are buying a new frame and can have the stiffness checked, record the measurement and track it every time you restring the frame. When you have lost 5 to 10 percent of the original stiffness, replace the frame, no matter how good it looks. Always have this check done in the unstrung condition.

Inertia

Inertia (or swing weight) is how a racket feels when you swing it. This is the most important way to understand just how the weight is distributed in the racket. Many refer to inertia as a racket's maneuverability. Try to understand the following example of inertia.

Two rackets are identical in most respects. They both weigh 300 grams and balance exactly in the middle. The first frame weighs 150 grams at the very top of the head of the racket and 150 grams at the extreme butt end. The other racket weighs 100 grams at the head, 100 grams at the butt, and 100 grams exactly in the middle. Both are 300 grams; both balance exactly in the middle. Which frame will feel heavier to swing? Why?

Obviously, the frame that weighs 50 grams more in the head will feel heavier when you swing it. This is how we explain inertia. Because the racket that weighs 50 grams more in the head is less maneuverable, it will feel slower to swing than the other racket. The frame that is heavier in the head will have more power and control but may be less maneuverable.

Remember the regular carpenter's hammer in the section on weight? You were feeling more than just a difference in weight distribution and balance. When you tried to swing the hammer in the two different conditions, you felt a difference in inertia.

With knowledge of the basics, it is possible to match a type of racket to a style of play. These generalized examples are intended to steer players with certain styles to specific types of rackets. Again, remember that there are no bad rackets, only bad choices.

Racket Head Size

Unfortunately, manufacturers have not agreed on a standard classification of head sizes. One manufacturer may refer to a racket with a head size of 98 square inches (632 sq cm) as a midsize, whereas another manufacturer would call the same frame a midplus. The following is helpful in classifying head sizes:

- Traditional size (older wooden frames): 60 to 79 square inches (387 to 510 sq cm)
- Midsize: 80 to 90 square inches (516 to 581 sq cm)
- Midplus: 91 to 100 square inches (587 to 645 sq cm)
- Oversize: 101 to 115 square inches (652 to 742 sq cm)
- Super oversize: more than 115 square inches (742 sq cm)

If you are not sure of your racket size, you can measure it by using the following calculation. Keep in mind that this will not be the exact size, but it will be close. You will need to measure the inside diameter of the string bed, both horizontally and longitudinally.

$$\text{Area (square inches)} = \frac{3.14 \times L \times H}{4}$$

Matching Frame Type to Playing Style

Tennis players are of three basic styles—baseliner, serve and volley, and all-court. The three basic styles of rackets are head heavy (HH), head light (HL), and even balance (EB). Let's look at the playing styles and how they differ.

Baseliners typically feel more comfortable staying back behind the baseline and hitting ground strokes all day long. They tend to come to the net only to retrieve balls or shake hands. If this is you, the contact point (where you most often hit the ball on the strings) is probably toward the head of the racket. Look for ball fuzz to determine this. Baseliners tend to hit most of their balls below the waist. Your contact point is farther away from your body and farther up the string bed of the racket. Baseliners tend to prefer a head-heavy racket because more of the weight is at the head (this will generally give it a higher inertia) and because the sweet spot will be higher, toward where the most head weight is. Baseliners hit more balls near the head and usually need a little more power because they play farther from the net. If this is your game style, a head-heavy racket will feel most comfortable to you.

Serve-and-volley players like to get to the net quickly and force opponents into a defensive position. These players hit most balls above the waist and usually contact the ball closer to the bottom of the string bed, mainly because their eye–hand coordination finds it more comfortable to play the ball closer. The serve-and-volley player usually does not extend the arm as fully as a baseliner does. A head-light racket is generally preferred here. With a head-light (HL) frame, the serve-and-volley player will have a more maneuverable racket with a sweet spot that is lower on the string bed.

The final style is a blend of the other two. The all-court player will feel comfortable playing either serve and volley or baseline depending on each point or the opponent. Because this player feels comfortable playing a blend of styles, the racket will tend to be balanced. An even-balance (EB) racket offers the diversity needed to hit balls from all contact points. The all-court player will have a variety of contact points but tends to hit most balls near the middle of the frame. The sweet spot of an even-balance racket will be toward the middle of the string bed, thus giving the all-courter a feel of an equal amount of power and control on contact.

Keep in mind that these are only examples of how to match a style of racket to a style of player. To determine what style of racket is best for you, try out a variety of frames to find which type best suits your needs.

Where L is the measurement of the inside longitudinal length from the tip to throat area of the string bed, and H is the measurement of the inside horizontal length of the middle of the string bed. Let's take a look at a sample racket that measures 13.5 for the inside longitudinal length and 10.25 for the inside horizontal length:

$$\frac{3.14 \times 13.5 \times 10.25}{4} = 108.7 \text{ square inches}$$

Deciding on the perfect head size is a complex subject. Use the 12 commandments of frames to help answer the following head-size questions:

If I find that	I should try:
I need more power	a larger head size.
I mishit many balls	a larger head size.
I have too much power	a smaller head size (if using a larger one).
my racket is too slow	a smaller head size (if using a larger one).

These are just a few examples. Remember that among rackets of various head sizes, every style of frame discussed earlier (head heavy, head light, and even balance) is available to meet your specific playing style.

Experimentation with different head sizes is crucial. Different head sizes of the same racket model will play much differently from one another. A general guideline is that the more help (power) you need from the racket, the larger the head size should be. Most professional players today use rackets that would fall into the midsize or midplus categories, whereas most recreational players use oversize or super-oversize frames.

Deciding on what length of racket to use wasn't an issue until a few years ago. Extra-long, stretch, long body, and extended length are examples of the terminology manufacturers use to highlight rackets that exceed the standard length of 27 inches (69 cm). The advantages and disadvantages of using a longer frame are listed in table 14.7. Remember that these generalized statements may not apply to everyone. Your personal results are

Table 14.7   Playability Characteristics Based on Racket Length

	Regular length	Longer length
Power	Less	More
Control	More	Less
Maneuverability	More	Less
Spin on ball	Less	More
Power on the serve	Less	More
Shock to arm	Less	More
Hitting late	Less	More
Reach to ball	Less	More

what matter. You should simply be aware that these differences can affect parts of your game. Note we are assuming that weight, balance, inertia, and flex are equal and that your ability to swing each frame is the same.

Racket Stiffness

The stiffness of the racket frame relates directly to how much power it delivers as well as how much shock is created on impact with a tennis ball. If you have to string your racket very tightly (over the highest tension recommended by the manufacturer) to gain the needed control, you probably have a frame that is too stiff for your style of play. On the other hand, if you need to string it very loosely (under the lowest tension recommended by the manufacturer), you should have a stiffer frame for your game. Examples of how stiffness affects your game are listed in table 14.8. Again, we assume that weight, balance, inertia, and flex are equal and that your ability to swing each frame is the same.

When manufacturers discuss the stiffness of a frame, it is usually in terms of RA units. This standard numbering system is determined by placing a racket (unstrung) on a piece of test equipment called an RA test. This device places a set amount of weight on a lever that makes the frame bend at its halfway point. The number read on the scale is the RA unit. The higher the number, the stiffer the frame. So a racket with an RA of 80 units is much stiffer than a racket with an RA of 60 units. Table 14.9 presents an unofficial classification chart that can help you understand stiffness.

These measurements are always recorded on an unstrung frame. Because of the added force placed on the frame at different tensions, the numbers will be lower when the racket is strung. If you check the stiffness both ways, you should expect to see that the strung frame will be two to six

Table 14.8   Playability Characteristics Based on Racket Stiffness

	Flexible frame	**Stiffer frame**
Power	Less	More
Control	More	Less
Maneuverability	Same	Same
Spin on the ball	More	Less
Power on the serve	Less	More
Shock to arm	Less	More
Comfort	More	Less
Sweet spot	Less	More

Table 14.9   Racket Stiffness Classification

RA value	Type of frame
0-55	Very flexible
56-60	Flexible
61-65	Medium stiff
66-70	Stiff
More than 70	Very stiff

units lower, depending on how the frame is strung and its construction. You should be aware of the stiffness of your frame so you can determine if fatigue is becoming a factor. If it is, you should replace the frame.

Highlights of Tennis Equipment Evolution

The following text briefly describes the changes made to tennis equipment throughout several decades, and how those changes subsequently affected how the game is played today.

1950s

In this era, rackets were made of wood and hand crafted. The racket head was a very small 50 to 60 square inches (323 to 327 cm) so the hitting surface sweet spot was about the size of two tennis balls, requiring very precise eye–hand coordination. The racket-head size affected swing style and how the player gripped the racket. Swing styles had to be very compact and classic and without much deviation. And because most tennis was played on grass courts, with a very low bounce, the players were forced to use a continental grip. Very little wrist was used in the swing, so the handles were very big to keep the wrist from moving freely. The lower-bouncing balls and lower power of the racket itself meant players used natural-gut strings because of the feel that players received from the natural fibers and because of the power the natural fibers provided. The rackets were extremely heavy to accommodate the needed power. This era required perfect technique in order to be successful.

1960s

Not much really changed in the 1960s except for Wilson's introduction of a steel tennis racket called the T2000. All strings, grip sizes, strokes, and weights of rackets primarily remained the same.

1970s

This was the tennis boom era, when equipment had its biggest change in technology. Aluminum was introduced, lighter than wood and more easily manufactured than wood or steel. Prince Tennis changed the game with the

Highlights of Tennis Equipment Evolution (continued)

first oversize tennis racket, which changed the sweet spot from the size of two tennis balls to the size of seven tennis balls. This made the game easier for everyone by eliminating the need for perfect technique and reducing injuries. For elite players, this oversize racket changed the way they played. Players put more spin on the ball, and eastern and semiwestern grips became more popular. Because of the more powerful racket and also because more tennis was being played on asphalt, concrete, or clay courts rather than on grass, the ball was now able to bounce normally. The result was a perfect storm of court construction, racket and equipment changes, and the popularity of the game itself. Strings were now made of synthetic fibers and were able to handle the stress of a larger tennis racket.

1980s

In the 1980s, the tennis racket took on space-age materials and designs. Arias, Krickstein, Courier, Lendl, Agassi, and Hooper were some of the players who started using carbon-fiber tennis rackets with such materials as graphite, Kevlar, boron, and titanium. Racket heads stayed between 90 and 107 square inches (581 to 645 sq cm), and power spin was the name of the game with players such as Agassi and Chang using the oversize Prince Graphite. The stiffer carbon fibers were lighter, faster, and easier for all levels to use. The Prince Graphite became the grandfather of all modern tennis rackets.

1990s

With power becoming a big part of the game, tennis companies started to look at ways to not only increase power but also give the player better leverage. Although the '80s were all about materials, the '90s were all about racket geometry: thicker cross-sections, bigger beams, tapered cross-sections for maximum power or control. Wide bodies gave weaker players a powerful shot and pro athletes lethal serves and ground strokes, which made it tough for the little guys to compete at the highest level. To make the game easier for average players, Prince started making longer rackets. This 1- to 2-inch (2.5 to 5 cm) extra length gave the weekend warrior more reach and leverage and gave the pro athlete more reach to counter the power of the new-age players.

Tennis strings needed a major change to increase durability. Once again, space-age material became a favorite. Kevlar and polyesters were combined to create durability and playability, which helped players control their powerful rackets.

These lighter, faster, more aerodynamic space-age rackets resulted in faster, slappier, and more explosive swings. Handle sizes started to come down, giving the wrist more freedom to move and be used for more power and spin. Of course all this came with more injuries, so tennis companies started looking for a way to reduce shock and vibrations—many types of strings have been invented to reduce the harshness of swinging from the hips. Multifilament strings combined with polyesters are now the staple of tennis strings.

2000-2010

This era was more about marketing than innovation. The tennis companies tried to capture the magic of the '80s with stories about materials—nano, liquid metal, triple threat—and although the hype was popular, it didn't really change the way people played. People just adjusted their style of play over time to better utilize what was invented in the '90s. The only real technology in this era was the Prince line of O3 rackets, which contained giant string holes that allowed the strings to move more freely.

2011-Present

The biggest equipment innovations in the last few years have involved tennis strings, tennis balls, and tennis string patterns. First, tennis strings now have different shapes—some are round, some are octagonal, and others are triangular. These shapes allow more spin to be placed on the ball, forcing the ball to jump higher on your opponent. The courts were slowed down to eliminate the "wham bam thank you ma'am" way the game was being played in the early 2000s. And grip sizes are even smaller than the past era. Also, because spin is very important in today's game, tennis companies are finding ways to make rackets with fewer strings so the ball has a chance to sink in through the openings on the string bed, allowing the string to better grip the ball on contact. The talk of the tennis world at this time for racket companies is spin, spin, and more spin.

Conclusion

With most items we buy, it seems that lighter, faster, stronger, and bigger are assumed to be better. Tennis rackets are no exception. The equipment available today is of better construction than the equipment of just a few years ago, but when is more power too much? When does lighter weight adversely affect your game? Remember that tennis has been around for a long time. Few changes have been made to court dimensions, ball specifications, or the way the game is played. If the size of a tennis court had increased along with racket technology, we would be playing the game on a football field with a net at the 50-yard-line.

Use the knowledge in this chapter to fine-tune your game. Forget what you see your favorite professional tennis players using. They don't choose their rackets by watching you play; neither should you by watching them. I like to use the following example to explain this: When watching professional car racing, say the Indy 500 or Daytona, we all marvel at the way drivers handle their cars at extreme speed. Not for an instant do we think we could do the same. Nor do we think that the Ford or Chevy we see on the track is available at the local dealer's lot.

Shouldn't you think the same way when buying a tennis racket? If manufacturers can make rackets that meet the specific needs of your favorite professional player, then be assured that they can make models suited to your needs. Experimentation coupled with proper knowledge is the fastest way to success. By addressing your specific needs, you will have more fun playing tennis, stay healthier, and win more matches. As with anything important to you, seek professional advice.

The Future of Tennis

Top players of the future will have to love the grind and work extremely hard to develop physically and mentally.

I am often asked to comment on the status of American tennis: Why there are so few Americans in the top 100, and why have Serbia, Spain, Switzerland, France, Russia and other nations overtaken the United States' dominating spot? I believe that there are many answers to these questions:

Scope

Tennis is now played on a global landscape. Several decades ago, the United States was one of only a few nations producing top players. Today, most countries, often with the support of their governments, are our competition.

Competition

In the early days of the now IMG Academy, we had the finest players in the world in one location competing against one another, such as Agassi, Courier, Wheaton, Sampras, Seles, Kournikova, Majoli. Although I didn't coach Pete Sampras, he and his coach, Tim Gullickson, were welcomed to my academy to train and compete against the best that the United States had to offer at the time. In the 1980s there were very few top-notch training facilities in the country. Now, with the popularity of training environments (dozens within a 10-mile radius of the IMG Academy alone), it is difficult for any one location to bring a critical mass of top players together.

Players

America's best athletes are not directed to tennis. Arthur Ashe recognized this problem more than 25 years ago: Junior high and high school physical education instructors throughout the school systems are, for the most part, coaches of basketball, football, baseball, and track and field. These are coaches who encourage their top athletes to compete in those sports. The USTA created the 10 and Under program, which is effective in introducing children to tennis, but the program is not available to the majority of kids in the school systems and public recreation systems.

Cost

The cost of becoming a top player is prohibitive. While children can learn to play in local programs (such as National Junior Tennis and Learning and not-for-profit programs) at little or no cost, becoming a highly ranked national tournament player is another matter. Instruction, court rental costs or club membership fees, clothing and equipment, travel, meals, hotels, coaches, and other expenses can cost as much as $150,000 per year. The median income for American families is just under $52,000, so only the top earners can afford to spend this kind of money without sponsorships. The most realistic approach to the development of American talent is a national scouting program. Once talent is identified through regional programs across the country, organizations like the USTA will need to support the players, both boys and girls, through the entire process. This is the only way to get our finest athletes, most without the financial resources to continue the development journey, to consider becoming world-class tennis players.

System

Unlike team sports like baseball and ice hockey, there are no farm teams in individual sports (that is, there are no minor-league environments where coaching and competition are available and the players receive nominal salaries and funds that sustain them while they continue to develop their skills). The USTA does have Challenger and Futures tournaments for sub-world-class players, but those are not enough. The idea of a minor-league team is that the major-league team funds it, having a vested interest in developing talented players and grooming them for the big stage.

Options

Let's face it: Most parents must be realistic and steer their kids toward college. It's also the most practical option, given the minuscule number of talented tennis players who sign professional contracts directly out of high school. Most kids have a better chance of becoming brain surgeons than signing pro contracts. The player ranked 161st in the National Football League receives an annual salary of $1.4 million. At the same time, the player ranked 161st on the ATP or WTA tour must spend about $100,000 to stay on the circuit. So, with college scholarships tucked in their back pockets, players question why they endure the pain of injuries, the increasing cost of competing, and the frustration of going at it alone.

In the 1990s I created a program called Tennis in a Can. This program was offered to municipal tennis facilities along with elementary, middle, and high schools so that their physical education teachers could teach the fundamentals of the sport to children as young as age five. It included 10 one-hour videos, a 350-page teaching manual, on-court teaching tools, and a traveling bag with the logos of the USTA and the USPTA, which endorsed the program. I made the entire package available for $295. We sold a few, but the public schools couldn't even afford this price. I approached some of my friends and raised enough money to send the Tennis in a Can program to nearly 4,000 schools at no cost, and it worked. When learning tennis is a fun experience, children love the game and look forward to it every day. I'd donate this program to the USTA and ask that someone on their staff oversee it at a national level.

To supplement the Tennis in a Can program, I'd encourage the growth of the USTA 10 and Under program and regional National Junior Tennis and Learning (NJTL) networks. This would provide avenues of advancement for those who want to take their tennis to the next level.

The USTA's NJTL engages thousands of kids through tennis, education, and life skills programming. While there are many outstanding NJTL chapters in several metropolitan areas, there are hundreds of major cities without any program at all. We would need to expand this program to make it more widely available.

We also need to understand that the game has changed dramatically over the past few decades. In the 1970s, '80s, and '90s, most players were making their break into the top 10 while they were still teenagers. Today, the top players in the world are a good decade or more older and physically more mature and fit. Venus Williams was born in 1980, Serena Williams and Roger Federer in 1981, David Ferrer and Li Na in 1982, and Maria Sharapova in 1987. In addition, size is now a factor. The average male on the pro tour is nearly 6 feet 3 inches, and many of the ladies exceed 6 feet. Because of these factors, we need to look at American tennis with a new set of eyes. First, let's take a look at the USTA's 10 and Under program:

Throughout my five decades in the business of tennis I have seen many changes in the sport and in the world. It's now common for both parents to work, and recreation centers and school physical education programs have been eliminated as the result of budget cuts. The popularity of computer games and lack of parental supervision have produced a generation of children sitting in front of screens and dealing with the challenges of drugs, alcohol, bullying, and sedentary lifestyles.

I am an innovator and have always been willing to explore various roads to success. I believe that the 10 and Under program deserves our earnest support. I'm aware of the supporters and critics of innovative thinking. They surfaced when I started my academy and when the USTA introduced the 10 and Under program. This initiative, designed to attract youngsters to tennis, introduced the following:

- Various sizes of smaller rackets
- Foam and low-compression balls
- Smaller courts
- Lower nets

The USTA came to the IMG Academy to demonstrate the program and to solicit my feedback. At the time, I responded quickly and withheld my endorsement, although it didn't take long for the program to spread. While it received mixed reviews, the positives far outweighed the negatives.

Over time, I gave the program further consideration and came to these conclusions:

- Young children need to be successful in their early tennis experiences. They need to look forward to their next lesson. Above all, they must have fun.
- The motor skills of children aged 10 and younger are changing dramatically. Increased strength and heart and lung capacity give children the endurance to improve their performance in athletic skills.

Holding a full-size racket in small hands and then having a full-size tennis ball come at them from 40 to 60 feet away are daunting experiences. It's a wonder how we ever expected them to deal with a projectile speeding toward them, make the mental calculation about where the ball would bounce, and adjust their bodies and get into the proper position to strike the ball. I have a new appreciation for the value of the 10 and Under program. I've seen it in action, and I know that the kids love tennis as a result.

Not everyone agrees with the philosophy of the 10 and Under program, the restrictions placed on the children at various levels of competence, or the use of balls of various compressions. Many argue that these changes, while designed to make the game easier to enjoy, actually make the transitions to regular-size courts and standard ball compression much more difficult.

I urge the USTA to remain open-minded and analyze the program on a continual basis and value the affirmative comments but give consideration to the negatives. Make the appropriate changes so we can continue to increase the number of children introduced to tennis. I feel certain that this program should continue, and I will provide personal assistance in any way that I can. After all, even if we don't create a pipeline of world-class players, we will provide kids with opportunities to receive college scholarships and help them keep their bodies in good health and enjoy tennis for a lifetime.

Index

About IMG Academy

With roots as a tennis academy dating back to 1978, today IMG Academy is the world's largest and most advanced multi-sport training and educational institution. IMG Academy helps countless youth, adult, collegiate, and professional athletes reach their full potential in and out of sport by providing world-class teaching and coaching, tailored programs, and professional facilities. 98 percent of IMG Academy's student-athletes matriculate into top universities, 60 percent of which are Division I; the remaining 2 percent historically turn pro. Based in Bradenton, Florida, IMG Academy also serves as a training and competition venue for amateur and professional teams, a host site for a variety of events, and a hub for sports performance research and innovation.

About the Author

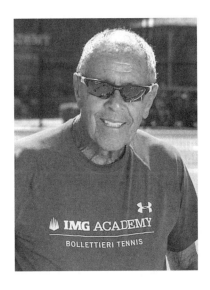

Nick Bollettieri is one of the most influential people in the world of tennis who is renowned for his passion for excellence and the game. His training program is recognized as one of the best systems for developing top players. It was this proven method that Bollettieri used to coach 10 top-ranked players in the world (Andre Agassi, Boris Becker, Jim Courier, Martina Hingis, Jelena Janković, Marcelo Ríos, Monica Seles, Maria Sharapova, Serena Williams, and Venus Williams) plus a multitude of other world-class players, including Petra Kvitová, Sabine Lisicki, Kei Nishikori, Nicole Vaidišová, Tommy Haas, Radek Stepanek, Ivo Karlovic, Mary Pierce, Jimmy Arias, and Anna Kournikova.

Bollettieri founded the world-renowned Nick Bollettieri Tennis Academy in 1978 to educate tennis student-athletes in a dual environment of intense athletic training and academics. Within 10 years, his vision expanded when IMG purchased the academy and helped evolve it into the elite academic and multi-sport training institution now known as IMG Academy. Bollettieri's insights into the game of tennis are sought by organizations around the world. He has written numerous books on tennis, contributed to many television and video programs, and is globally recognized for his overall promotion of the sport.

The Bollettieri name is synonymous with tennis excellence. The coach has achieved numerous honors and awards, including induction into the International Tennis Hall of Fame in 2014. He has also been inducted into the Florida Sports Hall of Fame (2004), honored with the prestigious Sports and Service Award by the Arthur Ashe Institute for Urban Health (2003), inducted into the Italian American Sports Hall of Fame (2002), and ranked as one of *Tennis Magazine*'s 50 Most Influential People in Tennis (2000) and as one of *Sporting Life*'s 25 People Who Have Influenced Tennis in the Past Century (2000). He was named National Coach of the Year for Tennis by the United States Olympic Committee and received the Tennis Educational Merit Award by the International Tennis Hall of Fame.